THE GONE FISHIN' PORTFOLIO

Get Wise, Get Wealthy . . . and Get On with Your Life

Second Edition

ALEXANDER GREEN

WILEY

Published by John Wiley & Sons, Inc., Hoboken, New Jersey.

Published simultaneously in Canada.

For general information on our other products and services or for technical support, please contact our Customer Care Department within the United States at (800) 762-2974, outside the United States at (317) 572-3993, or fax (317) 572-4002.

Wiley publishes in a variety of print and electronic formats and by print-on-demand. Some material included with standard print versions of this book may not be included in e-books or in print-on-demand. If this book refers to media such as a CD or DVD that is not included in the version you purchased, you may download this material at http://booksupport.wiley.com. For more information about Wiley products, visit www.wiley.com.

Library of Congress Cataloging-in-Publication Data

Names: Green, Alexander, 1958- author.
Title: The gone fishin' portfolio : get wise, get wealthy ... and get on
    with your life / Alexander Green.
Description: Second edition. | Hoboken, New Jersey : Wiley, [2021] |
    Includes index.
Identifiers: LCCN 2020053702 (print) | LCCN 2020053703 (ebook) | ISBN
    9781119795049 (hardback) | ISBN 9781119795056 (adobe pdf) | ISBN
    9781119794998 (epub)
Subjects: LCSH: Investments. | Portfolio management. | Finance, Personal.
Classification: LCC HG4521 .G693 2021 (print) | LCC HG4521 (ebook) | DDC
    332.6--dc23
LC record available at https://lccn.loc.gov/2020053702
LC ebook record available at https://lccn.loc.gov/2020053703

COVER DESIGN: PAUL MCCARTHY
COVER IMAGES: GETTY IMAGES: ©VMAKT (WATER) |
© SKODONNELL (BILLS)

SKY10022527_010421

This book is dedicated to the most inspiring and best man I've ever known, my father, H. Braxton Green.

If a man writes a book, let him set down only what he knows.
I have guesses enough of my own.

Source: Johann Wolfgang von Goethe

CONTENTS

FOREWORD

Money was big in my household in the 1950s and 1960s. We didn't have very much and my parents were children of the Great Depression. That meant financial doom was always near because if it happened once, it could happen again. Therefore, having money was ultra-important.

My father worked for Caltex, commuting into New York City for low wages. He worked in the oil company's treasury department. He kept track of money that flowed from the Persian Gulf.

My mother was a housewife on a budget. Tuna, boiled hotdogs, fish sticks and Mallomars were on the weekly menu. On weekends, my father grilled flank steak. The O'Reilly family had a used car, a manual lawnmower and a few chairs on the patio.

We lived in Levittown, New York. It was like communism. Everyone pretty much had the same resources. Which were not many.

I needed money for ice cream. The Good Humor truck. Bungalow Bar, Judy Ann. Occasionally, my mom would slip me a quarter for a toasted almond bar. Life was sweet when that happened.

At age 10, I recognized that my father was not going to give me the cash I needed to live in the style I wanted to become accustomed to. So I went to work. Cutting lawns in the summer, shoveling snow off driveways in the winter. My sister and I did not receive an allowance for chores. We did them *gratis* in return for Sugar Frosted Flakes.

My father was frugal. He was afraid. A big 6-foot, 3-inch former naval officer, he feared the worst. That he would lose his job and not be able to "provide." He saw plenty of Irish go under in 1930s Brooklyn. Until the day he died, he feared financial ruin.

So he saved, rarely spent. When I was 14, we took a bus from Long Island to Fort Lauderdale, Florida, during Easter vacation. About halfway down, in South Carolina, I said, "Hey, Dad, next time just shoot me, and you, Mom and Janet go."

I think he felt guilty about the bus ride, because he paid for a water skiing lesson in Fort Lauderdale. I got right up because I knew there would be no second lesson.

My teenaged years were spent playing sports and working. I slung ice cream at Carvel, was a swimming instructor and then hit the jackpot: I began my own business painting houses. Made nice money. Never asked my parents for a nickel. I'm proud of that to this day.

America is an exceptional place, and the socialists are full of it. If you work hard, get educated, and practice self-control and honesty, you will make money. There are more ways to do that here than anywhere else in the world.

But once money flows in, then a different set of problems develops. What do you do with your wages after taxes? Buy stupid stuff? Order $75 steaks? Zip around in a Ferrari?

Not me. Like my father, I saved and, fortunately, the money grew.

Then, my broadcasting and writing career exploded and capitalism paid me a serious visit. The only other neighborhood guy who had made it big was Billy Joel. I used to see him around wearing a leather jacket in July. Billy had that James Dean thing going on, and even dropped out of high school.

But he made huge money after "Piano Man." Problem was his manager stole a lot of it.

That didn't happen to me. I had honest representation. So my money accumulated. But I had no idea what to do with it. Because he feared losing money with stocks, my father bought municipal bonds. I bought a few as well. But I knew there was something more out there.

After flailing around with various financial newsletters, I stumbled upon Alexander Green and The Oxford Club in 2003. I analyzed what Alex was writing and bought some Berkshire B. Still have it, very strong return. Very strong.

So I stuck with Alex. Didn't know him personally but looked forward to his monthly newsletter. Didn't always make money but Alex's stock suggestions sure increased my net worth. I became a lifetime Oxford Club Member.

Then a couple of years ago, Oxford called me out of the blue. They wanted me to interview Alex for an infomercial.

Now, I *never* do that kind of thing. I am not a pitchman, I'm a journalist who delivers fact-based opinion. But after thinking it over, I decided to do business with Oxford and Alex. The reason is that I want people to succeed as I have in the markets. Alexander Green is a superb stock selector and a very smart guy. I want as many people as possible to know about him.

So that's my story, which leads into Alex's story. The book you are reading is subtitled *Get Wise, Get Wealthy . . . and Get On with Your Life*. It is well worth the time you are investing to read it.

So let's get going. There is wisdom to be had, and money to be made. You'll see.

Bill O'Reilly
Long Island
October 2020

PREFACE

In early 2003, I created a new investment portfolio for subscribers to *The Oxford Communiqué* and gave it a lighthearted name: the Gone Fishin' Portfolio. After a few years of market-beating returns, multinational publishing house John Wiley & Sons asked if I would write a book about it. I agreed.

I knew I had an excellent strategy to share with the world. However, I also realized that most financial advice has a short shelf life. Things change quickly in the world and in markets. Even the best investment letters written by the most insightful analysts are soon lining the reader's birdcage. A book, by contrast, gives an author the opportunity to make a considered argument, flesh out his or her case, and answer potential objections or criticisms.

But then, who needed another investment book, then or now? The shelves in my home were already groaning with titles on stock selection, value investing, trading strategies, asset allocation, global diversification and many other topics. I learned a lot from those books, but it wasn't always what the authors intended.

I discovered that no matter how smart, how experienced or how insightful the advice-giver, investment predictions—with the luxury of hindsight—can appear not just wide of the mark but foolish. Indeed, many investment books from years past stand out primarily as cautionary tales about pride and hubris.

The authors who made a compelling case for their investment approach were often short on specifics. For example, if high returns could be made investing in value stocks, great—but which ones? Sure, the author could offer a screen using price-to-sales, price-to-earnings, price-to-book, dividend yield or other financial metrics. But how many readers were actually equipped to do this—and to follow through with an equally rigorous sell discipline? Not many. The author could make specific stock recommendations, of course, but, in most cases, that is better done in an e-letter since the economy and financial markets change quickly.

The advice given in most investment books is either too ambiguous or, conversely, specific but soon dated. No wonder so few investment books are considered classics.

My goal was to break this trend and offer timeless investment advice that told readers exactly how and where to invest their money and in what percentages. And that's exactly what I did with the first edition of *The Gone Fishin' Portfolio*.

I soon learned there was an eager market for this kind of book. The week of its publication it soared to No. 2 on Amazon's list of nonfiction bestsellers and hit *The New York Times'* bestseller list the following week.

Timeless investment advice is an ambitious goal, however. And much has changed since the book's publication in 2008.

We witnessed the housing bust and the biggest financial crisis in nearly a century. Oil prices plunged as new technologies—horizontal drilling and hydraulic fracturing—made formerly inaccessible deposits economically viable. Interest rates dropped all the way to zero—and into negative territory in many countries.

We enjoyed the longest U.S. economic expansion and bull market from 2009 to 2019.

Eleven years of extraordinarily high stock returns were followed by a global pandemic, the greatest spike in unemployment since the Great Depression, the largest economic contraction ever, and the fastest—and shortest—bear market in history, quickly followed by the fastest market rebound and largest quarterly economic expansion in history.

With all these booms and busts, the Gone Fishin' Portfolio was truly put to the test. And it came through like a champ, delivering solid returns with less risk than being fully invested in stocks, and without a single modification to the original strategy.

This last point is key. The idea behind this investment system is to quit worrying about the economy, inflation, interest rates or the financial markets and instead use a strategy designed to grow your assets in good times and protect them in bad, despite the fact that we cannot know in advance when these expansions and contractions will arrive.

My goal with this book is to show readers the safest, simplest way to achieve and maintain financial independence.

I'm not talking about people with great connections, incredible talents or innate genius. I'm talking about everyday, ordinary people. People like Ronald Read.

Read, a longtime resident of Brattleboro, Vermont, died in 2014 at age 92. He lived modestly, as you might expect for a man who worked 25 years at a gas station and then 17 more as a janitor at a local J.C. Penney. Yet his relatives were shocked when they discovered that he left behind an estate valued at almost $8 million.

Read's story puts the lie to the conventional wisdom that to get rich you have to be well connected, highly educated or a successful entrepreneur with his or her own business. He made his fortune in the stock market, where anyone with even a modest amount of savings can take an ownership stake in many of the world's best businesses. He had no formal training in business or economics. But, as he proved with his own example, that's not necessary for long-term investment success.

How did a janitor and gas station attendant build a net worth that put him in the top 1% of the nation? Read was patient. He thought long term and wasn't buffeted by daily events or the regular caterwauls of market pundits. He didn't mistime the market because he never tried to time it. And he diversified broadly.

(Some investment pros will tell you the key to making a fortune in the stock market is owning a concentrated stock portfolio with just a small number of names. The assumption, of course, is this limited selection will do exceptionally well. But what if it doesn't? What if it does exceptionally poorly instead? A smart investor spreads his bets not only to reduce risk but to increase his chances of holding a lot of big winners. In the pages ahead, I'm going to show you how to own not just a few of the market's biggest gainers in the years to come but *every one of them*—and not just possibly but definitely. So stay tuned.)

Read kept his investment costs minimal. He didn't use a full-service broker or other high-paid advisor. He used a discounter only to execute his trades. And he lived frugally. Although his stock portfolio hit the multimillion-dollar mark many years before he died, he didn't flaunt his wealth. He was generally seen in the same flannel jacket and baseball cap. His most expensive possession was a 2007 Toyota Yaris valued at $5,000. He foraged for his own firewood and would often park several blocks away to avoid paying parking fees. As a result, he went from being a janitor to a philanthropist.

What did Read do wrong? From an investment standpoint, almost nothing. But from a commonsense standpoint, I question whether it was wise to live a life of such extreme frugality.

(As we'll discuss, that isn't necessary with the Gone Fishin' strategy. Living like a miser so you can spend your money in retirement is a bit like saving up all your sex for old age. It doesn't make a lot of sense.)

Read could have enjoyed some of the fruits of his success while he was alive, treating himself or someone he loved to something special every once in a while. Then again, that must not have been important to him. (And, after all, it was *his money*.) Clearly, he enjoyed the challenge of living modestly, something beyond the imagination of most Americans today.

On the other hand, his local library and hospital in Brattleboro are grateful. Read bequeathed them more than $6 million.

Why would I lead off with a story about a janitor and gas station attendant who accumulated a multimillion-dollar fortune? After all, someone like Read must clearly be the exception, not the rule.

Not so. I've met many men and women from humble circumstances who have developed sizable fortunes . . . and heard about many more. One of my regular golf partners recently told me he had just settled his father's estate.

"The man was a barber. He never made more than $10,000 a year. So I was surprised to find he left a seven-figure estate." How? By saving regularly and investing in stocks.

Read and my friend's father are typical of the thousands of men and women surveyed by Thomas Stanley and William Danko in *The Millionaire Next Door: The Surprising Secrets of America's Wealthy*. Stanley, and later his daughter, Sarah Stanley Fallaw (also a researcher), spent decades learning how middle-class workers and other men and women of modest means become rich.

The best part? It has nothing to do with founding a computer company in your garage, recording a platinum-selling album or playing third base for the Yankees. Rather, most people who achieve financial freedom in this country follow a remarkably similar path. They adopt work, spending, saving and investment habits that lead—almost inevitably—to a seven- or eight-figure net worth.

All you need are knowledge, discipline and patience. This book provides the knowledge. And in Chapter 15, I'll also address the factors that will challenge your discipline and patience in the months and years ahead.

The principles of wealth creation are well understood. But that doesn't mean that most people understand them. A few years ago, the Securities and Exchange Commission (SEC) released a wide-ranging report on financial literacy in the United States, and the conclusion was clear: We're not there. We're not even close. Yet the consequences of financial illiteracy have never been greater.

Corporate pension plans have gone the way of the passenger pigeon. And without serious reform, Social Security—according to the agency's own website—will eventually be bankrupted by time and arithmetic.

One health and retirement survey concluded that most Americans "lack even a rudimentary understanding of stock and bond prices, risk diversification, portfolio choice and investment fees." The most common response to most questions in the survey was "Do not know."

As a nation, our financial illiteracy is appalling. Even good students graduate from high school without understanding compound interest, IRAs and 401(k)s, or why we even have a stock market. And when it comes to money basics, ignorance gets expensive fast.

Here are just a few highlights from that SEC report.

When asked the primary benefit of portfolio diversification, respondents were given three choices: (a) risk reduction, (b) increased returns or (c) reduced tax liabilities. Only 56% knew the answer was (a). (Even if they had no clue, respondents still had a 33% chance of getting it right.) The reality is that most respondents didn't even know this most basic piece of financial knowledge.

When asked whether a young investor willing to take moderate risk for above-average growth should invest in (a) Treasury bills, (b) money market funds or (c) balanced stock funds, 63% of respondents chose the wrong answer—and even 49% of fund owners didn't know the correct answer was (c).

When asked whether a traditional IRA, a 401(k) or a Roth IRA offers withdrawals that are tax-exempt, only 44% knew the correct answer was a Roth.

This is really a shame, especially in a country like ours where citizens are given unprecedented freedom and opportunity to better their financial lives. Instead, too many learn the hard way, falling for the siren song of an expensive insurance agent or transaction-based broker . . . or committing hara-kari in a discount brokerage account.

What is the solution? Teaching basic financial literacy in every public high school in the country would be a good first step. But education reform is slow and difficult, not least of all because less than 20% of teachers polled said they felt competent to teach saving and investing.

This book intends to fill this gap. I'll cover the investment basics and unite them in a simple, straightforward investment strategy that will allow you to earn higher returns with moderate risk, ultra-low costs, and a minimal investment of time and energy.

Let me get started by telling you a little bit about my background and how I developed this investment system.

My circumstances were not as modest as Ronald Read's or my golf partner's father's. But I wouldn't call them privileged, either.

I grew up the second of four sons, in a middle-class family in the South. I lived in a house with no air conditioning and went to public schools without it. My family had little money to travel. A vacation was the six of us piling into an old station wagon and driving to Daytona Beach to see relatives. (It wasn't until two years after I graduated from college that I took my first commercial flight.)

As a young man, I worked a series of lousy jobs: maintenance on a truck terminal, night shift in an auto-parts warehouse and so on. I had no connections. I had no inheritance. But I worked and saved and invested. And things worked out, as they did for millions of other Americans who followed a similar path. I now spend my days trying to light that path for others.

My financial fortunes did get a tremendous boost when I got into the money management industry in 1985. The work suited me. Sixteen years later, I had gone from a net worth of approximately zero to financial independence. And I retired from the industry.

I was now free to do whatever I wanted, wherever I wanted, with whomever I wanted. It's called total financial freedom. And I can tell you from experience, it's a great feeling.

Unfortunately, many of my clients had not become financially independent. This was not because I advised them poorly. As an investment advisor, I dealt with my clients honestly and gave them the best advice and service I could.

Yet, in many ways, they operated at a disadvantage. Some clients had a poor understanding of investment fundamentals. Others found it impossible to commit to a long-term investment plan. Many were simply too emotional about the markets, running to cash at the first hint of danger.

Contrarian instincts are rare, too, I learned. Few people are emotionally stirred by low stock prices. But I am one of them. Every time there was a correction, a crash or a financial panic, I'd get an adrenaline surge, my pulse would rise, and I'd start buying.

My clients often did just the opposite. They were more inclined to curse loudly, sleep little and hurl epithets, some unrepeatable. Unfortunately, strong emotions like these are often a prelude to bad investment decisions.

Then there was the other small matter of my firm's fee schedule. Investment professionals don't get into the industry because the work is meaningful but low paying. You become a broker, a financial planner, an insurance agent or a money manager to get rich. And most of us do, eventually. In truth, what you're paying your financial advisor is probably too much. Many investors aren't doing that well because their advisors are doing *too well*.

This story is as old as Wall Street itself. In his book *Where Are the Customers' Yachts?*, originally published in 1940, Fred Schwed Jr. tells the story of a visitor to New York who is taken to the harbor and shown the impressive yachts that belong to the bankers and brokers. A tad naïve, the visitor asks, "But where are the customers' yachts?"

Where indeed.

I'm not suggesting that this is all Wall Street's fault. Clients are rarely abducted and forced at gunpoint to sign account-opening forms. Nor can advisors make important investment decisions without their clients' consent (not without landing in the hoosegow, anyway). We all need to take responsibility for the decisions we've made, including the decision to delegate important responsibilities.

Since retiring from life as a registered investment advisor 20 years ago, I've been busy living what I call "the second half of my life" as a financial writer.

For more than two decades I have been the Chief Investment Strategist of The Oxford Club, the world's largest financial fellowship with over 170,000 members. I am also an editor of *Liberty Through Wealth*, a free daily investment research service with over 600,000 subscribers.

Frankly, writing about investments rather than dealing with individual clients suits me better. I can give advice freely, and no one who heeds it has to wonder whether my real motive is to earn fees or commissions or capture their assets. I can offer opinions about the market without a compliance officer scrutinizing my words. And my readers don't have to worry about the objectivity of my analysis. I have no business relationships with the companies I cover, no investment banking colleagues seeking customers for new bond issues or secondary offerings, no reason to tell anything but the plain truth as I see it.

I don't mind telling you that many of these truths I learned the hard way. You can save yourself a lot of trouble—not to mention a boatload of money—by learning from my experience. As I've told my regular readers, "I've made the dumb mistakes so you don't have to."

In the pages that follow, I'm going to share with you the best long-term investment strategy I know.

The Gone Fishin' Portfolio will allow you to successfully manage your money yourself using a simple yet highly sophisticated strategy to increase your returns, reduce your investment risk, eliminate Wall Street's high fees and keep the taxman at bay, too. The idea is simple: Get Wise, Get Wealthy . . . and Get On with Your Life.

In Part I, **Get Wise**, we'll examine the challenges you face as an investor. I'll review the fundamental relationship between risk and reward in the financial markets. You'll also get an insider's view of how the investment industry *really* works.

Get Wealthy, discussed in Part II, means understanding and, I hope, adopting the Gone Fishin' strategy. You'll learn why this is arguably the safest and simplest way to reach your long-term financial goals. I will also address the financial and psychological challenges you're likely to face in the years ahead.

Get On with Your Life, which we will discuss in Part III, means taking your financial destiny into your hands and, at the same time, reclaiming your most precious resource—your time.

Setting up the Gone Fishin' Portfolio is a snap. Maintaining it takes less than 20 minutes a year.

You may not believe you're qualified to manage your money yourself. If so, I beg to differ. Investing can be made endlessly complicated, or paint-by-numbers simple. If you keep things simple, you're perfectly qualified to manage your money yourself—and in a highly sophisticated way.

As an investor, your overriding goal is to achieve and maintain financial independence. Your savings are the fuel. The Gone Fishin' Portfolio is the vehicle to get you there.

Let's get started.

ACKNOWLEDGMENTS

The Gone Fishin' Portfolio wouldn't have been possible without the help of countless people along the way.

It has been my exceptional good fortune to work with Bill Bonner, Mark Ford, Julia Guth, Steven King, and my other colleagues, mentors and good friends at Agora Publishing.

I'd like to thank Kristin Orman, Andrew Hubbarth and Nancy Hull for their many hours of research for the book.

Many thanks to Christina Grieves and Anne Mathews for their exceptional copyediting.

Thanks, too, to the folks at John Wiley & Sons for suggesting a revised and updated edition of the book and for reviewing the manuscript.

I would like to also express my gratitude to longtime subscriber Bill O'Reilly for his generous endorsement of my work and for writing the Foreword.

And thanks, as well, to our many Oxford Club Members and *Liberty Through Wealth* readers.

Carpe Diem,

Alex Green

PART I

Get Wise

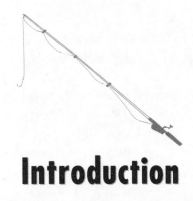

Introduction

As an investment analyst, I speak frequently at investment conferences across the United States and around the world.

The attendees come for a number of reasons. Some want to gain insights on interest rates, the dollar or the stock market. Others are seeking new investment strategies. Still others are looking for good investment ideas or, as one gentleman insisted, "just one great stock."

But before you can put your money to work effectively, you need something even more fundamental to your success: a philosophy of investing.

In her book *Philosophy: Who Needs It*, Ayn Rand argues that all of us have a philosophy of life, whether we know it or not. "Your only choice," she writes, "is whether you define your philosophy by a conscious, rational, disciplined process of thought . . . or let your subconscious accumulate a junk heap of unwarranted conclusions."

What's true of life is also true of investing.

Over the past two decades, I've dealt with thousands of individual investors, some highly astute, some rank novices. Many had only the foggiest notion of what they were trying to achieve— or how. In some ways this is understandable. World markets are complex and the investment process can be daunting.

Beginners often don't understand the fundamentals of saving and investing. And even more experienced investors are often stymied by the complexities and technical jargon surrounding the investment process. Many try (and inevitably fail) to outguess the markets—or simply wave the white flag and turn their portfolio over to "that nice young man down at Merrill Lynch."

Big mistake.

No one cares more about your money than you do. With a basic understanding of the investment process and a bit of discipline, you're perfectly capable of managing your own money, even your "serious money." *Especially* your serious money. By managing your own money, you'll be able to earn higher returns and save many thousands of dollars in investment costs over your lifetime.

The Gone Fishin' Portfolio rests on a powerful philosophy of investing. It's battle-tested. It's built on the most advanced—and realistic—theories of money management. And it works.

Moreover, this book does something that virtually no other investment guide does. I'm going to show you—very specifically—where to put your money. And then I'm going to show you how to manage it year after year.

Once you've set up your portfolio, the whole process will take less than 20 minutes a year to implement. This may sound like an audacious claim. But, as you'll soon see, the strategy itself is steeped in humility.

It is based on the only realistic premise for an investment philosophy—that, to a great extent, the future is unknowable. So don't expect me to draw on my gift of prophecy and tell you what's going to happen to the economy, interest rates, the dollar or world stock markets. (No one is more surprised than me how the market action unfolds each year.) Nor will we ignore uncertainty or pretend we have a system that has eliminated it. Instead, we're going to use uncertainty and make it our friend. In short, we're going to capitalize on it.

Investing is serious business. Getting it right is the difference between a retirement spent in comfort (or luxury) and spending your golden years counting nickels, worrying whether you'll have enough. The difference could hardly be starker.

Up until now, you may have been tempted to turn your investment portfolio over to someone else to manage. After all, your financial security is paramount. You may not think you can take the risk—or handle the responsibility—of running your money yourself. I fully intend to disabuse you of that notion. I also want to point out that there are serious risks to turning your money over to someone else. That person may manage it poorly. Or be terribly expensive. Or both.

If you're skeptical on this point, it may be that you've bought the story that Wall Street is selling: Investing is so complicated—or your personal circumstances so exceptional—that you should not be trusted to run your own money.

I'll concede that if you don't know what the heck you're doing, this is true. But one solution is learning what to do, rather than turning your financial welfare over to someone else.

When it comes to managing your money, there are plenty of potential pitfalls out there. However, those investors who wind up in retirement with less money than they need have generally fallen prey to one of four basic mistakes:

1. They were too conservative, so their portfolio didn't grow enough to begin generating the income required to meet their spending requirements.
2. They were too aggressive, so a significant percentage of their portfolio went up in flames along the way.
3. They tried—and failed—to time the market. Confident that they would be in for market rallies and out for market corrections, they ended up doing just the opposite much of the time.
4. They delegated unwisely. They turned their financial affairs over to a broker, insurance agent or financial planner who—over time—converted a substantial amount of their assets into the firm's assets. In addition, the advisor may have been too conservative, been too aggressive, or tried and failed to time the market.

If your nest egg is lying in pieces late in life, you don't have the opportunity—or the time—to build another one. The consequences, both personal and financial, can be devastating.

Planning your financial future is a momentous responsibility. The Gone Fishin' Portfolio will enable you to handle your serious money—the money you need to live on in retirement—in a serious way.

There are few guarantees in the world of investing. In fact, once you get beyond the risk-free world of Treasurys and certificates of deposit, there are virtually none. However, the Gone Fishin' Portfolio eliminates six major investment risks:

1. It keeps you from being so conservative that your long-term purchasing power fails to keep up with inflation.
2. It prevents you from handling your money recklessly.
3. It does not require you to own any individual stocks or bonds. So a single security—think Enron or Shearson Lehman—cannot cause your portfolio to crater.
4. It does not require a broker, financial consultant or anyone else to attach himself to your portfolio like a barnacle, siphoning off fees every year.
5. It doesn't require you—or any investment "expert"—to forecast the economy, predict the market or analyze competing economic theories about the future.
6. Perhaps most importantly, it guarantees that your time will be your own. Rather than spending countless hours evaluating stocks, market trends or fund managers, you'll spend your time as you please. While others struggle to manage their money effectively, you'll have "gone fishin'."

This last point means that instead of spending countless hours fretting over your investment portfolio, you'll be able to relax . . . play golf . . . travel the world . . . spend more time with your kids or grandkids . . . or just swing on a hammock in the shade with a glass of ice-cold lemonade. Because your investments will be on autopilot.

This is not just a strategy for today's markets, incidentally. The Gone Fishin' Portfolio is designed to prosper—and generate peace of mind—through all market environments. And I invite you to be skeptical. In fact, let me begin by asking you a question.

If I could show you a way to manage your money yourself, using a strategy that is as powerful and effective as any used by the nation's top institutions, that will allow you to outperform the vast majority of investment professionals, pay nothing in sales charges, brokerage fees or commissions, that will take less than 20 minutes a year to implement, and that is based on an investment strategy so sophisticated it won the Nobel Prize in economics, would you be interested?

I hope so. That, in a nutshell, is the Gone Fishin' Portfolio. It's about handling the money you intend to retire on simply, effectively and cost-efficiently, with the absolute minimum of time and attention.

If you're like most people I know, you have better things to do than watch your stocks bounce up and down all day.

Don't get me wrong. I'm not averse to trading stocks. (Long-term investing and short-term trading are not mutually exclusive activities.) But short-term trading strategies are beyond the scope of this book. Instead of focusing on trading or speculating, we're going to focus here on the money you intend to retire on—and perhaps ultimately leave to your kids, your grandkids or your favorite charity. This is money that shouldn't be treated like chips in a poker game.

Reaching financial independence is a serious goal, one that should be pursued in a disciplined, rigorous way.

That's why I recommend that you make the Gone Fishin' Portfolio the foundation of your long-term investment program. The philosophy behind it is based on the best investment thinking available. It has been tested in various economic conditions. It can increase your returns while reducing risk. And it will minimize your investment costs and annual taxes on your portfolio.

Best of all, it works. Investors who have put their money to work this way have enjoyed years of excellent returns while taking less risk than being fully invested in stocks.

I invite you to join them.

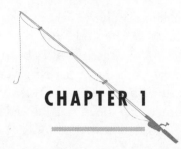

CHAPTER 1

The Unvarnished Truth About Your Money

I offer nothing more than simple facts, plain arguments, and common sense.

Source: Common Sense, Thomas Paine

A while back, some friends and I were vacationing in Key West and decided to do some deep-sea fishing.

We didn't have a boat, so we went to a local marina to see what we could charter. There were several boats available, so we began talking to various captains.

Most assured us that the fishing was excellent and encouraged us to hire them for the next day, before someone else booked them. But since we were in no hurry, we took our time and kept wandering down the dock chatting with the crews of different charters.

Near the end of the dock, we saw an older captain leaning back comfortably in his captain's chair with a beer in one hand and a cigar in the other.

"How's the fishin' been lately?" I asked.

"The fishin's been great," he said. "But the catchin'," he added with a shake of his head, "the catchin' ain't been so good."

"Why not?" we asked, a little surprised given the positive spin we had gotten from the other boat captains.

He said the weather had been unseasonably cool. That had affected migration patterns. The big schools of fish hadn't shown up yet. "Nobody's been catchin' much lately," he said.

We looked at each other in disappointment.

"It's still great weather to go out," he added. "And the fish *might* show up," he said after a long puff on his cigar. "You never know."

The prospect of spending the afternoon on the water without catching anything more than a bout of seasickness wasn't terribly appealing. So we huddled to talk about what we wanted to do. After a little discussion, we decided we were willing to risk going out. We also agreed we wanted to use the old boat captain.

Unlike the others, he hadn't blown any smoke up our skirts. He wasn't interested in talking us into a fishing trip. He didn't seem to particularly care whether we hired him or not. As a result, he did something nobody else did. He told us the truth. So we hired him.

We knew we were running the risk of paying to sit on the water all day without so much as a nibble. We could live with that. And, if we didn't catch anything, well, at least we went out with our eyes wide open.

The next day the weather was perfect. Despite his laid-back attitude, the captain and his mate were good company and gave first-rate service. And the "catchin'"? It was the best fishing I'd ever experienced—then or since.

A few hours after he got us out to his "spot," the ocean suddenly filled with so many dolphin—mahi—that the water turned yellow.

After a couple hours, our arms were tired. We literally couldn't hoist any more in. When we returned to port, we were giving away fish to the crew, other anglers who had come back empty-handed, even strangers on the dock. Our coolers weren't big enough to hold them all. (And, in case you don't know, fresh Florida mahi is just about the best-tasting fish around.)

What does this story have to do with your investment port-folio? Only this: I'd like to do for you what that boat captain did for us that day. I want to tell you the unvarnished truth, with no promises and no agenda.

I'd like to help you meet your long-term investment goals. But I don't want to sell you a financial plan, charge you a commission or wrap fee, or manage your money. I don't need you to subscribe to my investment letter or buy my other books. I just want to give you the straight dope with no strings attached. Believe it or not, that's a rare thing in the world of investing.

LAY CLAIM TO WHAT'S YOURS

Think about it. When was the last time you received investment advice from someone who was both qualified to give it and had nothing to sell? Not a mutual fund, a trading service, a financial plan, a software program, a brokerage account, an insurance policy, an annuity or a managed account. Nothing.

You might think you at least get independent investment advice from the national media, but think again. Cable television parades endless pundits across the screen, all with ever-changing opinions about the economy and the markets, all to sell advertising—much of it investment-related. The financial press maintains a circus of activity as well. Headlines shout, "Retire Rich," "Five Healthcare Stocks to Buy Today," "Double Your Investment Income," "The Shortcut to Seven Figures," "Is This Bull Market Over?" and so on.

The Gone Fishin' Portfolio is an antidote to all this noise and confusion. It is the distillation of much of what I've learned over more than 35 years as an investment analyst, portfolio manager and financial writer. It is the key to financial freedom—if you have the discipline to see it through. To benefit from this investment system, you need only follow three simple steps:

1. Read this book carefully to get a thorough understanding of how this strategy works—and why.
2. Put your money to work as I suggest in Chapter 10.
3. Take less than 20 minutes a year to keep this system on track, as I describe in the same chapter.

That's it. If you follow these three simple steps, you'll be on your way to meeting your long-term financial goals—and spending about as much time on your portfolio each year as you would eating lunch at McDonald's.

My objective here is not theoretical. I don't want you to simply read the book, nod your head and say, "Sounds good." My goal is to encourage you to use this system, to benefit from it. I want to set you on a path to a place where money and its management are no longer a concern in your life.

In essence, the Gone Fishin' Portfolio is about setting you free from concerns about your financial future. Don't get me wrong. The future, to a great extent, is always uncertain. But you'll enjoy the satisfaction and peace of mind that come from using an investment system that offers a high probability of success. That's not just my opinion, by the way. It's also the opinion of the Nobel Committee. (More on that in Chapter 9.) Trillions of dollars of institutional money are being run using systems similar to the one I'm about to describe.

Incidentally, I've also set up a special website devoted to this investment system. It will allow you to track your progress and will even remind you of the simple steps you need to take once a year to keep your portfolio on track. (Feel free to visit it at GoneFishinPortfolio.com.)

When you're done reading this book, there is only one commitment you'll need to make: a promise to take personal responsibility for your own financial freedom. I can't overemphasize how important this is.

LEAVE NOTHING TO CHANCE

Your employer and the federal government are not going to get the job done for you. Yet for more than two-thirds of elderly Americans, Social Security is their major source of income. (For a third of them, Social Security is their only income.) If you are retired or close to it, you can count on Social Security to help meet your financial needs. But it's tough to imagine living on nothing more.

For young workers, the program is a demographic time bomb. Americans are living longer and healthier lives than ever before. According to the Social Security Administration, the additional life expectancy of a 65-year-old in 1949 was not quite 14 years. Today it is more than 20 years.

By 2035, the number of Americans 65 and older will increase from approximately 56 million today to over 78 million. Yet there are currently 2.8 workers for each Social Security beneficiary. By 2035, there will be only 2.3 workers for each beneficiary.

There is no so-called trust fund. Current payroll taxes are being used to pay out current benefits. Without serious reform—long overdue—our federal pension program looks increasingly like a Ponzi scheme.

(The government's own publications have stated, "The current Social Security system is unsustainable in the long run.")

Sure, the nation's No. 1 entitlement program will survive in some form, but the solution to the problem is likely to come in the form of higher payroll taxes, an increase in the age of eligibility, and/or fewer benefits. Of course, most of us can only count on Social Security to cover a portion of our retirement expenses.

Private pension plans are going extinct, too. According to the Employee Benefit Research Institute, the share of private-sector workers covered by a defined benefit pension has fallen from 39% in 1980 to less than 4% today. Nationwide, state pensions are underfunded by more than $1.3 trillion. Many corporations have raided their own plans. Others have tried to chisel their way out of them. Some have simply waved the white flag and filed for bankruptcy.

Meanwhile, inflation—the thief that robs us all—is slowly but steadily driving up your cost of living. Your eroding purchasing power means you'll have to devote more of your budget in retirement to housing, utilities, insurance, healthcare costs and other monthly expenses.

This may sound depressing. But by facing the music, you can start making the choices that will provide a comfortable retirement.

Unfortunately, polls show that over half of Americans believe it is the responsibility of the government or their employer to take care of them in retirement. These folks are in for one rude awakening.

You may indeed get benefits from your employer and the federal government. But neither is likely to provide you with a cushy retirement.

That's up to you. As libertarians have insisted for years, responsibility is the price of freedom.

When you take control and accept full accountability for your own financial welfare, you let go of the idea that it is someone else's obligation to provide for you in retirement. You let go of the idea that your broker or financial planner will ensure your financial independence.

Ultimately, your financial welfare is up to you. You need to plan. You need to save. And you need to manage your money intelligently. These are just the topics I'll cover in the pages ahead.

REEL IT IN . . .

1. The Gone Fishin' Portfolio is a powerful and effective yet simple investment system to achieve financial freedom.
2. You can enjoy a high probability of success using this investment approach, one that has garnered recognition from the Nobel Committee and is being used—in similar fashion—by many of the world's biggest institutional investors.
3. The investing deck is fundamentally stacked against you. Brokers and financial advisors work for fees. The national media is dependent on advertisers. Accordingly, the Gone Fishin' Portfolio is designed for skeptical investors seeking objectivity—the unvarnished truth—about their investments.
4. Don't depend on Uncle Sam for all your retirement income. The federal government has said that the current Social Security system is unsustainable in the long run.
5. Americans are living longer than ever. To live well in retirement, you need your portfolio to last as long as possible, too. That's the objective of the Gone Fishin' Portfolio.

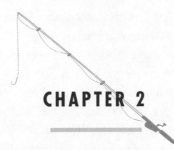

CHAPTER 2

The First Step on the Road to Financial Freedom

My problem lies with reconciling my gross habits with my net income.

Source: Errol Flynn

Before we explore the Gone Fishin' strategy, let's acknowledge a fundamental truth. There can be no investment without saving. I'm not talking about saving in terms of setting aside money for short-term goals like a new car or a down payment on a house. By saving, I mean giving up immediate spending in exchange for future income.

Saving for your future means setting aside enough money each month to reach your financial goals. Yes, it's partly about planning. But it's mostly about having the discipline to follow through.

According to a recent Federal Reserve report on the economic well-being of U.S. households, just 36% of nonretired adults believe their retirement saving is on track. A quarter of adults have no retirement savings or pension at all.

A few years ago, a survey by Bankrate.com found that 68% of adults avoid news about the cost of retirement. Why do so many Americans have their heads in the sand? There are various reasons. Some see their parents living fairly well on Social Security and pensions. Others simply lack the discipline to save. In a Fidelity survey, only about a quarter of respondents said they would make a lifestyle change now to save for later.

These folks might want to go back and read Aesop's fable about the ant and the grasshopper. As I stated in the previous chapter, Americans are living longer than ever thanks to healthier lifestyles and modern medicine.

If you're likely to live longer, you need a hardworking investment portfolio (one that can duck into a phone booth and come out with a red cape unfurled). But to truly maximize the size of that portfolio, you'll need to save as much as you reasonably can, as soon as you can, for as long as you can.

Most people know this, of course. They just have trouble doing it.

However, more Americans are saving and investing than the press might lead you to believe. Never at a loss for a sensational story, the national media creates the impression that Americans are spending everything, swimming in debt and saving nothing.

In truth, the personal savings rate in the United States in 2019 was 7.6%, according to Statista, a leading provider of market and consumer data. In June 2020, during the depths of the COVID-19 pandemic, it spiked to 19%.

These figures deal only with personal savings made after taxes. Most working Americans, however, sock away a portion of their paycheck each month in a 401(k). It comes out of their checks pre-tax, not after tax. So the federal government doesn't count that as savings.

If you and your spouse both work, you could be putting as much as $39,000 between you in a qualified retirement plan each year (plus another $13,000 if you're both over 50). Your employer may be providing thousands of dollars in matching funds, too. Yet, according to official government statistics, you've "saved" nothing.

When you get your paycheck, you probably make a mortgage payment. Part of that money goes to pay down the principal, which builds equity. (You may even pay off a little extra from time to time.) But Uncle Sam treats money you put into a mortgage as consumption. So, once again, none of this is "savings" according to official statistics.

If you're contributing to an IRA or 401(k), you're on the right path. If you can save 10% or more of your after-tax income, too, that's even better.

Of course, some Americans aren't funding a 401(k) or doing any other saving. Some don't own homes and, of those who do, many aren't paying down their mortgages. Rather, they've been borrowing against their equity, adding debt.

However, these folks don't represent the national trend. According to the Federal Reserve, U.S. households' 2019 total net worth—the total value of all assets, including stocks, bonds, bank accounts, houses and retirement funds, after subtracting debt— was over $100 trillion. That's $17.7 trillion higher than it was four years ago. And it's more than 12 times what total net worth was in the United States in 1980. Total American wealth is clearly rising, not falling.

But to join that group whose net worth is rising the fastest, you probably need to save more.

SOMETIMES LESS IS MORE

In *The Millionaire Next Door*, Thomas Stanley and William Danko reported that most Americans with a net worth of a million dollars or more follow a remarkably similar path. They maximize their earned income, minimize their expenses, live beneath their means and religiously save the difference. It may sound pedestrian, but do this long enough and one day you just may wake up with a seven-figure net worth.

It means making sacrifices, however. As we go through life, we quickly learn that expenses seem to rise to meet the income available. In our wonderful capitalistic society, there is never a shortage of fabulous products and services vying for our attention.

However, it *is* possible to say no.

Several years ago, I was invited to do a segment about saving and investing on Fox TV in Tampa, Florida. Near the end, the interviewer suddenly popped this question: "What do you say to those viewers out there who say they just can't save *anything*?"

As it happened, I had just returned from a two-week investment expedition to China. During my trip, I had visited with many laborers who made less than $150 a month. Yet the average Chinese worker—acutely aware that the government provides no social safety net—saves over 47% of his income. (I'm not suggesting for a moment that an American could live on anything close to this. But it was a powerful lesson in fiscal discipline nonetheless.)

"Too many Americans don't save anything," I reminded the moderator, half-jokingly, "because they're spending money they don't have on things they don't need to impress people they don't like." Judging by the look on his face, that wasn't the answer he was expecting.

Look, I realize that when you're young and starting out in life, saving may not be a priority. When you get older and you have kids (and perhaps elderly parents) to support, saving can be tough, too.

But most of us could get by—by hook or by crook—on at least 10% less than what we're living on today. If we pay ourselves that 10% (or more) first, it will make a world of difference 10, 20 or 30 years down the road.

Of course, it's not hard times that keep most Americans from saving what they should. It's a lack of discipline, something at which I used to excel.

As a young man in my 20s, I worked as a stockbroker in a local firm. I soon began earning a six-figure income. Not long after, I bought a spanking-new lakefront house, got the ski boat, the Jaguar XJ6 and all the other toys. I saved virtually nothing.

When my friends came over for parties—which were frequent—most of them assumed I was rich. I was nothing of the sort. Wealth is not the same thing as income. If you earn a lot of money and blow it every year, you're not rich. You're just living high. Wealth is what you accumulate, not what you earn. And it certainly can't be measured by what you spend.

Fortunately, because I was working in the financial services industry, I learned the importance of saving before it was too late. Take a look at Table 2.1, for example. It demonstrates the enormous advantage of beginning to save early. No matter what your age, it's never too late to begin.

TABLE 2.1 Effects of Saving $500 a Month at a 10% Annual Return

Year	Savings
1	$6,335.14
5	$39,041.19
10	$103,276.01
20	$382,848.45
30	$1,139,662.66

As Stanley and Danko wrote in *The Millionaire Next Door* . . .

Affluent people typically follow a lifestyle conducive to accumulating money. In the course of our investigations, we discovered seven common denominators among those who successfully build wealth.

1. They live well below their means.
2. They allocate their time, energy, and money efficiently, in ways conducive to building wealth.
3. They believe that financial independence is more important than displaying high social status.
4. Their parents did not provide economic outpatient care.
5. Their adult children are economically self-sufficient.
6. They are proficient in targeting market opportunities.
7. They chose the right occupation.

In short, they discovered that your net worth is essentially a result of the choices you make. To save as much as you can, you need to make the right career decisions, the right lifestyle decisions and the right spending decisions. It takes forethought. It takes discipline. And it means making hard choices.

If this sounds old-fashioned, so be it. Most of us are not talented enough to found and run some fabulous new technology company. Your income alone is not likely to make you rich. So the quickest way to jump-start your investment program is to start saving more.

A MATTER OF HOW WE VALUE THINGS

You do need balance in your, life too. You can't be happy—now or in retirement—living like a miser. The trick is to find the right balance between saving and spending. Each day there are choices you can make that will help you—or hinder you—on your way to financial independence.

If you keep in mind the choice between consumption and freedom, it becomes easier. Do you really need that new car—or would you rather keep the old one and become free to live where you want, with whom you want, doing what you want? Do you really need that new set of golf clubs—or would you rather keep your old ones and live where you want, with whom you want, doing what you want?

Ultimately, the choices are this stark. Because it doesn't matter how high the returns are on your investments if you haven't saved enough. Or, worse, if you're trying to dig yourself out from under a mountain of debt.

If you're looking for a bit of inspiration, consider Billy and Akaisha Kaderli. Years ago, they were profiled on both Kiplinger.com and Bankrate.com. The Kaderlis live in an active adult community in Mesa, Arizona, even though they didn't meet the community's minimum age requirements when they first moved there. The couple ditched the rat race when they were 38 years old and have already spent more than three decades in retirement.

When they first retired, the Kaderlis sold their home and simply explored the world, traveling between Venezuela, Mexico, Thailand and the Caribbean island of Nevis.

Most folks would say they are living the dream, playing golf, traveling the world and socializing with friends whenever they want. How did they do it? Not by striking it rich, but by being frugal.

They are an example of what some call "extreme early retirement." In their late 30s, Billy and Akaisha decided they were working too much, enjoying it too little and paying too much in taxes. Most of us would simply shrug and say, "That's life."

However, the Kaderlis decided financial freedom was a lot more important than accumulating more stuff. According to Akaisha, "Every time I looked at a latte or a new pair of shoes, I decided I didn't need them. If you're clear about what you want, it becomes easier. You can either buy this or be days closer to your goal."

Contrast this point of view with the materialistic mindset of many Americans, who often find themselves stuck on what psychologists call "the hedonic treadmill." Instead of thinking about financial freedom, they're obsessed with thoughts of a bigger house, a fancier car, the best new restaurants and, of course, the latest ultra-high-definition TV.

I won't argue that these things aren't desirable. And, who knows, a bigger house may be a great investment (although not if you pull the equity out and spend it). But if you want to enjoy extreme early retirement, the key is to earn as much as you can, spend more frugally, and religiously save and invest the difference.

The Kaderlis have set up a website (RetireEarlyLifestyle.com) to share their wisdom and experience. They list five sensible steps to early retirement:

1. **Track spending.** Take a close look at your spending on a daily basis. Once you start doing so, you'll be amazed at what you're spending your money on. It only takes a few minutes a day once you set up your system. After a month or two, you'll discover where you can reduce your expenses. Within a year, you'll be in control of future spending.

2. **Save a lot.** Once you have control of your spending, save that extra money for your future. If you're younger than 30 years old, a good target is to save 10% of your gross income—not your take-home pay, but the full amount of your salary before taxes and other deductions. After a short time, you won't miss the difference, but your savings will grow substantially. If you're over 30, increase your savings rate to 15% or more if possible. Take full advantage of employer-sponsored plans like 401(k)s, matching contributions and any other retirement benefits you receive—but don't include them in your savings percentages. That should be on top of what you're already saving on your own.

3. **Invest wisely.** Learn about investments, become your own expert, and keep things simple. You don't need to impress your friends with financial terms just so you can look knowledgeable . . .

4. **Put peer pressure into perspective.** Social pressure to spend can be subtle and pervasive, and it can divert you from your commitment to retire early. Marketing specialists

tell you that if you only buy this new product, car, house or membership, your lifestyle will improve. It's reasonably easy to tune out that marketing message, but you have to handle your friends with a little more tact. Trying to match the spending of your peer group is a surefire way to derail financial goals. Decide now that you don't have to keep up with their consumption to fit into the crowd. The choice is yours—not theirs.

5. **Keep your eye on the prize.** Set realistic goals and keep to your plan. The amount you save, how you invest, and when you plan to retire may differ from your colleagues and others. No one will be as dedicated or determined as you are to reach your objectives. Put these goals somewhere where you'll see them often, to remind you to keep on course. Every time you get sidetracked by spending a little bit more, succumbing to peer pressure or choosing not to put extra money into your retirement funds, you're literally delaying your retirement date by weeks, months, or perhaps even years. Stay focused.

This is good, commonsense advice. And unlike the performance of the stock market, saving is something that is under your control. It's guaranteed to have a significant impact on the long-term value of your portfolio. And—trust me—it's a whole lot safer than attempting something heroic with your investments.

In short, a successful investment program begins with disciplined saving. Regular saving remains the safest, easiest and most effective way to boost your portfolio. True, it means making hard choices. But, ultimately, you are the person responsible for your financial well-being.

Rare is the individual who stumbles on financial freedom accidentally. Unless you've got a rich relative with a bad heart—and a soft spot for you—whether you end up a slave to money or its master will depend mostly on you and the choices you make.

REEL IT IN . . .

1. There can be no successful investment program without saving. And significant saving requires fiscal discipline.
2. A high percentage of American workers are not adequately saving, which impacts their likelihood of a sound retirement.
3. Participating in a 401(k) or IRA program is a great route to savings. But you should also save at least 10% of your after-tax income.
4. Most high-net-worth individuals did not strike it rich, but, rather, had the discipline to live beneath their incomes and save the difference between their net income and expenses.
5. Finding that perfect balance between saving and spending is key to living happily now and in retirement.
6. Saving generally means prioritizing financial freedom over high living.

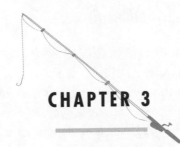

CHAPTER 3

Change Your Mindset, Change Your Life

The exceptional person has a vision—of great performances, of a great career, of a great something—and doesn't care what others may say or think.

Source: Bob Rotella, Bob Cullen, "How Champions Think: In Sports and in Life", Simon and Schuster, 2016.
© 2016, Simon and Schuster

During my 35-year career as an investment analyst, I've sought to discover how ordinary people in this country become wealthy, distill this knowledge to its essence and share it with others.

I'm now convinced that to reach your most important investment goals it's essential to develop what I call a "prosperity mindset." This is an investor's most critical asset.

Your mindset is the filter through which you see the world. It determines how you spend your time, what decisions you make and how you invest your money.

What is a prosperity mindset for investors? In my view, it rests on this foundation:

1. You understand the habits and choices that allowed tens of millions of ordinary Americans to become wealthy.
2. You recognize the major trends—historical, political, cultural, technological and financial—that are making things better for most people in most places in most ways.
3. Based on these trends, you maintain a rational optimism about the future, especially when the nation or the world experiences short-term setbacks, as we always do from time to time.
4. You have a coherent plan that gives you a high probability of achieving your most important financial goals.
5. And you are committed to following through to achieve those goals.

Let's start with understanding how most wealthy Americans got that way.

According to *The New York Times*, there were 18.6 million millionaires in the United States in 2019.

Spectrem Group reports that there were also more mass affluent households with a net worth between $100,000 and $1 million, excluding primary residences: 31.8 million, or nearly 1 in 4 households.

Yet a Federal Reserve survey that same year found that nearly 80% of Americans live paycheck to paycheck. Half say they would have trouble finding $400 to pay for an emergency.

This is a dramatic disparity, and it has hardly gone unnoticed. People tend to measure their well-being not according to their own material comfort against, say, their parents', but against their peers.

As a result, economic inequality has become an obsession in recent years. President Barack Obama called it "the defining challenge of our time." Pope Francis called it "the root of social evil."

Conventional wisdom holds that the richest Americans are hoarding the nation's wealth while everyone else stagnates or loses ground. This isn't just untrue. It's laughably wrong. Yet most people don't understand why.

Average U.S. household income and net worth hit all-time records in 2019. Things took a dip during the pandemic, but there have never been more households making over $100,000 a year. There has never been a smaller percentage of households earning less than $35,000 in inflation-adjusted terms. It's objectively untrue that the rich are getting richer and the poor are getting poorer. Every quintile has been moving up, not just over the last few years, but for decades.

Yes, the affluent have been getting richer faster than everyone else. But that's not terribly surprising in a knowledge-based economy, where education and specialized skills are in high demand.

However, economic inequality in itself is not morally objectionable. What is objectionable is *poverty*. Our goal should not be that everyone has the same. It should be that everyone has *enough*.

This confusion of poverty and inequality is due to what psychologists call the "zero-sum fallacy." This is the mistaken notion that wealth is a finite resource—like a pizza—that is divvied up in zero-sum fashion. So if Oprah Winfrey has more money, I necessarily have less.

That's not how the economy works. Wealth isn't just distributed. First it has to be created. Total wealth increases—and occasionally decreases—over time. The size of the economy, the amount of household income and total household net worth rise as the years go by.

A CAN-DO ATTITUDE

If you're a worker who would like to increase your pay, it's important to know that earned income is generally decided by nine factors:

1. Your educational attainment
2. Your chosen profession and specialization
3. Your years of experience
4. Your hours worked
5. Your work ethic
6. Your social skills

7. Your competence and proficiency in your job
8. Your ability to cooperate with, inspire and lead your co-workers
9. Your ambition to rise in the organization.

If you want to earn more, the choice is clear: Make yourself indispensable to someone.

Yes, some people are born with greater genetic gifts than others. You and I, unfortunately, were not born with the looks of Brad Pitt, the athleticism of LeBron James or the intellect of Isaac Newton.

Some of us are dealt better hands than others. Some are born with higher IQs or into high-income households (with all the advantages they confer) or to more nurturing parents. But we each need to play the hand we're dealt to the best of our ability.

From an economic standpoint, that means maximizing your education and marketable skills; showing competence, reliability and integrity at work; and doing whatever you can to rise in the organization. (Or seek out better alternatives elsewhere.)

Complaining that "capitalism is broken," "the system is rigged" and "life isn't fair" will not increase your income or net worth one penny. It is, however, guaranteed to make you bitter and unhappy.

Beyond income inequality, there is another form of economic disparity in this country. Some households have a much higher net worth than others. There is a significant wealth gap.

Is this unfair? Not necessarily. In my many decades as a money manager, investment analyst and financial writer, I've learned that wealth accumulation is based on six primary factors:

1. Your ability to maximize your income
2. Your propensity to save
3. Your appetite for risk
4. Your willingness and ability to let your money compound
5. The investment costs you absorb
6. The taxes you pay.

These factors are under your control. (Even the last one to a great extent, as I'll discuss in Chapter 13.)

Investment success is mainly about knowledge and personal accountability. It is only when we accept full responsibility for our choices and our actions that we take the giant step from childhood to adulthood.

Yet many choose to embrace the psychology of helplessness and victimhood, preferring to explain all their struggles in terms of the actions of others.

We often meet middle-aged men and women who are still grumbling about earlier unhappy experiences, who are still blaming their problems on other people or "the breaks." They are angry with their parents, fuming at an old boss, still simmering over their ex-spouse. They are upset about the injustice of it.

And you know what? They're right. Life isn't fair. There is no perfect justice. But fear, self-pity, envy, jealousy and anger hold us back, tie us down and suck the joy out of life.

Management consultant Brian Tracy points out that there is a simple antidote to the factors that create these negative emotions. You need only say three words: I am responsible.

Whether your problem is joblessness, addiction, overspending, obesity or poor finances, you move closer to a solution the moment you say "I am responsible."

It is impossible to say these words and still feel angry. The very act of taking responsibility short-circuits and cancels out negative emotions.

Yet many would rather train for the Boston Marathon in 3 feet of snow than utter these words. Why? Psychologists say human beings have a natural propensity to accumulate pride and shun regret. In other words, we tend to take responsibility for the positive developments in our lives and attribute unfavorable developments to others or circumstances.

This is not to say there aren't times when our lives are significantly influenced by outside forces. Maybe you are a great worker who lost your job due to corporate downsizing. Maybe your parents really were poor role models. But it is only when you choose to focus on what you can do and how you should act that you gain power.

Today, businesses and other organizations are looking for people who are willing and able to think, who are self-directing and self-managing, who respond to problems proactively rather than merely waiting for someone else's solutions.

A study done in New York a few years ago found that people who ranked in the top 3% in every field had a special attitude that set them apart from average performers in their industries. What was it? They chose to view themselves as self-employed throughout their careers, no matter who signed their paychecks.

These are people who set goals, make plans, measure progress and get results. Personal responsibility changes everything. It means you own your thoughts, impulses, feelings and actions. *You* are accountable for the consequences they bring and the impact they have on others.

This is not a burden, incidentally. It's a privilege and an honor to take ownership of your actions. It creates freedom and control. It gives meaning to life. Self-reliance is *the* great source of personal power. We create ourselves, shape our identities and determine the course of our lives by what we are willing to take responsibility for.

THE RIGHT MINDSET

If you want to do something about economic inequality in this country—especially as it relates to your own financial circumstances, the important thing is your mindset. How you handle your time, choices and money matters.

Too many people in today's society have little understanding of how wealth is created—how more than 11 million American households generated a seven-figure net worth.

These people optimized their education and marketable skills, maximized their incomes, lived within their means, saved regularly, invested smartly and let their money compound over a long period of time, generally decades.

Most of us work, of course, but many who could save *don't*.

Those who are physically or mentally disabled and cannot work deserve our sympathy and compassion. I support social welfare programs for the truly needy. But that cannot possibly describe most of us when the U.S. median household income was $68,703 in 2019.

Let's imagine that you and I are two hypothetical families earning exactly this median income—and watch how quickly our choices and habits change our economic circumstances.

I'm a spendthrift. I blow every dollar I make each year. You, on the other hand, are a little bit more prudent. You spend almost everything you make, but regularly save 4% of your monthly income—$229 a month—through a Roth IRA.

Let's further stipulate that you invest that money in a plain-vanilla S&P 500 index fund that generates nothing more or less than its average long-term return of 10%.

After the first decade, with dividends reinvested, you have $47,300. I have zero. As you can see, things are already unequal. In 20 years, you have $175,345. (Finding $400 for an emergency is not a problem.) I have nothing. In 30 years, you have $521,966. I still have *nada*. And in less than 38 years, your $229 a month has turned into more than a million dollars.

Plus, it's tax-free. (Let's recall that you were smart enough to invest in a Roth IRA where distributions are tax-exempt.)

Some readers may not have 30 or 40 years to save and invest, of course. In that case, they need to save more or earn a higher rate of return . . . or both.

Say, for example, rather than 4%, you saved 10% of that median income each month—or $572—and invested in the higher-returning Russell 2000 index of small cap stocks, which has returned 12% annually. You would have $132,898 in 10 years and more than a half-million dollars in 20 years. You would be a millionaire in less than 25 years.

Amp up the savings or the returns and you'll be there quicker still. In short, it's your behavior rather than luck, fortune or "the breaks" that ultimately determines your financial well-being.

This is how millions of ordinary Americans became millionaires. They weren't just lucky. They didn't inherit it. They had a plan. They stuck to it. And they reaped the rewards.

With time and discipline, you can, too. But first you need to understand how major trends underway are creating incredible progress for most of us.

REEL IT IN . . .

1. Successful investors develop a prosperity mindset.
2. The right habits and choices have allowed tens of millions of ordinary Americans to become wealthy.
3. There are major trends—historical, political, cultural, technological and financial—that are making things better for most people in most places in most ways.
4. Successful investors maintain a rational optimism about the future, especially when the nation or the world experiences short-term setbacks, as we always will from time to time.
5. A coherent plan—and commitment to that plan—gives investors a high probability of achieving their most important financial goals.

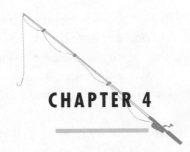

CHAPTER 4

Why Some Investors Succeed . . . But Most Don't

Success is only a matter of luck. Ask any failure.

Source: Earl Wilson

Have you ever wondered why some investors have tremendous success with their portfolios, meeting or exceeding their financial goals, while most struggle, earning low returns or actually losing money over the years?

You shouldn't.

Investing is essentially the transfer of wealth to those who have a process and can execute it from those who do not or cannot. Investors fail because they either aren't using a proven strategy or can't adhere to it.

There is more than just anecdotal evidence to support this.

Since 1984, analysts at the independent investment research firm Dalbar Inc. have published an annual Quantitative Analysis of

Investment Behavior report. The study examines investor performance in mutual funds. The findings are not salutary.

The study reveals that in the 20 years through December 31, 2019, the average mutual fund investor earned 4.25% annually versus more than 6.02% in an S&P 500 index fund and 8.03% in a global equity index.

That's a bigger difference than it may seem at first blush. The average investor turned a $100,000 mutual fund portfolio into $229,891. Over the same period, that sum would have turned into $321,926 in an S&P 500 index fund and $468,692 in a global index fund. The latter figure, of course, is more than twice as much—and would have required zero time and attention for 20 years. (And, incidentally, those were two decades when stocks performed poorly by long-term standards.)

The 2020 Dalbar study confirmed the conclusion it reached in previous years: Investment results are more dependent on investor behavior than on fund performance.

In short, most people are their own worst enemies when it comes to investing. They succumb to market timing, performance chasing and panic selling, thereby lowering—if not decimating—their returns.

To avoid this, you need a process, a coherent plan. Let me explain . . .

An investment recommendation is meaningless if it's divorced from a battle-tested strategy. (You should know exactly what you're doing and why.) That strategy in turn should be based on a proven investment philosophy. And that philosophy should reflect a particular sensibility, a way of seeing the world.

If this seems a bit complicated, it really isn't. Let me walk you through how it applies to the Gone Fishin' Portfolio.

As you'll soon see, the portfolio itself consists of 10 funds. Those recommendations are based on a strategy of asset allocation and annual rebalancing. That strategy in turn is undergirded by an investment philosophy common to sophisticated investors everywhere.

It's this: No one can tell you with any certainty what the economy or the stock market will do from week to week, month to month or year to year. People who say they do know are either fooling you or kidding themselves—or both. I am a militant agnostic when it comes to the future performance of the economy and markets. (I don't know and you don't, either.) This means we can avoid economic forecasters, market timers and the Psychic Network.

This philosophy is further underpinned by an optimistic, real-world sensibility—one that polls show is *not* shared by 94% of the American public. What is it? An acknowledgment that the world is getting better in most ways for most people in most places, thanks to the triumph of reason, science, democracy, innovation and capital markets.

Why do only 6% of Americans agree with that sensibility, the view that life is getting better for most of us? Because it runs totally against the mainstream media's metanarrative.

AN EMBARRASSMENT OF RICHES

Turn on the news and you'll hear stories of crime, war, terrorism, disease, natural disasters, corruption, domestic violence, poverty, economic inequality, nuclear proliferation, environmental degradation and political dysfunction.

Polls show Americans believe the American dream is fading, our children face limited opportunities and the country—if not civilization itself—is decidedly on the wrong track.

This is not just due to the health and economic crisis created by the coronavirus pandemic. Americans have been feeling this way for more than three decades.

Yet this dour perspective—one recycled 24/7 on cable news—is a gross distortion of the world we live in. For years I have tried to counter this depiction, to tell what radio broadcaster Paul Harvey used to call "the rest of the story."

I can already hear some readers objecting, insisting that the problems I just described here are quite real. And, of course, they are real. They're just given out of context and without a broader perspective.

Here's an analogy.

Imagine that I showed a roomful of high school students a five-minute video I've put together of a former basketball player. In clip after clip, he throws air balls, blows layups, misses rebounds, drops passes, clanks free throws, double dribbles and steps out of bounds.

When the film is over, I tell my young audience, "That player's name is Michael Jordan. What do you think of him?"

No doubt most would say, "He's terrible." The rest of us—especially those of us who had the thrill of watching Jordan play night after night—would strenuously object.

Not because the Chicago Bulls All-Star never shot air balls or clanked free throws. (As a longtime NBA fan and season-ticket holder, I saw him do both many times.) But because the video—though made up of actual events—was a gross distortion of the man's abilities and career. In short, I used real events to create a misleading impression.

The national media does the same thing, delivering the world each day through a dark prism of negativity. It's like Chinese water torture. Drip . . . drip . . . drip . . . drip . . . drip.

Yes, we live in a world with crime, war, poverty and other serious problems. Yet the news media makes no attempt to paint a faithful depiction of the progress we enjoy in most areas.

For example, war between nation-states, civil wars, terrorist incidents, violent crime, domestic violence, child abuse and even abortions are all down. (There hasn't been a war between the world's major powers since 1945.)

We in the West work shorter hours, have more purchasing power, enjoy goods and services in almost limitless supply, and have more leisure time than ever before.

The human life span has nearly doubled over the past hundred years. Living standards are the highest they have ever been. Literacy and education levels—even IQs—are at all-time highs. Technology and medicine are revolutionizing and saving our lives. All forms of pollution—with the exception of greenhouse gases—are in decline.

The pandemic was a significant step back in many ways. But by almost every standard, our lives today are wealthy beyond measure. We are cultural heirs to *an embarrassment of riches*. Yet, thanks in large part to continual, downbeat news coverage, most of us don't realize it. The average American is like an unwitting lottery winner whose ticket is lost in some upstairs drawer.

The consequences of adopting the popular but cynical world-view are many, including depressed mood, a shortened life span and, not incidentally, missed investment opportunities.

For two decades, I've tried to counter the media's narrative. And a few years ago, I gained a powerful ally: Steven Pinker. Pinker is a Harvard psychologist, bestselling author and one of the world's most influential thinkers, according to *Time* magazine.

His book *Enlightenment Now: The Case for Reason, Science, Humanism, and Progress* is a tour de force. Using objective data, evidence and reason—not to mention 75 mind-blowing graphs— he demolishes the pessimistic attitude that pervades today's public discourse by revealing how our lives are becoming, not worse as many feel, but longer, safer, freer, less violent and more prosperous.

Not just here but—with the exception of a few unfortunate spots around the globe—all over the world. The number and variety of ways the world is getting better should astonish you.

Despite the latest "crisis" in the news, our nation and the world are in far better shape than most folks realize. Multiple data points—from human life spans to living standards to incidents of war and violent crime—reveal that long-term trends in human health and welfare are strongly positive.

Seeing the true picture sharpens your perspective. It develops your prosperity mindset. And it makes you a more success-ful investor.

THE CASE FOR CAPITALISM

Capitalism is the greatest wealth creator—and antipoverty program—ever devised. It enabled the industrialization and inno-vation that has slashed poverty, fed billions, emancipated women, educated children and created widespread prosperity.

We count on corporations—large and small—to supply us with most of our wants and needs: the cars we drive, the planes we travel in, the clothes we wear, the homes we live in, the medicines that heal us, and the computers and smartphones that make our lives so much easier and more productive.

Investing in these companies not only fuels innovation and efficiency, it allows us to reach our financial goals. Yet I regularly talk to men and women who have nothing invested in stocks, often because of profound (and unjustified) anti-business attitudes.

Many can hardly utter the phrase *corporate profits* without a bit of spittle flying. Detractors, of course, argue that capitalism is all about selfishness, greed and exploitation. But that is a mischaracterization, as anyone would realize if they took even a moment to think about it.

True, men and women everywhere are self-interested. But businesspeople don't get rich by thinking about themselves. They get rich by thinking about other people, what those people want, and how they can deliver it better, faster or cheaper.

The beauty of capitalism is that you can have whatever you want if you just provide enough *other people* with what they want. You help yourself by helping others.

How about greed? I suppose for some folks there is no such thing as *enough*. That's unfortunate for them, since they'll spend their lives on a hamster wheel, always chasing more.

But here's a reality check: You can be the greediest businessperson in the world, but no one is going to give you a dime until you provide them with a product or service they want to buy.

Every free-market transaction is voluntary. If you don't want to work for a company, buy from a company, sell to a company or own its shares, you don't have to. Where is the exploitation in that?

Our economic system is about voluntary exchange for mutual benefit. That's why you hear "Thank you" twice whenever you make a store purchase. You say thanks because you want the merchandise more than the money. The retailer says thanks because he or she wants the money more than the merchandise.

Capitalism is not a zero-sum game—like checkers—where one side wins only when the other side loses. It's a win-win.

And there are strong incentives for companies to behave ethically. For starters, reputation is paramount.

Businesses focused solely on short-term profits don't last long. If they cut corners on quality, their customers leave. If they bargain with suppliers too hard, the suppliers won't sell to them. If they undervalue key employees, the employees will take their talents elsewhere. It is in the best interests of business owners to make sure all stakeholders—employees, suppliers, customers and communities—are satisfied.

Businesses are run by fallible human beings, of course. Sometimes they make mistakes, breach contracts, use poor judgment, harm individuals or damage the environment. When they do, they should be punished for their transgressions. But that doesn't make capitalism *wrong* any more than democracy is wrong when a congressman is found to have stacks of hundred-dollar bills in his refrigerator.

Most uber-wealthy Americans achieved their affluence not by inheritance or real estate speculation but by starting and managing profitable businesses. Most of us, of course, don't have the time, the investment capital or the experience necessary to found and run a successful business, but we can still own a piece of one through the quintessential expression of capitalism: the stock market.

With even a modest amount of money, an individual can accumulate a stake in many of the world's great businesses. And it's easy. A click of the mouse and you're in. Another click and you're out. (Compare *that* with your typical real estate closing.)

And owning a piece of a company is a whole lot simpler than running one. You don't have to sign personal guarantees, hire or fire employees, grapple with an avalanche of federal mandates and regulations, pay lawyers and accountants, or even show up for work. How great is that?

Some Americans today obsess over the issue of fairness. But the stock market shines here, too. If I own Amazon, for example, my gain over the next year will be exactly the same as the gain of the world's richest man, Jeff Bezos. Sure, he may own a few more shares than I do, but our percentage returns will be the same.

Some people worry about the environmental impact of capitalism. But there is good news on this front, too.

In recent years, seaborne oil transport has become immensely safer. (The annual number of oil spills is down from over 100 in 1973 to five in 2016.) And this is true even though vastly more oil is shipped today.

Thanks to habitat protection and conservation efforts, many species—including eagles, manatees, condors, pandas, rhinos and tigers—have been pulled back from the brink of extinction. (Some species remain in a precarious state, but, according to ecologist Stuart Pimm, the overall rate of extinctions has been reduced by 75%.)

Thanks to gains in efficiency and emission control, the modern world is also *decarbonizing*. Western countries have learned how to get the most energy with the least emission of greenhouse gases. As we climbed the energy ladder from wood to coal to oil to gas, the ratio of carbon to hydrogen in our energy sources fell steadily.

As a result, fewer cities are now shrouded in a smoggy haze. Urban waterways that had been left for dead—Puget Sound, Chesapeake Bay, Boston Harbor, Lake Erie and many others—have been recolonized by birds, fish, marine mammals and intrepid swimmers.

For decades, ecologists told us that environmental protection requires smaller populations, slower economic growth and lower living standards. It turns out that just the opposite is true. The wealthiest countries have the cleanest environments. And as the poor ones get wealthier, they get cleaner, too.

Once you see and understand the largely overlooked and unreported progress that goes on all around us every day, it inspires confidence in the future. That's key.

LOOKING ON THE BRIGHT SIDE

The greatest investors of the past century—men like Warren Buffett, Peter Lynch and John Templeton—didn't just maintain a positive long-term outlook. They maintained an optimism about the future that simply didn't have an off switch.

Some will insist that I'm viewing the world through rose-tinted glasses. Not true. I'm saying that most things are getting better for most people in most ways. I'm most definitely *not* saying that everything is getting better for everyone in every way.

(That wouldn't be progress. That would be fantasy.)

Some aspects of life are certainly getting worse. Tropical rainforests, the national debt and popular music spring immediately to mind. And even as the world progresses, some people are dealing with unfortunate breaks or tragic circumstances. And that's in addition to the work issues, health problems, relationship frictions and financial setbacks that we all deal with from time to time.

Of course, it's easy to be optimistic when the economy is strong, inflation is low, the country is at peace, corporate profits are up and stocks are trending skyward. The real challenge arises when the opposite occurs, which is often the case.

Here is a quick review of just a few of the hurdles investors have faced since I started in the money management business in 1985:

- On October 19, 1987, the stock market crashed. It was global, sudden, severe and entirely unexpected. Yes, program trading played a role, but analysts still argue about what caused it. After all, no politician was assassinated that day. No government failed. No currency collapsed. Yet the Dow finished the day down 22.6%. Many clients at the time told me it was the start of the "Greater Depression."

- In August 1990, Iraqi President Saddam Hussein decided he would like to own Kuwait and its tremendous oil wealth. As the tanks rolled into the country, energy prices spiked and U.S. stocks entered a bear market. It was the beginning of the first Gulf War.

- In March 2000, the bubble in internet and technology shares popped, sending the S&P 500 down 49% over the next 2½ years and the technology-heavy Nasdaq down 77% over the same period.

- On September 11, 2001, a group of religious zealots hijacked four commercial aircraft and crashed them into the World Trade Center, the Pentagon and a field near Shanksville, Pennsylvania. It was the beginning of the Afghan War, the Iraq War and the broad-based War on Terror, also known as the Forever War.

- In 2008, the housing bubble popped, leading to the collapse of Bear Stearns and Shearson Lehman. This kicked off the Great Recession. By March 2009, the stock market had lost more than half its value, unemployment peaked at 10% and household net worth took a 45% haircut. Many homeowners—especially those who hadn't made down payments on their purchases—mailed their keys to their banks. There were more than 200 bank failures.

- That same year, in response to the loss of business and consumer confidence, the Federal Reserve took interest rates to zero and embarked on ambitious large-scale asset purchases known as quantitative easing, eventually inflating its balance sheet by more than $5 trillion.
- In 2010, the Flash Crash took the value of the S&P 500 down 9.6% in less than an hour, as trading algorithms rocked the market, even disconnecting some exchange-traded funds (ETFs) from the value of their holdings.
- In 2011, a sovereign bank crisis roiled Europe. And, for the first time in history, U.S. Treasury debt was *downgraded*. (For the record, it has not been upgraded since.)
- In 2014, the Islamic State group (ISIS) gained global prominence after driving Iraqi government forces out of key cities and capturing a large swath of eastern Syria. At its peak, the world's largest and most powerful terrorist group ruled millions of people, controlled billions of dollars and maintained a force of more than 30,000 fighters.
- Also in 2014, oil and gas prices collapsed as formerly inaccessible deposits became commercially viable due to technological advances like hydraulic fracturing and horizontal drilling.
- In 2016, the United Kingdom—defying the pollsters— voted to leave the European Union. Stocks sold off on the Brexit news.
- As if pollsters didn't already have enough egg on their faces from Brexit, also in 2016, a celebrity real estate magnate— given no realistic chance of winning—captured the White House. Stock futures plunged on the news before recovering.
- In early 2020, the novel coronavirus began to circulate widely. The global pandemic forced a shutdown of most of the world economy, threw millions of people out of work, caused tens of thousands of small businesses to close their doors (many of them for good), was responsible for the biggest economic contraction in history and led to the fastest bear market ever.

In each case, the stock market bounced back—as it has every other time in history—demonstrating the incredible resilience of equities.

Through all of this, however, it took more than just intestinal fortitude to stay invested in stocks. It took a prosperity mindset, an abiding faith in the ability of entrepreneurs, investors, businesspeople and, yes, policymakers to tackle the problems of the present to create a more prosperous tomorrow.

During these crises, optimists didn't sell in a panic, run to cash, or hoard gold and silver. Rather, they patiently and selectively took advantage of some of the greatest buying opportunities of our lifetimes. And reaped the benefits.

DON'T MIND THE MEDIA

Most of the world's leading investors and business leaders understand the importance of a prosperity mindset.

Microsoft founder Bill Gates says,

> By almost any measure, the world is better than it has ever been. People are living longer, healthier lives. . . . You might think that such striking progress would be widely celebrated, but in fact . . . many people think the world is getting worse. [This] isn't just mistaken. It's harmful.

Benjamin Graham, the father of value investing and Warren Buffett's mentor, famously said, "Without a saving faith in the future, no one would ever invest at all. To be an investor, you must be a believer in a better tomorrow."

In a *Barron's* cover story, mutual-fund great Peter Lynch said, "The thesis underlying everything . . . is that the U.S. will be OK. If you don't believe that, you shouldn't be in the stock market."

And in a recent Berkshire Hathaway annual report, Buffett said,

> Many Americans now believe that their children will not live as well as they themselves do. That view is dead wrong: The babies being born in America today are the luckiest crop in history. . . . America's economic magic remains alive and well.

Clearly, the best investors understand that we will always have serious problems but that most things are getting better. Yet the overwhelming majority of us don't realize it.

This lack of understanding causes all sorts of negative consequences, from fear and anxiety to feelings of helplessness and depression. It also causes investors to misconstrue the economic outlook and believe that investment opportunities are far riskier than they really are.

What is the cure for this? A solid grounding in the facts is a good start. An understanding that "the daily news" is sensationalized and negatively biased is also helpful.

But the best piece of advice I can give you is this: Follow the trend lines, not the headlines.

To do this, you need to accept a few basic realities:

- Media stories, anecdotes and headlines are not necessarily accurate, objective or contextual.
- A "fact"—true or false—does not make a trend.
- Just because something isn't perfect today doesn't mean that it was better in the past or won't be improved in the future.
- What some people call problems or crises are often opportunities in disguise.
- Human beings, technology and capital markets operate today as a comprehensive problem-solving machine, improving our lives in almost every way imaginable: faster communications, more powerful computers, safer transportation, lifesaving drugs and medical devices, and so on.
- There is no limit to the betterments we can attain if we apply knowledge, innovation and free markets to enhance human flourishing.

I challenge you to approach everything you read and hear with a deep sense of skepticism—and a few basic questions like these:

- Is this story based on facts . . . or opinions?
- Does it include counterbalancing facts or just handpicked, one-sided ones?
- Has the journalist made a reasonable effort to tell multiple sides of the story?

- And—most importantly—could this narrative be overly pessimistic?

If you're going to invest money that you've earned, paid taxes on and saved instead of spending, you need to feel some sense of optimism about the future.

That's a tall order for people who consume the daily litany of sad, tragic or unfortunate events happening—or that could happen—in politics, economics and business.

Studies show that even highly educated individuals who watch cable news or read national newspapers hold worldviews that are unduly pessimistic.

If you kick yourself because you've been underinvested in a stock market that—with dividends reinvested—has more than quadrupled over the last decade, recognize that your failure to take advantage of these opportunities is due at least in part to saturation news coverage that is not just negative but perversely so.

Don't get me wrong. There will be more bad economies, awful uncertainties and even possible pandemics in the future. The question is, will you maintain a prosperity mindset and take advantage of the opportunities that unfold, or will you fall prey to the prophets of doom?

Heavy media consumption is a detriment to investors. Part of this is just due to the nature of the news, of course. Nobody wants to hear each day about all the buildings that didn't burn, the planes that didn't crash and the surfers who weren't bitten by sharks.

But cable channels highlight a fresh litany of woes each day, with stories ranging from political corruption to natural disasters to forecasts of impending doom. Human beings are hardwired to be on the lookout for threats, so these broadcasts attract eyeballs—and, more to the point, advertisers.

Combat these distorted views by acquainting yourself with the essential facts. You can do that by browsing websites like HumanProgress.org and OurWorldInData.org, or by reading books like *The Prosperity Paradox: How Innovation Can Lift Nations Out of Poverty* by Clayton Christensen; *It's Better Than It Looks: Reasons for Optimism in an Age of Fear* by Gregg Easterbrook; *The Rational Optimist: How Prosperity Evolves* by Matt Ridley; *Factfulness: Ten Reasons We're Wrong About the World—and Why Things Are*

Better Than You Think by Hans Rosling; *Ten Global Trends Every Smart Person Should Know: And Many Others You Will Find Interesting* by Ronald Bailey and Marian Tupy; and, of course, *Enlightenment Now*, which ought to be required reading in every high school in America.

Why am I making such a big deal about media negativity?

Because if we live in a horrible world at a terrible time and the country really is on the wrong track, why risk a dime of your hard-earned money in the stock market?

Some believe that whether the world is getting better is just a matter of opinion, like seeing the glass half-full instead of half-empty.

Not so. As Pinker points out in *Enlightenment Now*, to accept the reality of the world's profound progress . . .

> Requires only the convictions that life is better than death, health is better than sickness, abundance is better than want, freedom is better than coercion, happiness is better than suffering, and knowledge is better than superstition and ignorance.

The data shows that we have enjoyed fantastic improvements in all these areas over time. Denying this is not pessimism. It's ignorance.

REEL IT IN . . .

1. Investing is essentially the transfer of wealth to those who have a process and can execute it from those who do not or cannot.
2. Investors fail because they either aren't using a proven strategy or can't adhere to it.
3. The Gone Fishin' Portfolio is underpinned by a fact-based sensibility—that the world is getting better for most people in most places in most ways, as demonstrated by positive, long-term trends.
4. Due to a mediocre public education system and pervasive media bias, most people have a negative view of the world, and their investment returns suffer as a result.

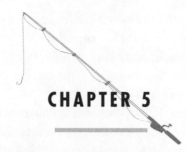

CHAPTER 5

Why Manage Your Own Money?

It is not easy to get rich in Las Vegas, at Churchill Downs, or at the local Merrill Lynch office.

Source: Paul Samuelson, Nobel Laureate

"I was spreading some risk around, and apparently it all wound up in your portfolio."

Cartoon by Leo Cullum. © 2003 The New Yorker Collection.

Many investment books contain a chapter about how to find a qualified investment advisor. This one doesn't.

As I mentioned earlier, no one cares more about your money than you do. You should manage it yourself. By the time you finish this book, you'll be perfectly capable.

I'm not suggesting that investment advisors who are competent and ethical don't exist. They do. I've worked with some of them. As you've already read, I was an investment advisor myself for 16 years. I'd like to believe I was one of the good ones. It's just that most investors don't *need* to pay for the services of a good one, either.

This flies in the face of what Wall Street often tells you, that investing is so complicated that you *require* their services. Or that the higher returns investment professionals can deliver will more than cover the cost of their services. More often than not, this is an empty promise.

You're busy. I get that. You have family and friends, work and hobbies, obligations and responsibilities. But this portfolio takes 20 minutes annually to maintain. I think anyone reading this book can spare that much time each year to reach their most important financial goals.

It's true that many people don't know enough to manage their own money. There is, however, a simple remedy for this. And this book aims to provide it. So don't let some full-service broker give you a low whistle and a shake of the head. Listen to those with a more independent frame of mind.

- Investment commentator Ben Stein writes, "Are you by chance wealthy? A 'high net worth' individual? That special handling everyone is giving you is merely the anesthetic that precedes the surgical removal of your wallet."
- In *What Wall Street Doesn't Want You to Know*, Larry Swedroe says, "Wall Street does not have the best interests of investors at heart. Wall Street wants to keep individual investors in the dark about both the academic evidence on how markets really work and the dismal track record of the vast majority of active managers."
- Bestselling author Michael Lewis wrote in *Portfolio* magazine, "Wall Street, with its army of brokers, analysts, and advisers funneling trillions of dollars into mutual funds, hedge funds, and private equity funds, is an elaborate fraud."

- Author and investment advisor Phil DeMuth writes on his website (PhilDeMuth.com), "Sadly, the high-net-worth individual is often treated as little more than a cow hooked up to Wall Street's milking machine."
- Not to be outdone, William Bernstein writes in *The Four Pillars of Investing: Lessons for Building a Winning Portfolio*, "The stockbroker services his clients in the same way that Bonnie and Clyde serviced banks."

You may find some of these judgments harsh. After all, most brokers and other financial advisors are good people who want to do right by their clients. They realize that a long-term relationship only results from a satisfied client. And, in a perfect world, perhaps both brokers and their customers could be fully satisfied.

Unfortunately, we don't live in a perfect world. There is a fundamental misalignment of interests here. As an investor, you want to earn the highest net returns. Investment advisors have a slightly different agenda. They want you to earn the highest return *net of their fees*. There's an important difference.

Most stockbrokers, for example, are better salespeople than investment advisors. (Or, as a friend at Morgan Stanley likes to say, "It's 97% of investment advisors that give the other 3% of us a bad name.") Virtually everyone on Wall Street—naturally—wants to earn as high an income as possible. Unfortunately, that can only be achieved by converting a significant percentage of client assets into the firm's assets. That's how the business works.

This would be perfectly fair if most investment advisors earned higher returns than you could achieve on your own. Alas, this is hardly the case.

LET THE BUYER BEWARE

As I've traveled around the world speaking at and attending seminars and conferences, I've heard a great deal of resentment from ordinary investors. They were angry at mutual fund companies that successfully marketed five-star performance and the notion that their firm's funds could beat the market over the long haul. They told me they were fed up with investment analysts who privately referred to their "Strong Buy" recommendations as "pigs," "powder kegs" and "pieces of junk."

They felt they had been had by brokers and financial planners whose interest in their own fees and commissions exceeded their interest in their clients' financial welfare. They were tired of insurance agents who tried to sell them more protection than they needed, at prices only the unknowing would pay.

They were angry, too, at corrupt or incompetent corporate chieftains—at companies like Enron, WorldCom, Bear Stearns, Shearson and others—who sold employees and shareholders down the river to satisfy their own lust for power and money.

And they were painfully aware that leading Wall Street firms had paid the biggest fines in SEC history—a total of more than $1.1 billion—for blatantly compromising their retail clients' interests while courting publicly traded companies for investment banking business.

Eventually, investors woke up to the simple fact that many of these folks were nothing more than self-interested parties whose overriding interest was separating them from their money. This is not always true, as I've said. But aside from ethical considerations, there is the question of competence.

You might imagine, for instance, that once a new hire becomes a stockbroker, his firm will teach him everything he needs to know about how to manage his clients' money intelligently. This is emphatically not the case. As Bernstein writes, "It is a sad fact that you can pass the Series 7 exam and begin to manage other people's life savings faster than you can get a manicurist's license in most states."

Plus, Wall Street firms give brokers—even brand-spanking-new ones—a great deal of leeway in determining how to invest their clients' hard-earned savings. Without a lot of personal experience to draw on, this can be a recipe for disaster. Just as a recent college graduate with a business degree is rarely qualified to set up or run his own business, a freshly minted registered representative is not the best-qualified person to manage the nest egg you've spent a lifetime accumulating.

"I lost a fortune in the market today. Yours."

When I worked in the investment industry, I was astonished to find how little some of my colleagues understood about the financial markets. It took me a while to realize this when I started because I often knew even less than they did. Yet these were my mentors. And the first thing I learned—something that sticks with me to this day—is how expensive (and painful) it is to learn Wall Street's lessons the hard way.

My associates were inveterate market timers. That means they had convinced themselves that they knew when to be in the market for the rallies and out for the corrections (and bear markets). Unlike the vast army of brokers on Wall Street, however, who are forever seeing nothing but blue skies ahead, my early colleagues were forever predicting that the stock market was on the verge of collapse.

When I joined the firm in 1985, the Dow Jones Industrial Average had just crossed the 1,400 mark. In hindsight, this was one of the great buying opportunities of the twentieth century. Although there would be many drops along the way—not least of all the crash of 1987, the dot-com collapse, the Great Recession and the coronavirus pandemic—the market had more than three decades of extraordinary performance ahead.

Yet our company chairman, who was also the head of "research," regularly warned us that the U.S. market was wildly overvalued and likely to plunge at any time. We were an international investment firm, and our outlook for Hong Kong, Australia, Switzerland and other foreign markets was, conveniently, more sanguine.

Experience has since taught me that many investors—and investment advisors—are what I call "apocaholics," folks who forever see financial catastrophe and economic collapse ahead. To many of them, this is not just an outlook or worldview, it's a religion, something they take on faith and feel in their bones. They can't be talked out of it and, frankly, why bother?

A TRIO WORTH LISTENING TO

In my early years in the money management business, I came to realize that there were a handful of investors whose investment returns were leaving everyone else on the roadside. These included Peter Lynch, the best-performing mutual fund manager of all time, who was managing the Fidelity Magellan Fund; John Templeton, pioneer of global investing and legendary manager of the Templeton Growth Fund; and Warren Buffett, chairman and CEO of Berkshire Hathaway.

These men didn't need publicity agents. Their audited track records spoke for themselves. As far as I was concerned, the three of them resided on Mount Olympus.

I began reading everything that I could find about them, anxious to learn how they knew exactly when to get into the market and when to get out. I didn't realize that this had absolutely nothing to do with their investment approaches. I was still so naïve at this point that, not only did I not know the answers, I wasn't even asking the right questions.

Fortunately, it wasn't difficult to figure out what these world-beaters were doing. Fidelity Investments was more than happy to send me plenty of information explaining Lynch's investment approach.

The Templeton organization was much the same, only better. It sent me regular updates on the Templeton Growth Fund strategy, as well as tapes of Templeton himself addressing groups of investors on his investment approach.

I remember listening to these tapes in my car over and over again. Once, a fellow broker riding with me, clearly uninterested in hearing Templeton expound on his investment principles, finally asked in frustration, "Hey, man, you got any Jimmy Buffett?"

"I've got some *Warren* Buffett," I answered.

"No," he responded with a sour look. "*Jimmy* Buffett."

"Sorry."

My favorite source of information on Buffett was his annual letter to shareholders. These clear, folksy, easy-to-read letters are chock-full of investment insights. It was hard for me to believe that the master himself was laying out the principles of successful investment for anyone to read. Best of all, it was free. All you had to do was call Berkshire and request an annual report. (Today you can access these reports online at BerkshireHathaway.com in a matter of seconds.)

These are still some of the best and most accessible writings on investing. They formed the foundation of much of what I found useful. And the principles are timeless.

As I studied the investment approaches of these three men, I was surprised to discover that none were market timers. Even though their approaches to buying and selling stocks were very different, they all approached the market with the same general philosophy. And that included a concession that they didn't have the slightest clue whether the market was about to go up or down. Instead, they made their money identifying companies that were trading below their intrinsic worth and selling them when the market recognized that value. (Easier said than done, by the way.)

So even the world's best investors understand you do not gain an edge by trying to time the market. If you remain skeptical on this point, listen to the words of some of the most successful investors of all time:

- Benjamin Graham: "If I have noticed anything over these 60 years on Wall Street, it is that people do not succeed in forecasting what's going to happen to the stock market."
- Buffett: "We've long felt that the only value of stock forecasters is to make fortunetellers look good. Even now, Charlie

[Munger] and I continue to believe that short-term market forecasts are poison and should be kept locked up in a safe place, away from children and also from grown-ups who behave in the market like children."

- Templeton: "I never ask if the market is going to go up or down because I don't know, and besides it doesn't matter."
- Lynch, in his book *One Up on Wall Street: How to Use What You Already Know to Make Money in the Market*: "Thousands of experts study overbought indicators, oversold indicators, head-and-shoulder patterns, put-call ratios, the Fed's policy on money supply, foreign investment, the movement of the constellations through the heavens, and the moss on oak trees, and they can't predict the markets with any useful consistency, any more than the gizzard squeezers could tell the Roman emperors when the Huns would attack."
- Lynch ends the book by telling readers, "The market ought to be irrelevant. If I could convince you of this one thing, I'd feel this book had done its job."

Why doesn't your investment advisor, obviously a smart guy, give up the economic forecasts and market predictions? Vanguard founder John Bogle put it best in *The Little Book of Common Sense Investing: The Only Way to Guarantee Your Fair Share of Stock Market Returns* when he wrote, "It's amazing how difficult it is for a man to understand something if he's paid a small fortune not to understand it."

This message also goes against the instincts—not to mention the hypercharged emotions—of most investors. They want to believe they are smart to move their money around in anticipation of the next big market move. But it boils down to this: You can listen to an investment advisor or stock market guru who has a service or system to sell. Or you can listen to the greatest investors of all time. The choice is yours.

Your broker or investment advisor is probably expensive. And you may imagine you're getting what you pay for. After all, this line of thinking is true in most aspects of life. You want to use the best builder for your home, the best accountant for your business, the best doctor for your surgery. But do you really need the best stockbroker?

No, you don't.

In this industry there are lots of investment complexities and jargon that can be off-putting to the average investor. But you no more need to master all this arcane knowledge to manage your money effectively than you need to understand how a combustion engine works to drive from here to the post office. Successful investing does not need to be complicated. It isn't necessary to do extraordinary things to get extraordinary results.

Simplicity and patience lie at the heart of the Gone Fishin' Portfolio. And you won't need an investment advisor to put it together—or to run it.

REEL IT IN . . .

1. History shows that Wall Street excels at salesmanship, not money management.
2. In most aspects of life, you get what you pay for. This is emphatically not the case with most investment advisors.
3. No one cares more about your money than you do. You should manage it yourself.
4. It makes sense to take investment cues from the world's great investors, like Peter Lynch, John Templeton and Warren Buffett.
5. These three investment icons understand that—whatever your investment approach—you do not gain an edge by trying to time the market.

CHAPTER 6

Know What You Don't Know

The greatest obstacle to discovery is not ignorance—*it is the illusion of knowledge.*

Source: Daniel J. Boorstin

We live in an uncertain world, especially when it comes to securing our financial well-being. The economy expands and contracts. Jobs are created and destroyed. Inflation ebbs and flows. Stocks rise and fall.

And then there is the occasional bolt out of the blue. Companies collapse. Governments fail. Markets crash. Terrorists attack. Pandemics arise. It's a bit unnerving for those of us seeking a bit of financial security and the peace of mind that comes with it.

Fortunately, the Gone Fishin' Portfolio takes life's unavoidable risks and uncertainties and turns them into your ally. It allows you to reach financial independence, not because of how much you know, but by conceding how much you don't.

To most investors, this is wildly counterintuitive. After all, we know there is a high correlation between education and income. (The average college graduate, for example, makes almost 70% more per year than a worker with just a high school diploma.) So when it comes to investing, it's natural to assume that the smartest investors are the most successful.

That's not necessarily true. Experience shows that it's humility and discipline—not superior knowledge—that lead to success in the world of investing.

Albert Einstein, for example, is the universal symbol of genius. He discovered the theory of relativity, won the Nobel Prize in physics, and made scientific advances in gravity, cosmology, radiation, theoretical physics, statistical mechanics, quantum theory and unified field theory. Wouldn't an investor be blessed to have an IQ like this?

Perhaps not. Einstein lost his investment capital—including his Nobel Prize money—on bonds that defaulted. For all his genius, he was a failure at investing.

Or take Long-Term Capital Management (LTCM), a hedge fund created in 1994 with the help of two Nobel Prize–winning economists. The fund incorporated a complex mathematical model designed to profit from inefficiencies in world bond prices. The brilliant folks in charge of the fund used a statistical model that they believed eliminated risk from the investment process. And if you've eliminated risk, why not bet large?

So they did, accumulating positions totaling $1.25 trillion. Of course, they hadn't really eliminated risk. And when Russia defaulted on its sovereign debt in 1998, the fund blew up. LTCM shareholders lost $4.6 billion in less than four months. To clean up the resulting mess, Federal Reserve Chairman Alan Greenspan had to orchestrate a buyout by 14 major investment banks.

Another example is Mensa. This society welcomes people from all walks of life, provided their IQ is in the top 2% of the population. But these folks could stand to pick up a copy of *Investing for Dummies*. During a 15-year period when the S&P 500 had average annual returns of 15.3%, the Mensa Investment Club's performance averaged returns of just 2.5%.

As Warren Buffett famously said, "Investing is not a game where the guy with the 160 IQ beats the guy with the 130 IQ."

Believing that you've got it all figured out or—just as bad—taking investment advice from those who think they do is a shortcut to disaster, not financial security.

Investment success comes from understanding basic investment principles, putting them to work in an effective strategy and staying the course. This idea is straightforward, but completely alien to most people. They figure that the best investors have uncanny insights about what's in store for the economy, interest rates, the dollar and the stock market. And, if you don't know, well—heck, you have to guess.

NO, YOU DON'T

You can generate superior returns without divining the future—and without guessing about it, either. You need only understand what part of the investment process is knowable and unchanging, and what factors, such as economic growth or market fluctuations, can never be known in advance.

Using proven investment principles in an uncertain world can provide you with outstanding long-term results. And that's just what the Gone Fishin' Portfolio does. It allows you to generate the returns you need without subscribing to *The Wall Street Journal,* without studying your investment holdings for long hours and without paying a high-priced financial advisor.

If you're like many long-term investors who are interested in financial security but uninterested in devoting time to studying the financial markets, this is all you need.

HUMILITY IS THE ONLY TRUE WISDOM

The philosophical foundation of the Gone Fishin' Portfolio goes all the way back to 327 BC, when one of the world's greatest investment books was written. For the record, that was a couple millennia before the founding of the London Stock Exchange. But some wisdom is ageless. That's certainly the case with Plato's *Apology.*

As you may recall, Socrates was on trial for corrupting the youth of Athens. He had done no such thing, of course. What he had done was educate them, teaching them to challenge arguments from authority and question what they believed to be true. In the process, he frustrated and embarrassed many powerful people with his persistent line of questioning, known today as the Socratic method.

It is a form of philosophical inquiry that consists of asking someone what he believes to be true, asking him to justify those beliefs and then challenging him to justify those premises further.

In Plato's *Apology*, the oracle at Delphi had pronounced Socrates the wisest man in Athens. No one was more astonished—or more disbelieving—than Socrates himself. So he immediately set out to disprove the oracle by finding a wiser man.

He started by examining a politician with a reputation for great wisdom and the ego to go with it. Not only was the old gentleman unable to validate his beliefs, but he resented Socrates' challenge to his authority.

"So I left him," says Socrates, "saying to myself, as I went away: 'Well, although I do not suppose that either of us knows anything really beautiful and good, I am better off than he is, for he knows nothing, and thinks that he knows; I neither know nor think that I know. In this latter particular, then, I seem to have slightly the advantage of him.' Then I went to another who had still higher pretensions to wisdom, and my conclusion was exactly the same. Whereupon I made another enemy of him, and of many others besides him."

In the end, Socrates discovered he was indeed the wisest man in Athens. Not because of how much he knew, but because he was the only one who understood how much he *didn't know*.

Perhaps nowhere is epistemic humility more valuable than in the world of investing. In the years I spent working with individual investors, I learned that the majority have a serious roadblock between them and financial independence: their own misconceptions.

Having read mainstream financial magazines, watched Jim Cramer's antics, or talked with their friends and neighbors about "hot stocks," many approach the markets with a poor understanding of basic investment concepts.

A perfect example is the day-trading mania that gripped thousands of otherwise clearheaded individuals during the great technology stock run-up of the 1990s, and then again when the market rebounded in the midst of the coronavirus pandemic.

Many of these investors sincerely believed that they knew what they were doing. They felt that they had a "system" for beating the market and creating short-term wealth. And, for a while at least, their monthly brokerage statements even confirmed it. But when the bear market shows up—as it always does eventually—they end up going back to their day jobs . . . or their bookies. No richer, but perhaps a little wiser.

As Buffett said, "It's only when the tide goes out that you learn who's been swimming naked."

In my experience, one of the biggest hurdles investors face is their own lack of skepticism—or doubt.

CERTAINTY—A FOOL'S PARADISE

Socrates made two important points. First, he told us to acknowledge our limitations, to face up to our own ignorance on certain matters. But he also admonished us to distinguish between those who speak well and those who speak the truth.

There are thousands of smart, articulate and highly persuasive men and women who make a comfortable living as financial pundits. Most of them sound highly knowledgeable when discussing financial matters. They seem to have mastered all the minutiae of investing. But do they really know what they don't know? Many of them, I can assure you from my years of experience in the investment industry, do not. Even those who have doubts often feel they have to present an all-knowing image to instill confidence in their clients.

The truth is, the economic and political world is too big, too dynamic and too complex to be predicted with any accuracy. The same is true of the stock and bond markets. The average investor's confidence in his or her own ability—or the advisor's ability—to predict the future is almost always misplaced.

Anyone can make a good market call. But no one—and no system—can accurately and consistently forecast the future. This idea makes some investors uncomfortable. But as French Enlightenment philosopher Voltaire said, "Doubt is not a pleasant condition, but *certainty* is an absurd one."

This is a hard concept for many investors to accept because there are so many brokers, advisors, analysts, newsletter editors and mass-media publications making predictions that are so confident that their opinions sound a lot like certainties—or at least strong probabilities. These folks are often credible and convincing. History demonstrates, however, that they are also quite wrong much of the time.

Ask a market timer to provide an audited track record of past forecasts and you're likely to get nothing more than a glib line or a blank stare. There's a good reason, too. *Money* magazine's senior editor wrote about the experience of Philip Tetlock, a psychiatrist and professor at the University of California–Berkeley and one of the world's foremost authorities on *experts*:

> Starting in the 1980s, Tetlock surveyed professional know-it-alls, including academics, think tankers and journalists, and asked them to make predictions about future events around the world.
> The results, published . . . in his book *Expert Political Judgment*, are pretty humbling. The experts he surveyed did no better with predictions in their field of study than "dilettantes," experts from other fields who were just drawing on their general knowledge. Some, in fact, did significantly worse.
> "The moderately attentive reader of good newspapers can do as well as someone who devotes many years of study to predicting whether, say, Chinese growth rates will continue or Japan's Nikkei index is going up," says Tetlock.

Ouch.

One reason the experts get away with dubious results is that we let them. Our craving for predictions seems to be more deeply entrenched than any innate sense of skepticism.

Even the most experienced economists can't tell you how fast the economy is likely to grow, where interest rates are going or where the dollar is headed. The best investors know this. Peter

Lynch says, "If you spend 13 minutes per year trying to predict the economy, you have wasted 10 minutes."

The mass media is in on it, too. For example, *The Wall Street Journal* polls more than 60 economists each month to see what lies ahead for the GDP, interest rates and other economic variables. Most of them get it wrong. Their consensus isn't so hot, either.

It got to the point where even the *Wall Street Journal* staff was having a laugh. Reporter Jesse Eisinger wrote, "Pity the poor Wall Street economist. Big staffs, sophisticated models, reams of historical data, degrees from schools known by merely the name of the biggest benefactor . . . and still they forecast about as well as groundhogs." (Punxsutawney Phil may actually have an edge on most of them.)

History also demonstrates that if your portfolio is being run by a market timer—that is, someone who plans to have you invested during market rallies and out during the sell-offs—you are wasting both your time and your money. Unfortunately, time and money are exactly the two ingredients required to reach financial independence. You cannot afford to waste either.

Yet eager to trust someone with their savings, too many investors look for a broker, a money manager or a television pundit who can tell them what the future holds.

Consciously or unconsciously, they imagine the investment process works something like this: "First you make an educated guess about what the economy is likely to do. Based on this, you have a hunch about where the market is likely to go. And based on that, you have a theory about what sorts of investments you should be buying."

But a theory that's based on a hunch—that's based on a guess— isn't the best foundation for your investment portfolio. So how do you reach your financial goals? By facing facts, by using a system— like this one—that doesn't rely on guesses about the economy or the stock market, and by knowing what you don't know.

Investment success begins with a strong dose of humility—not just about your own knowledge but, just as importantly, about the knowledge of the so-called experts.

You're on the right track the day you say to yourself, "Since no one can tell me with any certainty what the economy or the stock market is going to do next year, how should I run my portfolio?"

Some would call this a confession of ignorance. In truth, it is the beginning of investment wisdom. Because no matter how much you know, or how well informed your advisor is, the reality is that uncertainty will always be your inseparable companion.

I understand how intense this yearning to know can be. But in order to embrace the Gone Fishin' philosophy, you have to let it go. Rather than pretending to have answers we don't have, we accept the uncertainties. We deal with them. We capitalize on them.

The Gone Fishin' Portfolio skips the guesswork and endless analysis—and allows you to focus on the important business of meeting your financial objectives.

REEL IT IN . . .

1. You don't need to predict the future to generate first-class returns.
2. No one—and no system—can accurately and consistently forecast the economy or the financial markets.
3. Experience tells us that it's humility—not superior knowledge—that paves the way to successful investing.
4. Making investment decisions based on hunches or guesses— whether made by you or an expert—is not intelligent risk taking.
5. The Gone Fishin' investment philosophy is based on the notion that nobody knows what the market is likely to do next. This system doesn't eliminate uncertainty. But it does allow you to capitalize on it.

PART II

Get Wealthy

CHAPTER 7

Common Stocks

The Greatest Wealth Creators
of All Time

I know of no way of judging the future but by the past.

Source: Patrick Henry

In 1988, Charles Givens published a bestseller called *Wealth Without Risk*. I can only assume it was about inheritance, because I know no other way of getting wealthy without taking risk. (Even the Mega Millions lottery—one of the world's worst bets with 300-million-to-1 odds—requires that you risk two bucks.)

Successful investment is about the intelligent management of risk. You can't avoid risk or eliminate it. You have to take it by the horns and deal with it.

Every investment choice entails risk. Even if you're so conservative that you keep all your money in cash investments like T-bills and certificates of deposit—not a terribly good idea, incidentally—you are taking the sizable risk that your purchasing power fails to keep pace with inflation.

Yet, terrified of seeing the value of their investments decline even temporarily, plenty of investors do exactly this. This is understandable at first blush. After all, it's not easy watching your nest egg get scrambled as the stock market spasms in reaction to every piece of bad business news or new government statistic.

But history shows that over the long run, you are well compensated for withstanding the vicissitudes of the market. If, by contrast, you seek stability in your investments first and foremost, your returns are guaranteed to be low. Investments in money market funds and certificates of deposit return very little after taxes and inflation. Over the past 90 years, T-bills have returned approximately 3.8% per year. And, of course, even that return seems triumphant compared with today's ground-scraping yields. Most short-term bond funds and money market accounts pay essentially nothing and offer a negative real (after-inflation) return on your money.

Don't get me wrong. If you're saving for a short-term goal like a new car or a down payment on a house, you can't get safer than 30-day T-bills. Unless the American flag is no longer flying over the White House a month from now, your investment is secure. Over the long haul, however, this kind of safety comes at a steep price. Paradoxically, a portfolio that takes a conservative approach to market risk is often exposed to a high degree of shortfall risk. (This is the risk that you'll run out of money before you run out of heartbeats.)

Stocks have given far superior long-term returns. Yet many investors are frightened of them. They view the market as a giant casino (and it often acts that way from hour to hour and day to day). But, over the long term, nothing could be further from the truth.

Historically, the odds of making money in the U.S. stock market are 50-50 in one-day periods, 68% in one-year periods, 88% in 10-year periods, and 100% in 20-year periods.

This should not surprise you. Stocks are not simply slips of paper with corporate names on them. A share of stock is a fractional interest in a business. When a corporation issues stock, it is offering each purchaser the right to share in the fortunes of the business.

Once the initial stock offering is complete, shares are then bought or sold on an exchange.

That's when things get interesting. Stocks move each market day based on news or investor perceptions about inflation, interest rates, economic growth, commodity prices, the dollar, consumer confidence, technological developments, business conditions, government policies and many other factors.

This causes a company's share price to fluctuate more dramatically than the prospects for the underlying business. That's because stock prices are determined "at the margin." Only a small fraction of a company's shareholders sell their shares in the market each day. Yet that tiny fraction determines the value of the entire company—at least temporarily. Sudden imbalances in buy or sell orders can quickly push a stock dramatically higher or lower.

Sometimes these price swings are triggered by a change in the company's fundamentals. But a company's daily share price can rise or fall for reasons that have nothing to do with the outlook for the company, or even the economy. Individual stock prices can be pushed around, for example, by rumors, official buy or sell recommendations by major wirehouses, short sellers, high-frequency traders, tax selling, good or bad publicity, insider transactions, fads, takeover speculation, or bad news elsewhere in the sector. Short-term momentum traders often pile on, too, creating even more volatility.

For short-term traders, these are issues that must be understood and dealt with. But for long-term investors—like those using the Gone Fishin' Portfolio—daily trading activity can be conveniently ignored.

Why? Because over the long term there is one thing about equities that you can safely take to the bank: Share prices follow earnings. (Earnings, of course, are the net profits of a business.) Look back through history and try to find even a single company that increased its earnings quarter after quarter, year after year, and the stock didn't tag along. Conversely, try to uncover one whose earnings declined year after year and the stock continued to move up. It just doesn't happen.

That's why Benjamin Graham famously said of the stock market, "In the short run it's a voting machine, but in the long run it's a weighing machine." And what it weighs is corporate earnings, both actual and prospective. Regardless of what the market does next week or next month, you can count on it to reflect earnings over the long haul.

When results are measured not in months or years but decades, nothing has rewarded investors better than common stocks. Not cash, not bonds, not real estate, not gold, not collectibles, nothing. That's why I call common stocks the greatest wealth creators of all time.

THE BEST INVESTMENT . . . EVER

Jeremy Siegel, a professor of finance at the Wharton School of the University of Pennsylvania and author of *Stocks for the Long Run: The Definitive Guide to Financial Market Returns and Long-Term Investment Strategies,* has done a thorough historical study of the returns of different types of assets over the past couple hundred years.

What he discovered (extended through 2019 by my research team) is dramatic: $1 invested in gold in 1802 would have been worth $75 at the end of 2019. The same dollar invested in T-bills would have grown to $4,430. A $1 investment in bonds would have been worth $34,198. And $1 invested in common stocks with dividends reinvested—drum roll, please—would have been worth $29.7 million (see Figure 7.1).

The odds are good, of course, that you weren't around a couple hundred years ago. And, unless something truly exciting happens soon in the field of cryogenics, you won't be around 200 years from now, either.

However, it's not necessary to think *that* long term. Start whenever you want and you'll find that when measured in decades, the investment returns for different asset classes are remarkably consistent. Stocks are the big winner. Since 1926, the stock market has generated a positive return in 69 out of 94 years.

But those inevitable down years quickly take the fun out of the stock market for most investors. Since 1945, the S&P 500 has tumbled 26%, on average, in the periods leading up to and during recessions.

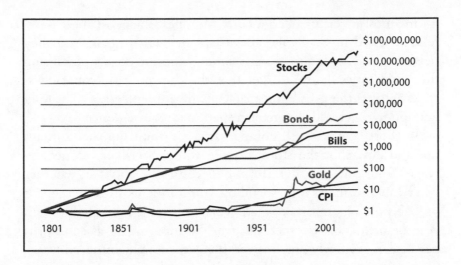

FIGURE 7.1 Total Nominal Return Indices (1802–2019)

Source: Jeremy J. Siegel, "Stocks for the Long Run, 4th Edition: The Definitive Guide to Financial Market Returns & Long Term Investment Strategies", McGraw Hill Professional, 2007. © 2007, McGraw Hill

That often drives investors to the sidelines, where they miss the ensuing rally. Running to bonds or cash when a recession looms might be a fine idea, if only recessions were predictable. They're not. Statistics show that recessions tend to be identified weeks or months after they begin. By the time headlines confirm that a recession has arrived, the damage in the stock market is usually done.

Even if you somehow knew what was going to happen in the economy, you still wouldn't necessarily know what was going to happen in the stock market. Perversely, stocks often fall during the good times and rally during the bad times. Money manager Ken Fisher doesn't call the stock market "The Great Humiliator" for nothing.

And even if you make a good call and get out of the market before a downturn, how do you know when to get back in? Wait too long and you can miss a substantial part—or all—of the next bull market. That can be costly.

It is clear to anyone who takes the time to investigate that stocks have outperformed all other liquid investments—and illiquid ones, too, including real estate and other tangibles. And while no one can tell you with certainty what investment returns will be in the future, most investors need a fairly high percentage of their portfolio invested in stocks to meet their long-term goals. And they need to stick with this stock market exposure to avoid missing the good times. Never forget that the greatest risk you face as an investor is the possibility that your investments won't last long enough to meet your long-term spending requirements.

In short, you are well compensated for enduring the constant ups and downs of the stock market. Yes, you're likely to get the sweats from time to time. But when you think about it, whether you're able to meet your spending commitments in retirement is probably more important than what the stock market does this year or next. This is especially true because, while asset returns have been relatively stable over the past couple hundred years, human life spans have lengthened dramatically.

What does this have to do with your investment strategy?

Quite a bit, actually. The whole point of financial planning is to make sure your investment portfolio doesn't kick the bucket before you do. If you're in good health, you may live a lot longer than you think—or than you're counting on, financially. This means that unless you're independently wealthy—and can live happily ever after with your money tucked away in triple-A, insured, tax-free bonds—stocks should play an important part in your retirement planning.

This thought scares the bejesus out of novice investors—and a few old hands as well—especially when the market, with no notice whatsoever, begins rumbling like Krakatoa.

This is the norm, however. Investors who expect to earn the generous returns only a diversified stock portfolio can deliver while watching their net worth rise as smoothly as a bank balance are either uninformed or unrealistic. "Steady as she goes" has never described long-term equity investing.

DON'T GET CAUGHT ON THE SIDELINES

Despite the inevitable volatility, there are good reasons to be grateful for the stock market. Capitalism does a better job than any other economic system of alleviating poverty, raising our standard of living and creating prosperity. The essence of capitalism is the private ownership of the means of production and distribution. Most of us, however, don't have the capital or the experience to run our own business. (And statistics show that less than half of all new businesses survive the first five years.) Enter the stock market, the mechanism that makes capitalism truly democratic.

Virtually anyone can still own a piece of a thriving business through the quintessence of capitalism: the stock market. With even a modest amount of money, an individual can accumulate a stake in many of the world's greatest companies and most profitable businesses.

Yet how quickly this notion of owning great companies gets lost in the daily headlines, where the focus is constantly shifting from Fed policy to Wall Street downgrades to the latest hedge fund blowup. Yes, the stock market can be frightening at times. But it is essential that you understand that nothing offers you the prospect of earning higher long-term returns. That's why stocks are a key component of the Gone Fishin' Portfolio.

"What about the looming bear market?" some may ask. "Shouldn't we wait until the coast is clear?"

Waiting for everything to look better before you invest is a bit like waiting for all the traffic lights to turn green before you pull out of your driveway. It isn't going to happen. No one ever sounds an "all clear" for the stock market.

To successfully time the market requires you to buy low, sell high and then buy low again (while covering all spreads, trading costs and taxes on capital gains). Fail, and you'll get left behind while the equity train rumbles on.

For example, Putnam Investments calculated that for the 15-year period between January 1, 2005, and December 31, 2015—a period that included The Great Recession—a $10,000 investment in the S&P 500 with dividends reinvested would have turned into $36,418.

But if you invested the same amount and missed the market's 10 best days, it would have grown to only $18,358. If you missed the 20 best days, the number is just $11,908.

And the numbers turn negative if you spent more time out of the market. That same $10,000 shrank to $8,150 if you missed the best 30 days and plunged to $5,847 if you missed the best 40 days.

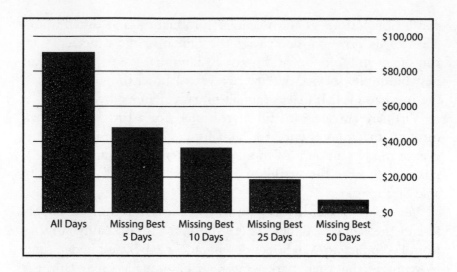

FIGURE 7.2 Hypothetical Growth of $10,000 Invested in the S&P 500 from January 1, 1990, to December 31, 2019

Note: This example does not include dividend reinvestment or tax implications.

This period was no anomaly. Looking back at the performance of the S&P 500 from 1990 through 2019, if you had missed only the five best-performing days in the market you would have ended up with a portfolio worth 47% less than the one that was fully invested. Even more surprising, missing the 25 best days since 1990 would have reduced the value of your portfolio by 79% (see Figure 7.2).

Clearly, attempting to move in and out of the market to catch the best possible returns can easily derail your investment plans.

Of course, bearish commentators—some of whom have held the same negative outlook on stocks, not just for years but for decades—will argue that the coming market decline will be so painful that you'd be better off getting out altogether.

Ironically, these "permabears" make a living telling you to sell the securities they never recommended you buy in the first place. As for them telling you when to get back in the market, I'll let you in on a little secret: That day never comes.

If you're wondering whether your bearish advisor is a real dyed-in-the-wool grizzly, see if he is suggesting your money should be primarily invested in gold. (This sounds suspiciously similar to the "investment" advice my wife gets at the jewelers.)

Permabears don't give up easily, though. For those who remain skeptical of their arguments, they aren't afraid to pull out their trump card, the Great Depression.

A REASON FOR OPTIMISM

The Great Depression occurred when the United States and other developed economies were on the gold standard. This greatly restricted the government's ability to respond in the face of an economic crisis. A paper money standard, properly managed, can prevent the severe depressions that plagued the gold standard while keeping inflation moderate, as we've seen over the past several decades.

Still, every stock investor should understand the Great Depression and how it affected investors. For example, in all five editions of *Stocks for the Long Run,* Siegel has told the infamous story of John Jakob Raskob.

In the summer of 1929, *Ladies' Home Journal* interviewed Raskob, a senior executive with General Motors, about how the typical individual could build wealth by investing in stocks. In the article published that August, titled "Everybody Ought to Be Rich," Raskob claimed that by putting $15 a month into high-quality stocks, even the average worker could become wealthy.

His timing left something to be desired. Just seven weeks after the article appeared came Black Friday, the stock market crash of 1929. And it wasn't until July 8, 1932, that the carnage finally came to an end. By then, the market value of the greatest corporations in America had declined an astonishing 89%. Millions of investors were wiped out. Thousands who had bought stock on margin (with borrowed money) went bankrupt.

Raskob was held up as an object of ridicule. Yet Siegel points out that had you followed Raskob's advice, patiently putting $15 a month in stocks beginning in August 1929 (the equivalent of roughly $220 today), within just four years you would have earned more than someone who put an identical amount in T-bills over the same period. That's right—after just four years, during the worst period of stock market performance in U.S. history.

After 30 years, your portfolio would have grown to $60,000, the equivalent of $313,000 today. That's a 13% annual return, far more than investors would have earned had they switched into T-bills, bonds or gold at the very top of the market.

Some might argue this was a fluke. So let's take a look at another extreme scenario: Germany and Japan after World War II. As Siegel writes . . .

> In the 12 years from 1948 to 1960, German stocks rose by over 30% per year in real terms. Indeed, from 1939, when the Germans began the war in Poland, through 1960, the real return on German stocks nearly matched those in the United States and exceeded those in the U.K. Despite the total devastation that the war visited on Germany, the long-run investor made out as well in defeated Germany as in victorious Britain or the United States. The data powerfully attest to the resilience of stocks in the face of seemingly destructive political, social, and economic change.

The story in Japan was similar. By the end of 1945, stock prices stood at about a third of their level just prior to the empire's surrender. Over the next 40 years, the Japanese market returned more than 20 times its American counterpart.

Often, the very best periods of stock market performance come during periods of negative sentiment and high volatility. In fact, the best five-year return in the U.S. stock market began in May 1932—in the midst of the Great Depression—when stocks returned 367%. The next best five-year period began in July 1982, during one of the worst recessions in the postwar period. As you can see in Table 7.1, it has paid off to stay invested in U.S. stocks during troubled times.

The lesson is this: Over the long haul, stocks have consistently delivered superior returns, throughout expansion, recession, inflation, deflation and war. Waiting until the backdrop feels "safe" has never been an effective way to earn high future returns.

Of course, the market can always go lower than you think it will—and for longer than you think it will—before a major

TABLE 7.1 Investing in Stocks During Troubled Times

Year	Event	Subsequent Five-Year Return
1932	Great Depression	194%
1982	Dramatic Tightening of Interest Rates	183%
2002	Collapse of Internet Stocks	101%
2009	Financial Crisis and Great Recession	177%

uptrend appears. For this reason alone, you should not have money invested in stocks that you need in less than five years.

But for your serious, long-term money, there are good reasons to maintain a significant exposure to high-quality stocks. Yes, the stock market will be unnerving and unpredictable in the near term. But inflation makes your future financial requirements unpredictable, too. That's why you need to generate the higher returns that only equities can give.

When Siegel's book first came out, detailing the returns of various asset classes, it caused a bit of a sensation. Not because he pointed out that stocks have given the best historical returns. That was already common knowledge, at least among students of the market.

The real bombshell was the following statement from the first edition, based on a thorough examination of two centuries of financial data:

> Although bonds are certainly safer than stocks in the short run, over the long run the returns on stocks are so stable that stocks *are* actually safer than either government bonds or Treasury bills. The constancy of the long-term, after-inflation returns on stocks was truly astounding, while the returns on fixed-income assets posed higher risks for the long-term investor.

Stocks are safer than T-bills? To many investors, that sounded like lunacy. But for long-term investors who measure their returns in decades, it has been the case for more than two centuries now. Is it likely to remain that way in the future? It is safe to assume so. Let me explain why, not in financial terms but in human ones.

USING THE PAST TO SAFEGUARD YOUR FUTURE

We all have economic needs: food, clothing, shelter, utilities, healthcare and so on. It is business—not government—that fills those needs. As long as there are human beings, businesses will prosper by filling those needs. Many investors would benefit from thinking not about the stock market, but about the advantages of owning a portfolio of thriving businesses. This is likely to remain the most assured route to financial independence.

Any academic can tell you how much stocks have returned in the past. No one can tell you exactly what stocks will return in the future. But when estimating future returns, it is reasonable to expect that they will not be significantly higher or lower than long-term historical returns.

History clearly demonstrates that no other asset class returns more than stocks over the long haul. Once you understand this—and accept the steep odds against timing the market—you've made the first step toward adopting an investment strategy that can generate high returns with an acceptable level of risk.

Given equities' superior long-term results, a few bold investors may ask, "Why not invest 100% of my portfolio in stocks?"

The answer can be found in human psychology. People are not unfeeling automatons. You have to consider the likelihood that you will stay the course after you've set up a workable strategy. My many years as an investment advisor clearly demonstrated to me that most investors have a low pain threshold when it comes to tolerating market declines.

Many felt an overwhelming urge to "do something." And that something was invariably to "Sell!" when most of the damage was already done. However, there are ways to reduce the volatility of your portfolio—and thus your propensity to panic—and still meet your most important investment goals.

That is the subject we will turn to next.

REEL IT IN . . .

1. Shortfall risk—the risk of outliving your money—is the biggest threat to your long-term financial security, not stock market fluctuations.
2. The investment that has given the best long-term returns after inflation is common stocks. They should make up the core of your long-term portfolio.
3. It isn't possible to know in advance the best times to be in the market. For this reason, you need to maintain a consistent long-term exposure to equities.
4. The trade-off for investing in stocks is greater volatility than bonds or bills. However, there are ways to reduce this risk. (More on that in the next chapter.)

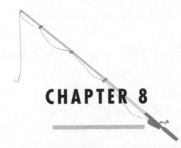

CHAPTER 8

Don't Buy What Wall Street Is Selling

The most costly of follies is to believe in the palpably not true.

Source: H.L. Mencken

History clearly demonstrates that common stocks should provide the foundation of any portfolio designed to maximize total returns. The first question, of course, is how many stocks should you own, and which ones? For the Gone Fishin' strategy, the answer is simple: *all of them*. We're going to capture the performance of every major public company on the world's leading stock exchanges.

This may come as a surprise to regular readers of my newsletters and trading services. After all, I spend several hundred hours a year researching, recommending and monitoring a few dozen individual stocks that I believe are the best of the best. And not without success.

So why are there no individual stock picks in the Gone Fishin' Portfolio? This strategy is about long-term investing, not trading. It's about meeting your most important financial goals, not pursuing short-term gains. It's also about spending as little time as possible on your investments and getting on with your life.

For this strategy we're going to skip buying and selling individual stocks, which requires a lot more time and attention, and own mutual funds or exchange-traded funds (ETFs) instead.

THE MUTUAL FUND ADVANTAGE

According to Statista, nearly half of American households own mutual funds. Most investors are already familiar with them. As you may know, they offer several important advantages:

1. **Diversification.** The risk of owning a whole portfolio of stocks is considerably less than the risk of holding any one individual stock. But it can take quite a bit of money to build a diversified portfolio of stocks or bonds. You get instant diversification with each mutual fund share.

2. **Professional management.** Whether you own an index fund or an actively managed fund, there is a professional manager overseeing the portfolio.

3. **Low minimums.** Each fund establishes its own investment minimum. But minimums have come down dramatically over the past few years. And ETFs have no investment minimums. (More on that in Chapter 11.)

4. **No financial advisor required.** You can buy mutual funds that charge no loads (commissions) directly from the fund companies.

5. **Liquidity.** Mutual fund companies will allow you to redeem (sell) all or part of your shares on any day the market is open for trading.

6. **Automatic reinvestment.** You can arrange for all your fund's dividends and capital gains to be automatically reinvested in the fund—or directed to other funds—without charge.

7. **Convenience.** You can buy and redeem fund shares online, by phone or by mail. You can arrange automatic purchases from your bank account or you can arrange regular periodic withdrawals. You can also arrange that the proceeds from your funds' redemptions or distributions be deposited in your bank account.

8. **Simplified recordkeeping.** You will receive regular statements showing the value of your account and any activity. At the end of each year, you'll receive the tax-reporting information you need, too.

9. **Customer service.** If you have a question or a problem, or need to make changes to your account, you can call your fund's toll-free customer service line and get the help you need at no additional cost.

10. **Time.** Owning shares of a mutual fund saves you the trouble of researching, constructing and monitoring a portfolio of individual stocks.

THE WISER BET

There are essentially two types of mutual funds—index funds and actively managed funds:

1. **Index funds.** With indexing, the fund manager attempts to replicate the return of a particular benchmark, such as the S&P 500 or the Bloomberg Barclays Aggregate Bond Index. Index fund managers generally do not buy stocks or bonds that are not included in the benchmark.

2. **Actively managed funds.** Active managers try to outperform a benchmark by selecting the best-performing securities or trying to time the market. Or both.

Some readers may question why any investor would settle for the performance of an index when you can opt for a fund manager who is willing to swing for the fences.

However, you may not realize just how exceptional—and rare—great managers are. Investing in actively managed funds is generally an exercise in futility. The overwhelming majority of actively managed funds fail to beat their benchmark.

Need proof? There's plenty of it.

In June 2020, Berlinda Liu, director of global research and design at S&P Dow Jones Indices, published a report showing how active fund managers' track records stack up.

Eighty-two percent of small cap equity fund managers failed to beat their benchmark over the previous 15 years. Eighty-two percent of mid-cap equity fund managers failed. Ninety-one percent of large cap equity managers failed. And so did 82% of real estate investment trust (REIT) managers.

Of course, some foreign markets are less efficient than the U.S. market. That would lead many to believe that active fund managers excel in that arena.

The same report found that 83% of global funds, 88% of international funds and 90% of emerging market funds also underperformed over the last 15 years.

I wish I could tell you the story was different with fixed income funds, but it's not. Eighty-six percent of investment-grade short-term bond fund managers underperformed their benchmark—and so did a whopping 98% of government long fund managers over the last 15 years.

Is this just a recent phenomenon? An aberration, perhaps? Hardly.

In 1967, academic Michael Jensen decided to evaluate mutual fund managers, testing for evidence of the ability to consistently beat the stock market averages. What he discovered—and scores of studies have subsequently confirmed—is that the average fund produces roughly the same gross return as the market. Unfortunately, the average investor receives a *net* return that is lower, thanks to expenses. As you'll see, those costs add up quickly, dramatically reducing the final value of your portfolio. Expenses alone prevent most actively managed funds from keeping pace with index funds.

(It's also worth noting that even world-beaters like Bill Miller can lose their magic touch. The former manager of the Legg Mason Capital Management Value Trust was once famous for beating the S&P 500 for 15 consecutive years, a feat few fund managers can match. But he went off the rails—off the cliff, really—during the financial crisis and Great Recession, destroying his market-beating track record. He ultimately left the fund in 2011. He was the last household name in the U.S. mutual funds industry.)

In *What Wall Street Doesn't Want You to Know*, Larry Swedroe writes, "Mark Carhart conducted the most comprehensive study ever done on the mutual fund industry. He found that once you account for style factors (small-cap vs. large-cap and value vs. growth) the average actively managed fund underperformed its benchmark by almost 2% per annum." That's nearly 20% of the market's long-term return.

Some financial advisors simply shrug and tell you, "Don't buy the average funds. Buy the good ones." But there's the rub. Studies show that a fund that beats the market one year is no more likely than its competitors to outperform it the following year.

In *The Little Book of Common Sense Investing*, John Bogle quotes David Swensen, chief investment officer of the Yale University endowment fund: "A minuscule 4% of funds produce market-beating after-tax results with a scant 0.6% (annual) margin of gain. The 96% of funds that fail to meet or beat the Vanguard 500 Index Fund lose by a wealth-destroying margin of 4.8% per annum."

When the fund industry prints its famous disclaimer, "Past performance is no guarantee of future results," that's not just boilerplate. Past is not prologue when it comes to the performance of the best actively managed funds. That's why it's estimated that more than half of all institutional monies are now invested using indexing strategies.

In an earlier chapter, I quoted top-performing investment managers like Warren Buffett and Peter Lynch. Yet even they agree with the power of indexing. In the April 2, 1990, issue of *Barron's*, Lynch said, "[Most investors would] be better off in an index fund." In his 1996 letter to Berkshire Hathaway shareholders, Buffett said, "The best way to own common stocks is through an index fund."

The question you should ask yourself is, "If the nation's most sophisticated institutions and the most successful investors of our era are advocating an indexing strategy, should I be using one?"

The answer is an unequivocal yes. Actively managed funds are laden with higher management and administrative fees. These funds may also charge front-end or back-end loads and 12b-1 fees (annual marketing or distribution fees)—expenses that will make your head spin. There are other costs, too. And oftentimes they are not itemized neatly for you. Instead, the specifics are buried in fine print in the prospectus.

Of course, selecting the so-called "best performing" funds may be the way your broker or financial advisor makes a living. But the sooner you realize these funds are unlikely to outperform their benchmarks, the quicker you'll be on your way to securing your financial freedom. It's a straightforward equation, really. The fees you pay directly reduce your investment portfolio's returns. More money in expenses means less money in your pocket. It's that simple.

THE LOW-FEE WAY TO BEAT THE STREET

Arthur Levitt, the longest-serving chairman of the Securities and Exchange Commission (SEC), published a bestselling business book exposing Wall Street's agenda, *Take On the Street: What Wall Street and Corporate America Don't Want You to Know; What You Can Do to Fight Back.*

In it, he declares:

> Investors today are being fed lies and distortions, are being exploited and neglected. In the wake of the last decade's rush to invest by millions of households, a culture of gamesmanship has grown among corporate management, financial analysts, brokers, and fund managers, making it hard to tell financial fantasy from reality.

If this all sounds a bit depressing, cheer up. The Gone Fishin' Portfolio offers an effective solution. The portfolio consists entirely of low-cost funds that charge no loads and no 12b-1 fees. In fact, you'll pay the lowest fees in the entire industry either through Vanguard mutual funds or ETFs.

I could have chosen any of dozens of mutual fund groups to implement the Gone Fishin' Portfolio. However, The Vanguard Group is special. It is among the nation's largest mutual fund groups. When the first edition of this book came out in 2008, Vanguard had just over $1.1 trillion in assets under management. Today it has well over $6.2 trillion. Such a large asset base allows the company to enjoy economies of scale that enable it to maintain its position as the lowest-cost fund family in the industry.

And that's not all. This fund manager's structure is unique. The Vanguard Group is owned entirely by its individual funds, and, ultimately, the shareholders. It operates the funds "at cost"—charging only the amounts needed to cover operating costs and extracting no profits. That means no fund family is likely to seriously challenge Vanguard's low-cost leadership.

Vanguard also embodies a particular philosophy of investing, one that, in many respects, dovetails nicely with our Gone Fishin' Portfolio. The story of this fund family and its founder, John Bogle, is one worth telling.

In 1949, Bogle was a graduate student at Princeton University who needed a topic for his thesis. He stumbled on an article in *Fortune* magazine about the mutual fund industry, an industry so small and young at the time that Bogle had never heard of it. Since no academics had researched or published on the topic, Bogle decided to lead the way. And lead he did.

Bogle earned an A+ on his thesis, "The Economic Role of the Investment Company." It included a number of revelations that would change the face of personal investing. He pointed out that the vast majority of mutual fund managers did not beat the market with any consistency. (A reality—as we've seen—that has not changed over the last 70 years.) In fact, most performed worse than a random sample. He also found that mutual fund fees were too high, especially the front-end sales loads. Some investors may ask, "Why didn't the fund family lower them to increase investor returns?"

That's not how the mutual fund business works.

Bogle showed that lowering the loads led to a loss of interest from salespeople and resulted in lost business for the fund companies. He further concluded that a perfect fund, one with the benefits of the shareholder in mind, would follow an index and charge the lowest fees possible. This would provide a higher long-term net return to the shareholder. This, as we now know, was a revolutionary idea.

A job offer based on the strength of his thesis soon followed. Bogle went to work at Wellington Management Company straight out of college and was running the company by age 36. He was let go after the early 1970s market crash. Nine months later, however, he founded a fund company based on his own investment principles. The Vanguard Group was born.

It's worth noting that Bogle wrote up his discoveries in 1951. Yet for 25 years, no one started an index fund. Today, the mutual fund industry is enormous. In 2018, U.S. mutual funds had more than $17.7 trillion in assets under management. Yet, despite load funds' high costs and poor performance, investors still plunk hundreds of billions of dollars into them every year. In fact, broker-sold stock and bond funds regularly attract more money than lower-cost no-load funds.

LOWER COSTS, HIGHER RETURNS

Bogle, who died in 2019, devoted his career to steering investors in the right direction, arguing that "the central principle of the mutual fund business should be, not the marketing of financial products to customers, but the stewardship of investment services for clients." To Bogle, stewardship didn't mean just charging more competitive fees. It meant delivering higher returns by charging the lowest fees possible. It meant not bamboozling clients with deceptive claims. Most importantly, it meant putting the interests of shareholders first.

The average Vanguard mutual fund and ETF expense ratio is 85% less than the industry average (see Table 8.1). That's because with actively managed funds, there are actually three more layers of expenses beyond the fund's expense ratio listed in the prospectus and annual reports.

TABLE 8.1 Vanguard Fees Versus Industry Average Fees

Fund	Vanguard Fee	Average Fee
Small Cap Index	0.05%	1.10%
Emerging Market Index	0.14%	1.32%
European Stock Index	0.10%	1.24%
Short-Term Bond Index	0.20%	0.72%
Real Estate Investment Trust Index	0.12%	1.19%
Inflation-Protected Securities Fund	0.20%	0.72%
Pacific Stock Index	0.10%	0.97%
Total Stock Market Index	0.04%	0.91%
High-Yield Corporate Bond Fund	0.23%	1.01%

The expense ratio merely comprises administrative expenses plus management fees. But actively managed funds incur many other costs that shareholders ultimately bear.

For example, funds must pay commissions on transactions. With actively managed funds, these can be substantial. As an individual investor, you can enter an online order with your discount broker and pay no commission to have them execute it. But things aren't so simple in the fund industry. Funds need specialists to handle the large transactions that they make. And even the best-informed investors generally don't know their funds' trading costs. That's because, while the SEC requires that they be reported to shareholders, the presentation is generally so obscure that you're unlikely to find them unless you're a CPA.

Another cost fund shareholders must absorb is the bid–ask spread on each security. A stock is always offered slightly higher than it is bid. And the bid–ask spread is often wider in foreign markets. Clearly, a fund that is trading actively has high hurdles to clear.

Yet another cost to shareholders is what is known as market impact cost. This is not reported and difficult to estimate. Impact costs arise when large blocks of stock are bought or sold by institutional investors, like pension plans, hedge funds and mutual funds. Bear in mind, if you're a manager running hundreds of millions or billions of dollars in client assets, you can't simply click a mouse and liquidate your holdings at the market. Such a huge sell order would temporarily wreck the price of the security you're trying to sell, reducing shareholders' returns. The same is true if you're accumulating a position in a stock. You would bid up the price of the securities as you bought them. Typically, a fund manager needs days or weeks to accumulate or unwind a position. Who gets stuck with the market impact cost? Go look in the mirror.

A NEEDLESS DRAG ON PERFORMANCE

This mountain of costs is unrecognized by most fund investors. It is also substantial. In *The Intelligent Asset Allocator: How to Build Your Portfolio to Maximize Returns and Minimize Risk,* William Bernstein estimates that the expense ratio, commissions, bid–ask spreads and impact costs of actively managed funds total 2.2% for large cap funds, 4.1% for small cap and foreign funds, and a whopping 9% for emerging market funds. These costs are a serious drag on performance and yet another reason to favor index funds over actively managed funds.

Especially since Vanguard's costs are going down, not up.

Clearly, you have an enormous cost advantage using Vanguard. This is no industry secret, by the way. Vanguard has been named "Best Buy" by *Forbes* magazine, "Best Fund Family" and "Best Discount Broker" by *Worth,* and "Best Fund Family" by *Smart Money.* Vanguard also received Morningstar's inaugural Award for Investing Excellence for Exemplary Stewardship in 2019.

With Vanguard, you know exactly what you're getting. Vanguard stock and bond funds stay fully invested in their target markets. Their managers do not try to time the market. Vanguard does not advertise its funds' past returns or peer rankings, which are based on past performance and can mislead investors.

In short, the interests of Vanguard shareholders and fund managers are completely aligned. That means lower fees, less hassle, no sales pressure and higher net returns. That's why The Vanguard Group is the best mutual fund family for constructing the Gone Fishin' Portfolio, which I'm about to unveil. However, when speaking at conferences about this portfolio, I often have investors tell me something like, "The bulk of my money is in my 401(k). And my 401(k) plan doesn't offer Vanguard funds. What should I do?"

401(k) plans are great for encouraging saving and investing. But the downside may be a lack of flexibility. Yours may offer a limited number of investment choices determined by your plan provider. You may or may not have a choice of investing in Vanguard funds. If Vanguard is available, by all means take advantage of it. If not, you can substitute other no-load funds based on the asset allocation model in Figure 9.2 and achieve much the same results.

If you have any reservations about relying on index funds rather than using an active manager, heed the words of Douglas Dial, who was portfolio manager of the CREF Stock Account, the largest pool of equity money in the world.

Dial is a former active manager who had a conversion. "Indexing is a marvelous technique. I wasn't a true believer. I was just an ignoramus. Now I am a convert. Indexing is an extraordinarily sophisticated thing to do . . . If people want excitement, they should go to the racetrack or play the lottery."

Why don't you see more about this in the mass media? You do, occasionally. But the overriding goal at *Forbes, Fortune, Businessweek* and similar publications is not to make readers wealthy. Their goal is to gain subscriptions, rent lists and sell advertising. Actively managed funds and brokerage firms are among their largest advertisers. Why alienate them? And how can these publications devote space to a complete investment strategy like this one every month, when the goal is to keep tantalizing readers with ever-new ways of getting rich?

Sadly, few stand to profit from telling the truth. Not brokerage firms. Not the mutual fund industry. Not the mass media. Everyone has an agenda, it seems. You, however, have an agenda of your own: financial freedom. And that requires shutting out the noise and confusion created by the mainstream media, Madison Avenue and Wall Street's attempt to grab your assets.

As I'll describe in the next chapter, the Gone Fishin' Portfolio will give you all the tools you need.

REEL IT IN . . .

1. The easiest and most convenient way to own common stocks is through mutual funds. They offer diversification, professional management, low minimums, automatic reinvestment and other conveniences.

2. Index funds are preferable to actively managed funds. Over time, they are likely to deliver higher net returns to shareholders.

3. The Vanguard Group is one of the nation's largest fund groups. Its size and unique structure allow it to offer mutual fund investors the lowest costs in the industry.

4. For these and other advantages, you should construct the Gone Fishin' Portfolio using Vanguard mutual funds or an alternative I'll discuss in Chapter 11.

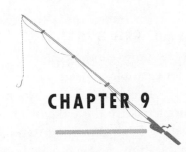

CHAPTER 9

Your Single Most Important Investment Decision

Everything should be as simple as it can be, but not simpler.

Source: Albert Einstein

The Gone Fishin' Portfolio has two primary objectives. One is to help you earn a higher return within an acceptable level of risk. The other is to simplify your life and save you time.

However, the investment community and financial press spew out so much analysis and so many opinions each week, it's easy to lose sight of the big picture.

This is particularly true with the rise of so much financial journalism on TV. Turn on CNBC or Fox Business and you'll see every major corporate announcement scrutinized and every important government statistic examined with an eye toward how investors should react.

If you are a short-term trader, there is occasionally news that you should understand and respond to. But for the long-term investor, the day-to-day noise can be conveniently ignored.

A few years ago, for example, a major television station called my office and asked if I would appear on its news show to recommend the steps investors should take in the wake of a major hurricane. My publisher at The Oxford Club thought it would provide valuable exposure for our organization and encouraged me to do it. I refused.

True, the storm caused a real mess. But it had come and gone. Damage to commercial properties and oil refineries was already reflected in share prices—and in some cases before the hurricane even made landfall.

To go on national TV and suggest that investors should begin rearranging their portfolios made no sense. (Of course, the station had no problem finding another commentator eager to fill in.)

Long-term investors are better off watching reruns than listening to most talking heads on the investment shows. At least *Seinfeld* won't persuade you to cash out of stocks in a panic.

Adopting an accurate, fact-based view of the world is your first step toward becoming a successful investor. The second step is to discern what you can control. Figure 9.1 is helpful.

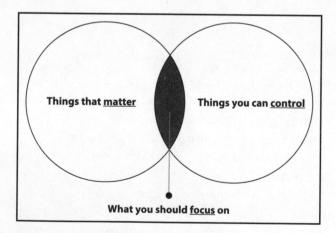

FIGURE 9.1 What You Should Focus On

SEVEN CRUCIAL FACTORS

So now that we've gotten past this week's money supply figures and today's advance-decline ratio, let's get down to brass tacks. There are only seven factors that determine the long-term value of your investment portfolio:

1. How much you save
2. How long your investments compound
3. Your asset allocation
4. Your security selection
5. How much your investments return
6. How much you pay in annual expenses
7. How much you pay in taxes

That's it. Whether you're investing $10,000 or $10 million, these seven factors will determine what your net worth eventually becomes. So let's take a closer look at each.

How Much You Save

I've already devoted a chapter to saving and told you it's important to save as much as you can, as soon as you can, for as long as you can. Understand, too, that it's tremendously beneficial to keep saving even as your portfolio takes wing.

Realize that you can have the world's most sophisticated investment strategy, but if you've saved only a pittance, it won't make much difference. Before you can invest seriously, it is essential to forgo nonessential spending.

It's also important to save in a qualified retirement plan first, where your money compounds tax-deferred and your contribution may be tax-deductible. This is especially true if you contribute to an employer-sponsored plan that provides matching benefits.

How Long Your Investments Compound

There are two ways to let your investments compound longer. You can start investing sooner or work and save longer. Or both. If you're 20 years old, for example, you need only have $31,327.88

TABLE 9.1   Amount Needed to Reach $1 Million by Age 65 at 8% Annual Return

Age	Investment
15	$21,321.23
20	$31,327.88
25	$46,030.93
30	$67,634.54
35	$99,377.33
40	$146,017.90
45	$214,548.21
50	$315,241.70
55	$463,193.49
60	$680,583.20

Source: John C. Bogle (2006), The Boglehead's Guide to Investing © 2006, John Wiley & Sons.

compound at 8% to accumulate $1 million by age 65. But to fully appreciate the high cost of waiting, look at Table 9.1. At 40, you need to have $146,017.90 compounding at 8% to reach $1 million by age 65. At 55, the number turns into $463,193.49. Clearly, it's in your interest to let money start compounding as soon as you can—and leave it alone as long as you can.

This requires more than a little discipline. But it's imperative that you adopt a hands-off mentality toward your investments. You can't enjoy the benefits of compounding if you interrupt the process by tapping your portfolio from time to time to buy the latest and greatest object of fascination.

Albert Einstein famously said that the most powerful force in the universe is money compounding. Let the force be with you.

Your Asset Allocation

Investors are often surprised to learn that their most important investment decision is not the securities they own but the asset allocation they represent. Your asset allocation is how you divide your portfolio among different imperfectly correlated assets like stocks, bonds, real estate investment trusts (REITs) and so on. (By uncorrelated, I mean they don't necessarily move in the same direction at the same time.) As we've seen, stocks give the greatest return over the long haul. The trade-off is high volatility. Blending different types of stocks with safer assets can generate excellent returns with less risk than being fully invested in stocks.

Your Security Selection

Once you've decided on your asset allocation, you have to select the mutual funds and/or exchange-traded funds that represent it. Hard as it is to believe, there are broker-sold mutual funds that represent various indexes but have front-end or back-end loads, 12b-1 fees, and high annual costs.

Owning these makes zero sense. (Unless, of course, you're the broker and your client is too naïve to understand how expensive it is to invest this way.)

Ideally, you want to own the securities that best represent the various asset classes and that have the lowest cost and most tax efficiency. (More on both in a bit.)

You could asset allocate your portfolio using individual stocks and bonds, but that requires quite a bit more time, money and analysis and so is outside the scope of this book.

However, I do want to point out that some individual investors have outperformed the market over the past decade by owning the best-performing stocks of the past several years. You probably know them as the FAANG stocks: Facebook, Amazon, Apple, Netflix and Google's parent, Alphabet. (Microsoft is sometimes added to this list as well.)

I'm all for owning outperforming stocks. After all, I've researched and recommended them for years. But to buy and hold a stock just because it has been going up—even if it has been going up for a long time—is not a prudent investment strategy.

There is a strong consensus that the tech giants will continue to dominate their markets—and the annual lists of top-performing stocks—forever. But forever is a long time. And history shows that chasing the outperformers generally fails in the end.

You may remember the "Nifty Fifty" from the 1970s. This was an elite list of 50 stocks that propelled the bull market early in that decade. They were often described as one-decision stocks— Buy!—since they were viewed as extremely stable over long periods of time.

A few of them did do well in the decades ahead, including Anheuser-Busch, Coca-Cola, Johnson & Johnson, McDonald's, and Merck.

But others most definitely did not, including International Telephone and Telegraph, Louisiana Land and Exploration, Eastman Kodak, and General Electric.

Many leading technology companies also generated great returns for a while but then generated years—or even decades—of serious underperformance. Just a sampling includes names like IBM, AOL, Yahoo, Cisco Systems, BlackBerry and Ericsson.

How Much Your Investments Return Annually

This is the great unknown, of course. Outside of low-returning, risk-free assets, you cannot know with any certainty what your returns will be in any year or even decade. But over the long haul, the returns on various asset classes are remarkably stable. Our goal with the Gone Fishin' Portfolio is to generate higher than average returns while keeping risk carefully controlled.

How Much You Pay in Annual Expenses

All things being equal, the higher your investment costs, the lower your annual returns and the longer it will take you to reach your financial goals. Keeping investment expenses to a minimum is crucial, although I can guarantee it's not your investment advisor's biggest priority. Sure, he wants you to earn decent returns. But he may have an eye on that new BMW, too.

How Much You Pay in Taxes

The government requires revenue to fund its various spending programs. But regardless of how patriotic you are, when financial independence is your goal, the IRS is not your friend. The taxman can take good returns and make them mediocre very quickly. Yet many investors fail to consider the tax consequences of their actions. They needlessly fork over many thousands of dollars each year by failing to tax-manage their investments. Doing this requires you to take a few steps to minimize the annual tax bite to your portfolio. (This is an important topic that I'll cover in more detail in Chapter 13.)

THE IMPORTANCE OF THESE FACTORS IN THE GONE FISHIN' PORTFOLIO

These seven crucial factors will determine both the long-term value of your portfolio and your quality of life in retirement.

Note that of these seven factors only one is beyond your control: No. 5. No matter how proficient you are as an investor, you cannot control your portfolio's annual investment returns. Yet this is the factor so many investors spend their time fretting about. What will the stock market do? When will my bonds bounce back? Are gold stocks finally set to rally? You might as well ask what the weather will be six weeks from Saturday. Nobody knows.

The Gone Fishin' Portfolio eliminates the perpetual guessing game about what lies ahead for the economy and the markets. Instead, you accept what you don't know (and can't control) and focus on those things you do know and can control—specifically, saving, compounding, asset allocation, security selection, costs and taxes.

Of the six factors we can control, the most important is your asset allocation. It is your single most important investment decision. That's a bold claim, so let me provide the evidence.

In the 1980s, Gary Brinson, a noted money manager and financial analyst, published two sophisticated studies in *Financial Analysts Journal,* analyzing the returns of pension fund managers. They clearly demonstrated that—over the long term—asset allocation accounted for more than 90% of the total return of a diversified investment portfolio. The rest was due to other factors, including security selection, costs and taxes.

These results—which have been confirmed by many other studies—are startling. They show that over the long term, your chosen asset allocation is nine times as important as everything else combined.

HIGHER RETURNS WITH LESS VOLATILITY

The goal of asset allocation is to create a diversified portfolio with the highest possible return within an acceptable level of risk. You achieve this by combining noncorrelated assets, like stocks, bonds and REITs. Academics call it building an efficient portfolio.

When I talk to investors about asset allocation, they are often dismissive. "Oh, I understand asset allocation," many of them say. "That means you should diversify. I do that already."

But asset allocation is more than simple diversification. If you own an S&P 500 index fund, for example, you are broadly diversified. (After all, you own a piece of 500 different companies.) But you aren't properly asset allocated, unless your goal is to be 100% invested in U.S. large cap stocks.

Other investors tell me they don't even have an asset allocation. They do, of course. Everyone does. (They just don't know what it is.) Even if all your money is in Treasury bills, you have an asset allocation. It's not a particularly good one, however. It's 100% cash.

As we've discussed, U.S. stocks have historically returned more than bonds. So, for example, a portfolio with 80% of its assets in bonds and 20% in stocks will behave very differently than one with 80% in stocks and 20% in bonds. Over time, the latter portfolio is likely to generate far superior results.

Of course, in today's ultra-low interest rate environment, high-quality bonds don't yield much of anything. However, we will use a strategy that allows us to capture higher yields when they become available in the future.

(I know that the conventional wisdom is that interest rates will stay low for many years into the future. And this may be true. But, again, we don't do any economic forecasting here. Rates could stay low or begin moving up sooner than expected. Today's common belief about perpetually low rates could turn out to be just as wrong as the widespread investor belief in the early 1980s that hyper-inflation and double-digit interest rates were here to stay.)

To determine your asset allocation, simply total up the value of all your liquid assets—stocks, bonds, mutual funds and bank accounts—and then determine what percentage of your total portfolio is in stocks, what percentage is in bonds and what percentage is in cash. Those percentages make up your basic asset allocation.

If you are uncertain which asset classes the funds you own fall into, contact the funds themselves. They'll be happy to tell you.

THE GONE FISHIN' ASSET ALLOCATION MODEL

In essence, the Gone Fishin' Portfolio is an asset allocation model. Its goal is to generate high returns without enduring the hair-raising volatility of a 100% stock portfolio.

Although I will describe each of the funds in detail in the next chapter, here is a list of the 10 asset classes that make up the Gone Fishin' Portfolio:

1. **U.S. large cap stocks.** Large cap is short for large capitalization. (A company's market capitalization is calculated by multiplying the number of shares outstanding by the price per share.) Large cap stocks are the biggest companies, typically ones with a market capitalization of $10 billion or more. Historically, they have returned an average of 11% per year. This category includes blue-chip household names like Intel, Amazon, Chevron, Procter & Gamble, Visa, and Apple.
2. **U.S. small cap stocks.** Small cap stocks are smaller companies, generally with a market capitalization that puts them in the bottom 20%, by size, of the New York Stock Exchange. (These are companies with a market capitalization of $3 billion or less.) Historically, they have returned 12% per year. These returns are slightly better than those of large cap stocks, but the price of admission is higher volatility. During rocky periods in the market, small cap stocks will make you feel like you've entered a bull-riding competition.
3. **European stocks.** Western Europe, of course, has both large and small companies, just like the United States. For the purposes of the Gone Fishin' Portfolio, we'll be using European large caps.

4. **Pacific Rim stocks.** Here we'll be focusing on large cap stocks, primarily in Japan, but also in Australia, Hong Kong, Singapore and New Zealand.

5. **Emerging market stocks.** These are shares of the leading companies in developing markets, primarily in Latin America, Eastern Europe and Asia.

6. **Precious metals equity (PME).** These are the world's largest gold mining companies. Many of them also produce silver, platinum and industrial metals.

7. **Real estate investment trusts (REITs).** These are companies that trade like stocks but invest in commercial properties—shopping centers, hotels, apartment complexes, office parks and warehouses. REITs avoid corporate income taxes by distributing more than 90% of their net cash flow to shareholders each year.

8. **Short-term corporate bonds.** A corporate bond is a company's IOU, a debt security that represents a promise to repay a sum of money at a fixed interest rate over a certain period of time. Short-term bonds generally yield less than long-term bonds. (Although when the yield curve is inverted, they may yield more.) Their shorter maturities make them less volatile than long-term bonds and less susceptible to price depreciation when interest rates rise.

9. **High-yield bonds.** High-yield bonds, or "junk bonds," are corporate bonds that do not qualify for an investment-grade rating. These bonds pay higher rates of interest because the issuers are less creditworthy. Default rates are higher on these than on investment-grade bonds as well. (According to Moody's, the annual default rate for BB/Ba bonds is about 1.5%.)

10. **Inflation-adjusted Treasury bonds.** These are U.S. government bonds where the principal increases with inflation, as measured by the consumer price index. The interest rate is fixed (and can be negative), but if there is an increase in the consumer price index—and you can pretty much bank on that—you earn that rate on a higher principal value, so your payments actually rise.

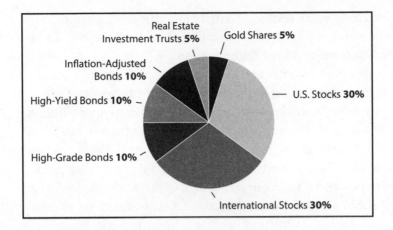

FIGURE 9.2 The Gone Fishin' Asset Allocation

As seen in Figure 9.2, our basic asset allocation is 70% equities and 30% bonds. But the suballocation—the types of stocks and bonds we'll use—varies from traditional models. It is designed to be both aggressive enough to boost your long-term returns and uncorrelated enough to smooth out the inevitable bumps along the way.

In any given year, these assets will generate returns that may be greater or less than their long-term averages. No one can tell you for certain what any of these asset classes will return next year or over the next 10 years. In certain years, the returns for some asset classes will be negative. We may even experience the occasional down decade, as we did for U.S. stocks from 2000 to 2009.

Going forward, however, it is reasonable to expect that the long-term returns will be close to their historical averages. Furthermore, by combining these assets, we can look forward to earning a return that comfortably exceeds inflation without taking the risk of being fully invested in stocks. That's because these asset classes are not perfectly correlated. In technical terms, when some zig, others will zag. This reduces the swings in value you'd otherwise see on your account statement month to month and year to year.

For instance, foreign stocks may climb when our domestic market is tanking. U.S. stocks and short-term corporate bonds are actually negatively correlated. That means these bonds are more likely to be rising if U.S. stocks are falling. Gold shares and REITs may rally when inflation is higher. And so on.

When you blend assets that give uncorrelated results, you take your first step toward what I call the holy grail of investing.

Why the holy grail? Not because you'll generate eye-popping returns, although that may happen from time to time. I call it the holy grail because investing in the Gone Fishin' Portfolio will enable above-average returns with below-average volatility. And it allows you to spend your time doing what you want, secure in the knowledge that you are using a system that comes as close to guaranteeing long-term investment success as anything else available.

This is not just my opinion, by the way.

A NOBEL PRIZE–WINNING STRATEGY

In 1990, the Nobel Prize in economics was awarded to Harry Markowitz, Merton Miller and William Sharpe. They understood that financial markets are extremely efficient at pricing securities. (That means share prices generally reflect all material, public information.) Markowitz's groundbreaking paper "Portfolio Selection," published in *The Journal of Finance,* laid the foundation for much of today's asset allocation strategies, including the Gone Fishin' Portfolio.

Of course, neither Markowitz nor anyone else can eliminate uncertainty in the investment process. However, he won the Nobel Prize for showing how a portfolio constructed of uncorrelated assets can allow you to master uncertainty and generate excellent investment results. He helped define and develop the concept of the efficient frontier, the point where you generate the best returns within a given level of risk. (It is important to understand that no one can show you the "optimal asset allocation" in advance. This is something that can be recognized only in hindsight.)

Higher returns with less risk. That's the holy grail, the goal of the Gone Fishin' Portfolio. Conventional wisdom says it isn't possible. The Nobel Committee and decades of experience say it is.

The work done by pioneers such as Brinson, Markowitz and others provides the philosophical underpinnings of the Gone Fishin' strategy. And there is a mountain of statistical evidence supporting this approach.

In sum, there are two primary reasons you should asset allocate properly. One is to increase returns. The other is to lessen the volatility of a stock portfolio. However, market volatility is not your biggest risk. Not having enough money to live on is. Volatility can never be eliminated completely without resorting to super-safe investments that leave you vulnerable to this greater risk. Like a slow leak in your pool, inflation gradually drains your purchasing power. You don't feel it in your gut like a bear market in stocks. And you may not notice inflation in the short term. But it's there year after year, gnawing at your purchasing power like termites in a historic mansion.

If you shrink from risk and volatility and keep your money invested in Treasury bills, certificates of deposit and other cash investments, inflation will win. That creates a diminished standard of living.

Cash investments are fine for setting aside an emergency fund or reaching short-term investment goals. But susceptibility to inflation makes them unsuitable for reaching your long-term investment goals.

THE BEAR MARKET PROTECTION KIT

As we've seen, stocks usually give superb returns when results are measured over decades. Yet from personal experience, I know that many individual investors are unable to patiently ride out the inevitable downturns in the stock market. They become restless. Or get fearful. For this reason, it makes sense to diversify a portion of your investment portfolio into assets that do not move in sync with the stock market. That is why 40% of the Gone Fishin' Portfolio is divided among alternative investments that include REITs, gold shares and three different types of bond funds. Here's the breakdown.

- REITs: 5%
- Gold mining shares: 5%
- Short-term corporate bonds: 10%
- High-yield bonds: 10%
- Inflation-adjusted Treasury bonds: 10%

Let's look at these asset classes in more detail.

REITs

A REIT is a company that derives its revenue from the management of commercial property. Think of a REIT as a mutual fund made up of hotels, office parks, apartment buildings, shopping centers or warehouses. Ordinarily, you may find commercial properties like these difficult investments to make, provided your last name isn't Trump or Rockefeller.

But REITs make it possible. These trusts have historically returned 8% a year, a little less than common stocks. But they return more than bonds and don't move in unison with either stocks or bonds. So they reduce the overall volatility of your portfolio.

Incidentally, REITs are required to distribute at least 90% of their net income to shareholders each year. (That's how they avoid paying corporate income taxes.) So most of your return will come from dividends.

Bear in mind, there is no guarantee that REITs—or any asset class—will move up when stocks move down. But historically, REITs have often risen—or fallen less—when stocks were going lower.

Gold

We also have a 5% gold allocation. Not to the metal itself, but rather to shares of precious metals mining companies.

The physical metal—especially in the form of bullion or numismatic coins—is lovely to behold. But keeping a large quantity of the metal at hand is risky. If you store it safely, there are costs associated with that, too.

Unlike gold, mining stocks produce economic value by profiting from the extraction and processing of the metal. Shareholders receive this value through appreciation in the share price and the distribution of profits via dividends.

Blue-chip mining shares have returned more than gold over time. And they are a leveraged play on the price of the metal. If gold moves up 10%, gold mining shares often rally 20% or more. That's because the gold business is pretty straightforward. Miners pull the metal out of the ground and sell it at market. There are cash costs for exploration and extraction and noncash depreciation costs as the value of the mines decreases. After overhead and interest costs, the rest flows to the bottom line. So even a fairly modest increase in the spot price of gold can have a significant impact on earnings.

But here's the top reason I like gold shares: They are an excellent portfolio diversifier. They are negatively correlated with bonds. And gold stocks have less than a 0.2 correlation with the S&P 500. That means they also move independently of other types of equities. That's good news when the broad market is moving south—as it will from time to time.

Gold mining stocks are volatile. In 2012 and 2013, for instance, they fell by more than half. They are also infamous for sometimes generating negative returns for several years in a row.

So why include them in the portfolio? Not just for the diversification value but also because when they move, they can *really* move. Precious metals equities went up 46% in 1964, 57% in 1967, 128% in 1979, 67% in 1980, 66% in 1987, 62% in 2002 and 56% in 2003, to give just a few examples. When you rebalance your portfolio, you'll be able to capitalize on these big moves and buy lagging assets with the profits.

Bonds

Lastly, let's look at bonds. When you purchase a bond, you are actually lending money to the issuer. When you do, you're promised a return on your investment—the bond's yield to maturity—and the return of the face value of the bond (usually $1,000) at a specified future date, known as the maturity date.

The maturity date may be as far off as 30 years or less than a year away. In essence, a bond is simply an IOU, a promissory note that pays interest (usually every six months) until maturity.

Over the long haul, bonds don't generally return as much as stocks, although they have on occasion. (You'd have to go back to 1831 through 1861 to find a 30-year period when the return on either short- or long-term bonds exceeded the return on equities.)

Edward McQuarrie, a professor emeritus of the Leavey School of Business at Santa Clara University, spent years reconstructing the history of stock and bond returns going back to 1793. He found that bonds outperformed stocks in 38.7% of all 10-year periods since then. And in many additional decade-long periods, bonds lagged stocks by less than 1% a year.

However, the primary benefit of bonds is their imperfect correlation with stocks. That gives them a stabilizing effect.

The Gone Fishin' Portfolio employs three types of bonds:

1. **Short-term corporate bonds.** Corporate bonds offer a fixed interest payment over time. That payment does not vary with the profitability of the firm. We will use high-quality corporate bonds instead of Treasury bonds because they yield more due to slightly higher credit risk. In fact, by owning high-grade, short-term corporate bonds, you can essentially get the same returns as long-term government bonds without the volatility of long-term bonds. As long as we're using bonds to reduce the swings in our portfolio, why not choose the less volatile option?

2. **High-yield bonds.** High-yield bonds, also called non-investment-grade bonds or junk bonds, are also corporate bonds. These are bonds rated BBB- or lower by rating agency Standard & Poor's. They are issued by companies less creditworthy than those that issue investment-grade bonds and are considered speculative. But don't let the name junk bond throw you. A diversified portfolio of these bonds, even after accounting for defaults, has returned more than either Treasurys or high-grade corporates. And while they do tend to be more highly correlated with the stock market than other bonds, they do not move in lockstep with equities, giving you some diversification advantage.

3. **Inflation-adjusted Treasury bonds.** These bonds, more commonly referred to as TIPS (Treasury inflation-protected securities), are the only bonds that guarantee you a return that is at least equal to inflation, as measured by the consumer price index. (Unless, of course, the bonds sport a negative yield.) TIPS pay interest every six months, just like a regular Treasury bond. The interest you receive is exempt from state and local (but not federal) income taxes. And as with other Treasurys, your investment is backed by the full faith and credit of the U.S. government. TIPS are less volatile than traditional bonds. And they are great portfolio diversifiers because they tend to rise when traditional bonds—as well as stocks—are falling.

There has been a long-running debate in the investment community on whether it is better to own bonds individually or through a mutual fund. Both have their advantages.

If you buy an individual bond, you're guaranteed the return of your principal at maturity. Plus, if you own a bond, there are no ongoing expenses as there are with bond funds. For these reasons, some investors insist on owning bonds outright instead of through a mutual fund.

But there are disadvantages to owning individual bonds that can make bond mutual funds the better choice. For example, buying (or selling) a bond requires a broker and can involve commissions. Putting together a diversified bond portfolio requires a much larger investment. There are often hidden markups, markdowns and spreads when you trade bonds in the secondary market. And, of course, you cannot automatically reinvest the interest payments. You would have to find a place to put the interest payments to work when you receive them. That may entail still more commissions or markups.

If you stick with no-load bond funds, as we will with the Gone Fishin' Portfolio, it's true there are annual expenses you will absorb. But they will be ultra-low. And there will be no costs for buying or selling your bonds. You will also enjoy lower minimums, instant diversification and professional management, and you can arrange to have your fund dividends automatically reinvested.

These conveniences make your fixed income investments both simple and convenient. So we'll make good use of low-cost bond funds in our Gone Fishin' Portfolio. But we won't overdo it. Stocks are the greatest wealth creators of all time. So our Gone Fishin' Portfolio will have greater exposure to them than bonds.

Owning bonds means you're realistic. It takes nerves of steel—something lacking in mere mortals—to place your liquid net worth in a pure stock portfolio and ride out severe bear markets, especially as your portfolio grows in value and the dollar fluctuations become more extreme. For that reason, we'll balance our volatile stock holdings with investments that will act as shock absorbers in the portfolio.

Asset allocating this way will lower your risk and allow for plenty of shut-eye at night.

REEL IT IN . . .

1. There are seven factors that will determine the long-term value of your investment portfolio: how much you save, how long your investments compound, your asset allocation, your security selection, how much your investments return annually, how much you pay in annual expenses and how much you pay in taxes.
2. Of these seven factors, only one is out of your control: your portfolio's annual return. So we'll concentrate our efforts on the other six.
3. Your asset allocation is your single biggest investment decision. Studies show that more than 90% of your portfolio's long-term return is due to this factor alone.
4. Asset allocation is not just diversification. It means having a strategic mix of noncorrelated assets that will boost returns while lowering risk.
5. The Gone Fishin' Portfolio's basic allocation is 70% equities and 30% bonds. But its suballocation, which includes REITs, gold shares and three different types of bonds, is aimed at boosting returns while reducing volatility.

CHAPTER 10

The Gone Fishin' Portfolio Unveiled

Simplicity is the ultimate sophistication.

Source: Leonardo da Vinci

You now understand the investment philosophy that underpins the Gone Fishin' Portfolio. In this chapter, I'm going to describe exactly where to put your long-term capital to work (and in what percentages)—and what you need to do to keep your investments on track year after year. The adjustments you need to make to your portfolio will take less than 20 minutes a year.

Advice this specific is virtually unheard of in the world of investing books. Ordinarily, the author describes general principles and techniques—which may or may not be sound—and then leaves the reader to apply them.

It becomes your responsibility to do the legwork, uncover the right stocks, analyze the right funds, and buy and sell when the time is right. You're left to survey the investment landscape and make important decisions. But since there are no specific instructions, most readers probably do little or nothing.

My goal here is different. I'm not going to lay out a smorgasbord of choices. Instead, I've kept it dead simple. I'm going to present a single portfolio designed to meet your long-term investment goals.

Let's get down to the nuts and bolts.

HOW TO PUT YOUR MONEY TO WORK

As I've made clear throughout the book, a key component of any long-term portfolio is a healthy exposure to stocks. The asset allocation model I created recommends that you have 30% of your portfolio invested in U.S. stocks, 30% in foreign stocks, 5% in real estate investment trusts (REITs) and 5% in gold shares. The remaining 30% we'll divide evenly between three different types of bonds.

As mentioned in Chapter 9, the U.S. stock allocation (30%) should be divided evenly between large cap and small cap stocks.

Why are we dividing our money between large and small stocks rather than just buying a single fund? The answer is because these two asset classes behave differently and often give widely varying returns. From January 1, 1980, to January 1, 2000, for example, the S&P 500 returned 1,261% while the small cap Russell 2000 returned 810%. But for the 20-year period between January 2000 and January 2020, small cap stocks returned 330% while the S&P 500 returned only 224%.

Clearly, there are distinct periods—sometimes years, sometimes a decade or more—when one group leads the other. Over long periods, however, small stocks have generally outperformed large ones. True, they're more volatile, but they compensate for it with superior returns.

The international stock allocation (30%) we're going to divide geographically, with one-third going into European stocks, one-third into Pacific Rim stocks and one-third into emerging market stocks.

TABLE 10.1   The Gone Fishin' Portfolio

Holding	Symbol	Allocation
Vanguard Total Stock Market Index Fund	VTSAX	15%
Vanguard Small-Cap Index Fund	VSMAX	15%
Vanguard European Stock Index Fund	VEUSX	10%
Vanguard Pacific Stock Index Fund	VPADX	10%
Vanguard Emerging Markets Stock Index Fund	VEMAX	10%
Vanguard Short-Term Investment-Grade Fund	VFSTX	10%
Vanguard High-Yield Corporate Fund	VWEHX	10%
Vanguard Inflation-Protected Securities Fund	VIPSX	10%
Vanguard Real Estate Index Fund	VGSLX	5%
VanEck Vectors Gold Miners ETF	GDX	5%

Table 10.1 shows how to implement the Gone Fishin' strategy using Vanguard mutual funds (and one exception).

- **Invest 15% of your portfolio in the Vanguard Total Stock Market Index Fund (VTSAX).** This fund tracks the broad market, but returns are determined primarily by the performance of U.S. large cap stocks. Its benchmark is the CRSP U.S. Total Market Index. (This index is considerably broader than both the Dow Jones Industrial Average and the S&P 500.) The fund holds a blend of both growth and value stocks ranging from small to large.
- **Invest 15% of your portfolio in the Vanguard Small-Cap Index Fund (VSMAX).** This fund captures the performance of U.S. small cap stocks. Like the Vanguard Total Stock Market Index Fund, it holds a blend of both growth and value stocks. Its benchmark is the CRSP U.S. Small Cap Index, a broadly diversified index of smaller U.S. companies.

Next, we move to international stocks, where you should have 30% of your portfolio invested. Again, we're dividing our investment into separate parts—rather than investing in a single diversified international fund—because the movement of these different assets is often uncorrelated. (This lack of correlation will pay off when we make our annual adjustment to the portfolio, which I'll describe in a moment.)

- **Invest 10% of your portfolio in the Vanguard European Stock Index Fund (VEUSX).** This fund's benchmark is the FTSE Developed Europe All Cap Index, which measures the performance of stocks in more than 15 developed European markets. It holds both growth and value stocks.
- **Invest 10% of your portfolio in the Vanguard Pacific Stock Index Fund (VPADX).** This fund's benchmark is the FTSE Developed Asia Pacific All Cap Index, which tracks equities from developed markets in Asia, Australia and other parts of the Pacific Rim. It, too, holds both growth and value stocks. (This equity asset class has significantly under-performed the others over the last couple decades. But these markets should ultimately "revert to the mean," giving higher returns in the future.)
- **Invest 10% of your portfolio in the Vanguard Emerging Markets Stock Index Fund (VEMAX).** This fund captures the return of major equity markets in Latin America, Eastern Europe and Southeast Asia. This fund's benchmark is the FTSE Emerging Markets All Cap China A Inclusion Index.

Now let's move to the fixed income side, which is 30% of the portfolio. We know that bonds return less than stocks over time. But they also provide balance and reduce risk in your portfolio. Our asset allocation model suggests that you have 10% of your portfolio in high-grade bonds, 10% in high-yield bonds and 10% in inflation-adjusted Treasurys.

- **Invest 10% of your portfolio in the Vanguard Short-Term Investment-Grade Fund (VFSTX).** This fund invests in a variety of high-quality and medium-quality fixed income securities. (At least 80% are short- and intermediate-term investment-grade securities.) The fund maintains a dollar-weighted average maturity of just one to four years.
- **Invest 10% of your portfolio in the Vanguard High-Yield Corporate Fund (VWEHX).** This fund invests in

a diversified group of high-yielding, higher-risk corporate bonds with medium- and lower-range credit quality ratings. At least 80% of its assets are in corporate bonds that are rated below Baa by Moody's Investors Service. Maturities range from short to intermediate term.

- **Invest 10% of your portfolio in the Vanguard Inflation-Protected Securities Fund (VIPSX).** The fund invests at least 80% of its assets in inflation-indexed bonds issued by the U.S. government and its agencies. It can invest in bonds of any maturity. However, its average maturity will be between seven and 20 years.

Now we will move on to REITs. As I described in Chapter 9, these trusts allow investors to own an interest in commercial properties, including shopping centers, office parks, hotels, warehouses, industrial centers and apartment complexes. REITs offer several benefits over traditional real estate investments. They are highly liquid, trading on an exchange like a stock. They allow an investor to own a diversified portfolio of properties in a single investment. They also have a fairly low correlation with the stock market, making them a great portfolio diversifier.

- **Invest 5% of your portfolio in the Vanguard Real Estate Index Fund (VGSLX).** The fund's benchmark is the MSCI US Investable Market Real Estate 25/50 Index, which measures the performance of publicly traded equity REITs and other real estate–related investments.

In the first edition of this book, I suggested you invest 5% of your portfolio in the Vanguard Precious Metals and Mining Fund (VGPMX). At that time, the fund closely tracked the performance of the S&P Global Custom Metals and Mining Index. And it did the job for us for over a decade. But in 2018, the fund changed its name and its objective (although the fund's symbol remained the same). It became the Vanguard Global Capital Cycles Fund. Its new benchmark is the Spliced Capital Cycles Index. And it has a new manager: Wellington Management Company LLP.

The old fund invested at least 80% of its assets in shares of U.S. and foreign companies in the mining industry. It could also invest up to 20% of its assets directly in gold, silver and precious metal coins. The new fund, by comparison, will invest at least 25% of assets in the metals sector and up to 75% in other natural resource companies and infrastructure-related firms, including telecommunications and utilities. Clearly, the fund is no longer suitable for investors wanting a 5% interest in precious metals mining companies.

When Vanguard first announced the change, critics came out of the woodwork to claim that the company made the change because gold was out of favor. (The metal peaked at $1,917.90 an ounce in August 2011 and then spent several years in the doldrums before finally surpassing that high in July 2020.)

However, Vanguard does not follow fads or try to make money off its investors. It did not change the fund's investment objective because gold was less popular.

When gold was streaking higher more than a decade ago, Vanguard closed the fund to new investors because it became increasingly difficult to put massive inflows of cash to work in the relatively tiny gold equities sector.

Why is it so small? According to the World Gold Council, approximately 197,576 metric tons of gold have been mined over the course of human history. If that were melted down and cast into a cube, it would measure just 71.2 feet per side.

Indeed, the total value of all globally traded gold and silver mining companies is just a tiny fraction of the market capitalization of a single large company like Apple, Microsoft or Amazon. Moving large sums into and out of the sector is tricky indeed—and can easily move prices up or down.

Vanguard's official reason for changing the fund's objective was to stabilize the fund's performance and seek broader opportunities for growth. But the change in objective made it ill-suited for investors seeking broad exposure to the world's top gold mining companies.

There are other mutual fund alternatives available, including Fidelity Select Gold Portfolio (FSAGX) and U.S. Global Investors Gold and Precious Metals Fund (USERX). But both have substantially higher expenses than Vanguard. So here's my suggestion . . .

- **Invest 5% of your portfolio in an exchange-traded fund: VanEck Vectors Gold Miners ETF (GDX).** (More about it in the next chapter.)

Each of these funds has an initial investment minimum of $3,000 and a subsequent investment minimum of $1. Since there are nine Vanguard funds in the Gone Fishin' Portfolio, this means you will need a minimum of $27,000 to get started (or more to achieve the desired asset allocation). Plus, approximately another $1,500 to invest in VanEck Vectors Gold Miners ETF to maintain a 5% asset allocation.

Small investors who can't meet this minimum need not despair. I have an ETF solution for you in the next chapter that will allow you to use the same Gone Fishin' strategy and start with virtually any amount.

You will find more complete information about each of these funds in Appendix A.

YOU MAY QUALIFY FOR EVEN LOWER COSTS

As I've pointed out, Vanguard funds have annual expenses that are the most competitive in the industry. In fact, the average mutual fund has expenses that are several times those of Vanguard's. This makes a tremendous difference over time. However, you will save even more if you qualify for Vanguard's Admiral Shares.

Admiral Shares are a class of Vanguard funds created to recognize and encourage the cost savings realized from large long standing accounts. Vanguard passes these savings on to the shareholders who generate them. The ultra-low Admiral Shares expense ratios can be 18% to 50% below the already low cost of ordinary Vanguard shares.

There are Admiral Shares available for every fund selection in our Gone Fishin' Portfolio.

Five of our nine recommended funds are only available as Admiral Shares with a $3,000 minimum investment. For the remaining recommendations, you are eligible for Admiral Shares if you invest in Vanguard's index funds and maintain a minimum investment of $50,000. In fact, Vanguard automatically converts qualifying accounts to Admiral Shares on a quarterly basis.

Admiral Shares provide you with further significant cost savings. And you will benefit from these savings year after year, because these are not just temporary fee waivers. Admiral Shares are a long-standing Vanguard policy. Lower costs mean higher net returns to you.

To create your Gone Fishin' Portfolio, you need only visit the Vanguard website (Vanguard.com) or call the company toll-free at 877.662.7447. Vanguard customer service representatives will be happy to answer any questions you have and make sure you receive a prospectus for each of the funds, including the applications. Fill out the applications, and return them to Vanguard with your check.

Incidentally, do not call Vanguard and say, "I'd like to invest in the Gone Fishin' Portfolio." This is my strategy, not theirs. And with trillions of dollars under management, it is unlikely that the customer service agent you reach will have the foggiest notion how this portfolio works. Vanguard provides the investment vehicles, not the strategy or recommendations.

When you've set up and funded your account, you're on your way to handling your serious money smartly and effectively. I'd love to tell you that there's nothing more to do. (Yes, the Gone Fishin' Portfolio is simple. But it's not quite *that* simple.) There is still one more step you'll need to take, one that will take just a few minutes a year. It's called rebalancing. And it's an important part of our strategy.

HOW TO KEEP YOUR PORTFOLIO ON TRACK

Each fund in the Gone Fishin' Portfolio represents a specific percentage of your total portfolio. But over time, those percentages will fluctuate with the performance of the financial markets. For instance, high-grade bonds may finish the year higher, and stocks may be lower. REITs may have appreciated, and gold mining shares may have fallen. And so on.

The job of rebalancing is to bring your asset allocation back to the original target percentages. This controls risk. Over the years, it will also deliver a significant performance boost. Why? Because rebalancing requires you to reduce the amount you have invested in the best-performing asset classes and add to those that have underperformed. Since all assets move in cycles, rebalancing forces you to sell high and buy low.

There are essentially three ways to rebalance:

1. You can add new money to those funds that have fallen below your target asset allocation.
2. You can sell a portion of the funds that have risen above your target percentage and add the proceeds to those funds that have fallen below it.
3. If you are taking out annual distributions to spend, you can pull money from the funds that have appreciated the most, thereby bringing your asset allocation back into alignment.

Here's an example. Let's say your initial investment in the Gone Fishin' Portfolio is $100,000. That means you start with the following:

- $15,000 in the Vanguard Total Stock Market Index Fund (15% in U.S. large cap stocks)
- $15,000 in the Vanguard Small-Cap Index Fund (15% in U.S. small cap stocks)
- $10,000 in the Vanguard European Stock Index Fund (10% in European stocks)
- $10,000 in the Vanguard Pacific Stock Index Fund (10% in Pacific Rim stocks)
- $10,000 in the Vanguard Emerging Markets Stock Index Fund (10% in emerging market stocks)
- $10,000 in the Vanguard Short-Term Investment-Grade Fund (10% in high-grade bonds)
- $10,000 in the Vanguard High-Yield Corporate Fund (10% in high-yield bonds)
- $10,000 in the Vanguard Inflation-Protected Securities Fund (10% in inflation-adjusted Treasury bonds)
- $5,000 in the Vanguard Real Estate Index Fund (5% in REITs)
- $5,000 in the VanEck Vectors Gold Miners ETF (5% in gold shares).

At the end of the year, the total value of your portfolio will have changed, and so will the percentage you hold in each fund. Let's say, for example, that your portfolio ends the year worth $122,000.

Your Vanguard Total Stock Market Index Fund may have grown from $15,000 initially to $21,960, for example. That's a nice return. However, U.S. large cap stocks now represent 18% of your portfolio instead of your target percentage of 15%. And if some assets are now a bigger percentage of your total portfolio, that means other assets are now a smaller percentage.

The real estate fund or the precious metals equity fund may represent less than 5% of your total portfolio value. If you have enough cash to make up the difference, you can simply add money to each fund that has lagged until it reaches our original target allocation.

This way is preferable because it means you're not creating a taxable event by selling something. (Taking profits involves paying capital gains taxes, unless you hold this portfolio in a qualified retirement account.) It's also positive because, as I mentioned in the chapter on saving, it really pays to keep adding to your investments over time. It is one of the few steps you can take that is guaranteed to help you reach your financial goals more quickly.

However, if you didn't have the cash to invest, you would need to redeem $3,660 worth of the Vanguard Total Stock Market Index and put the proceeds into those funds that have fallen below your target percentages. (You would do this by simply calling Vanguard's toll-free number and asking the representative to make the changes for you.)

To rebalance your portfolio each year without adding money to your account, you simply redeem part of those funds that have risen above your target percentages and add the proceeds to those that have declined below your target percentages. It's as simple as that.

The Beauty of Rebalancing

How often should you do this? Approximately once a year. The exact date you do it is not important. But there needs to be an interval of at least a year and a day between each time you set your portfolio and rebalance.

Why? Because you'll avoid paying short-term capital gains taxes by waiting at least a year and a day. (The IRS gives more favorable tax treatment to long-term capital gains.) Unless you hold these investments entirely in a qualified retirement plan—like an IRA or 401(k)—where a fund redemption is not a taxable event.

As your portfolio grows in value, it becomes increasingly unlikely that you will save enough each year to avoid selling something during the rebalancing process. (Unless your income and/or savings rate grows dramatically.)

Adding to those sectors that are down sounds simple enough. But I can tell you from working with hundreds of investors that most have a strong compulsion to add to those assets that are performing best, not those that are performing worst. Forget what the hot asset class is doing. You want to buy what's cheapest for the long-term advantage it confers.

As investment great John Templeton has said, "To buy when others are despondently selling and to sell when others are avidly buying requires the greatest fortitude and pays the greatest reward."

Don't thwart the power of this strategy by succumbing to the temptation to buy more of your winning funds (or bail out of your lagging ones). Given enough time, each asset class will experience a down cycle. That's when you'll add to them, when they're cheap and out of favor. Not when they're popular and expensive.

The beauty of our rebalancing strategy is that it provides you with a clear discipline of what to sell and when. Remember, it's impossible to predict which asset class will be the best- or worst-performing in any given year. International stocks, for example, may have underperformed last year. But there is no way of being certain that they won't be one of the top performers this year or next. And even if an asset class experiences several years in a row of lackluster performance, which is not uncommon, it's important that you not stray from your discipline.

Regardless of what happens from one year to the next, the advantages of rebalancing are much clearer over a decade or more.

By adding to your lagging assets, you may occasionally feel like you're throwing good money after bad. You're not.

Rather this practice forces you to sell high and buy low, every investor's objective. That's essentially what rebalancing is: shifting money from the assets that have appreciated the most to the ones that have lagged the most.

Research from Ibbotson Associates conclusively demonstrates that the strategy of rebalancing reduces the level of portfolio risk in both market upturns and downturns. But it found that the risk reduction is greater during market downturns.

It's not hard to understand why. Stocks give the best returns over time. But when the stock market is performing poorly, a rebalanced portfolio is less likely to experience negative returns than one that isn't rebalanced.

There is a lot of debate among asset allocators about how frequently you should rebalance. Some say once a year, some say every 18 months, and still others argue some other time period works best.

In *Rational Expectations: Asset Allocation for Investing Adults*, William Bernstein describes how he spent years studying a multitude of rebalancing intervals, ranging from one month to four years. He concluded that "there was less than a quarter of a percentage point difference between the best and worst strategies. At that level, the small difference would take centuries to reach statistical significance."

The important thing is that you do rebalance. Buying funds and just holding them through thick and thin isn't the wisest course. Since stocks appreciate the most over time, they will eventually make up the overwhelming majority of your portfolio. Without rebalancing, the older you get, the riskier your portfolio will become. That's not what you want.

In short, the Gone Fishin' Portfolio requires you to take only one action a year: rebalancing. It not only reduces volatility but will boost your returns. (Studies show that annual rebalancing can enhance portfolio returns by about 1% a year.) It also helps instill the discipline required for investment success.

So do it. And keep doing it, year after year.

PUTTING THE GONE FISHIN' PORTFOLIO TO THE TEST

As you can see from Figure 10.1, the Gone Fishin' Portfolio—rebalanced on December 31 of each year—performed better than the S&P 500 over the 20-year period from 2000 to 2019. And this was with far less risk than being fully invested in stocks. (After all, 30% of our portfolio is in bonds.)

This outperformance was partly because there were years when the strategy returned more than the broad market. And partly because there were years when it declined less.

If you had owned the Gone Fishin' Portfolio in the bear market of 2000 to 2002, for example, you would have seen it decline 6.1% in 2000, 2.7% in 2001 and 5.4% in 2002. These are temporary declines that most investors can live with. The S&P 500, by contrast, fell harder: down 9.1% in 2000, down 11.9% in 2001 and down 22.1% in 2002.

The Gone Fishin' Portfolio did suffer a more dramatic decline during the financial crisis in 2008. It returned a negative 31.7%. But the S&P 500 performed even worse, down 36.6%.

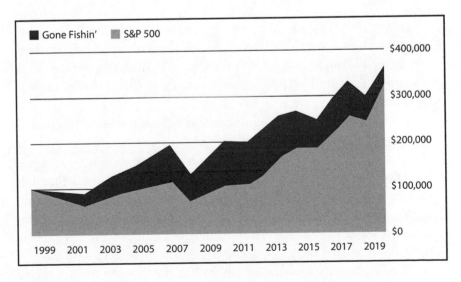

FIGURE 10.1 Gone Fishin' Portfolio Versus S&P 500 From 2000 to 2019

Note: Returns from 2000 to 2002 are based on back-testing of the Gone Fishin' Portfolio.

TABLE 10.2 Annual Return of the Gone Fishin' Portfolio Versus S&P 500

Year	Gone Fishin' Portfolio	S&P 500
2000	−6.1%	−9.1%
2001	−2.7%	−11.9%
2002	−5.4%	−22.1%
2003	32.7%	28.3%
2004	15.3%	10.9%
2005	12.0%	4.8%
2006	17.1%	15.6%
2007	9.7%	5.6%
2008	−31.7%	−36.6%
2009	34.4%	25.9%
2010	16.4%	14.8%
2011	−3.1%	2.1%
2012	13.5%	15.9%
2013	12.5%	32.0%
2014	3.9%	13.5%
2015	−3.5%	1.4%
2016	11.1%	11.8%
2017	16.4%	21.6%
2018	-8.8%	−4.2%
2019	20.4%	31.2%

Note: Returns from 2000 to 2002 are based on back-testing of the Gone Fishin' Portfolio.

In the decade from 2010 to 2019, however, the S&P 500 out-performed our strategy. There are various reasons. For starters, yields on all bonds came down significantly over this period. That was good for bond prices, but it lowered the distributions on our income funds.

As well, international equity markets—and especially emerging markets—underperformed the U.S. market dramatically over the past 10 years. The decade that ended in 2019 was one of the best ever for the U.S. stock market. From January 2010 through December 2019, the S&P 500 returned 13.5% annually. If you go back and include 2009 as well, the 11-year annualized return was a mouthwatering 14.6%. That's much better than the S&P 500's long-term annual return of about 10% (see Table 10.2).

What investors may not recall is that the decade from January 2000 through December 2009 was one of the worst on record. The Dow hit a peak of 11,722 in March 2000 and bottomed out at 6,547 in March 2009, 44% lower. The S&P 500 delivered a negative return over the decade. The Nasdaq declined a jaw-dropping 66.5%.

But 10 years of negative returns set us up for the decade of extraordinary returns that followed. No doubt many investors wish they could turn back the hands of time and load up on U.S. stocks when they were cheap. Alas, that's not possible. However, you have a similar opportunity today in the emerging markets of Asia, Eastern Europe and Latin America.

For example, from January 2010 through December 2019—that period of blockbuster U.S. equity returns—emerging markets eked out a low single-digit annual return. The MSCI Emerging Markets Latin America Index returned 29.4%. As with the U.S., it was a rare down decade.

Just as U.S. stocks were ultra-cheap in 2009, so are emerging market stocks today. Figure 10.2 shows a comparison of emerging markets versus the United States.

As I write this, emerging markets are quite the bargain, selling for roughly half the valuation of the U.S. market. Yet many investors question whether emerging markets deserve a place in their portfolios. The answer is a resounding yes.

Let me start by making the macro case. Emerging markets make up more than 160—or 80%—of the approximately 200 nations in

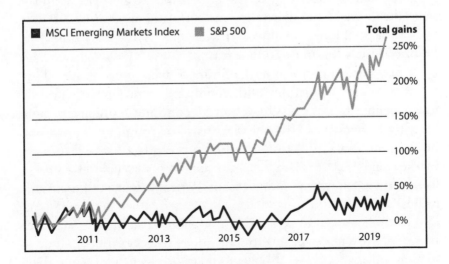

FIGURE 10.2 Total Gains of Emerging Markets Versus United States

Source: Bloomberg, Total Gains of Emerging Markets Vs. United States. © Bloomberg L.P.

the world. These countries contain 77% of the world's land-mass and more than 85% of its population. China and India alone have over 2.7 billion citizens, or more than one-third of the planet's population of 7.8 billion. And here's something that may surprise you. These countries represent 59% of total global GDP, up from less than half a decade ago and just 23% two decades ago.

Investors in developed markets may not realize it, but emerging markets today are the world's primary drivers of both global growth and wealth accumulation. They comprise the dominant share of the world's population and natural resources and the largest reservoir of future consumers.

One of the biggest economic developments of the next few decades will be the emergence of a new "world middle class." Fortunes will be made meeting the wants and needs of the 6.6 billion citizens residing in emerging markets.

Yet when I talk to most Americans about how much exposure they have to emerging markets in their portfolios, the typical answer is somewhere between 0% and 5%. That's far too little. Our Gone Fishin' strategy places 10% of your portfolio in this sector. And if history is any guide, what caused the portfolio to lag the S&P 500 over the last several years should cause it to outperform in the future, as all asset classes eventually revert to the mean.

Returning to our long-term performance, I have not emphasized the Gone Fishin' Portfolio's outperformance of the S&P 500 over the last 20 years—indeed this chapter is the first time I've mentioned it—for an important reason.

It may not outperform in the future. I make no promises. This is a conservative portfolio with significant exposure to safe but low-yielding bonds. If U.S. equities continue to deliver their long-term average of 10% per year, it will be tough for an investor holding 30% in bonds to keep up. On the other hand, if foreign markets and U.S. small caps deliver annual returns closer to their long-term averages, the Gone Fishin' Portfolio may well continue to beat the S&P 500.

However, this strategy is really not about "beating the market." It's about growing your investment capital in good times and protecting it in bad. It's less about winning the investment game than making sure you never lose.

A SIMPLE STRATEGY IN A COMPLEX WORLD

I don't pretend that the Gone Fishin' Portfolio is the only way to manage your long-term money effectively. I only claim that it works. I don't know an alternative strategy that has a greater probability of success—or requires less time.

Incidentally, there is a limit to how far back you can test the Gone Fishin' Portfolio—and for a simple reason. This strategy requires you to invest 10% in inflation-adjusted Treasurys (TIPS). However, Uncle Sam only created these securities in 1997. (And Vanguard did not introduce its first TIPS mutual fund until 2000.)

You cannot know for certain what this portfolio (or any other) will return in the future, no matter how much back-testing you do. Historical asset class returns are a valuable guidepost. But they are no guarantee.

However, it's not just the attractiveness of past or future returns that makes the Gone Fishin' Portfolio such a compelling choice. It's also that it requires so little attention.

I have a tennis pal, for instance, who spends hours each day trading. Is he making money? He says he is. But then, traders rarely talk about their losses. More to the point, is he making enough to justify the hundreds of hours he spends doing it each year? I wonder. (And I notice he hasn't given up his day job.)

The Gone Fishin' Portfolio is designed for those who want a powerful and sophisticated system for managing their money, but who prefer to dedicate their time and energy to the things they value most, whether that's growing prize tomatoes, playing Pebble Beach or reeling in marlin off Costa Rica's Pacific coast.

If this strategy is so great, you may wonder why your investment advisor hasn't recommended it. I tried to make that clear in the early chapters. The Gone Fishin' Portfolio makes them obsolete. It generates no brokerage commissions, no planning fees, no sales loads and no wrap fees.

It's true we all need to rely on banks and insurance companies for some financial services. But do you need to use them—or anyone else—to manage your money, too?

Absolutely not. Armed with the investment basics and a little discipline, you can manage your serious money yourself—and save many thousands of dollars in the process. The folks on the other side of the desk may argue that the world of investing is so complicated—and your financial circumstances so distinctive—that it's foolhardy to consider managing your money yourself.

Investing can, of course, be a complicated subject. But you also have the choice of keeping it simple. That's what the Gone Fishin' Portfolio does. It keeps effective, sophisticated money management simple.

If you like short-term stock trading as a hobby, by all means, continue to enjoy it. I do it myself. This is something you don't generally hear from hard-core asset allocators, incidentally. But you can invest your long-term growth money safely and have some fun in the market, too. The two activities are not mutually exclusive.

It is important, however, to separate your long-term core portfolio (like the Gone Fishin' Portfolio) from your short-term trading portfolio. This keeps things uncomplicated. Plus, it ensures that you don't start trading your long-term positions or find yourself clinging to your short-term trades.

In my view, even the most dedicated short-term traders need an effective long-term strategy like Gone Fishin' for their serious money. But my hunch is that the vast majority of folks have better things to do than watch the stock market bounce up and down all day. It's for these folks that I've written this book. And for those, too, who want some insurance to back up their trading activities.

With the Gone Fishin' Portfolio you can manage your money yourself. You can accomplish this with just as much sophistication as the country's leading money managers—and get better results than the vast majority of them. You will do an end run around Wall Street's marketing machine that wants to "capture your assets" and live off your investments. Best of all, the whole program requires a commitment of less than 20 minutes a year. That's not much to ask when the goal is financial freedom.

Managing your money this way is likely to lead to superior long-term investment returns. And the strategy is designed to make sure you never lose. After all, you have removed three layers of risk—active manager risk, individual security risk and high expenses—that could potentially derail your retirement plans or cause you to fail to meet your investment objectives.

Our goal here is not to beat the market by the largest margin in the shortest period of time. Rather, it's to allow you to achieve financial independence and its important byproduct: peace of mind.

WHAT TO TELL THE NAYSAYERS

There are some aspects of the Gone Fishin' strategy that critics—and fee-oriented investment advisors—may find controversial. I want to address those potential objections now. Some, for example, may object to the inclusion of asset classes like gold shares and junk bonds. Others will question the weightings of different asset classes. Still others will question the one-size-fits-all nature of this strategy. I'm happy to rebut them all.

Unusual Success From Unusual Assets

Let's begin by looking at the reasons for the inclusion of more controversial asset classes like gold shares, foreign stocks (particularly emerging market stocks) and high-yield bonds. In my view, the key to diversifying wisely is including investments that tend to be out of sync with the rest of your holdings.

Many asset allocation models have not performed particularly well over the years, partly because their makeup is so conventional. Indeed, many have nothing but a U.S. stock fund, a U.S. bond fund and cash.

Holding a lot of cash is like dragging an anchor. If it makes you feel comfortable, keep enough cash in the bank to cover a year's worth of living expenses. But don't include it in your long-term portfolio. Cash does nothing to boost your long-term returns.

And that plain-vanilla approach is unlikely to do as well in the future as our Gone Fishin' strategy. It doesn't allow you to benefit from investment opportunities overseas, the inflation protection available from TIPS, or other alternative investments like junk bonds, gold shares and REITs.

Excluding these lesser-owned assets is a shortcoming of other investment models. For example, a 10% exposure to the high-yield bond market enables higher returns while taking less risk than being fully invested in stocks. Despite the pejorative name "junk," these bonds offer a number of advantages.

First, high-yield bonds have traditionally returned more than investment-grade bonds. Second, high-yield bonds have a fairly low correlation with investment-grade bonds, like Treasurys and triple-A corporates. That's what we want when we asset allocate. Third, owning a broadly diversified portfolio of high-yield bonds is a lot less risky than owning just a handful of individual bonds.

Blending high-yield bonds with the other nine asset categories actually reduces your overall portfolio volatility while increasing your returns.

Still, many asset allocators give them a pass. Here are the three leading objections, along with my responses:

1. **You invest in bonds for safety**. That's true, but putting riskier assets in your portfolio increases the return of the portfolio as a whole. (And, technically, junk bonds are safer than stocks because they represent a senior claim on the assets of the company.)

2. **High-yield bonds are extremely tax-inefficient**. Yes, their interest payments are taxed at your marginal tax rate, not the lower capital gains rate. But you can avoid this problem by owning them in your IRA or other qualified retirement plan, as I describe more fully in Chapter 13.

3. **High-yield bonds are more closely correlated to stocks than investment grade bonds**. True again. But so what? The two asset classes don't move in lockstep and there are plenty of periods when high-yield bonds perform better than equities.

To those who insist high-yield bonds are simply too risky to include, remember the words of former junk bond king Michael Milken: The rating on triple-A bonds only has one way to go—down. Sure, most investment-grade obligations maintain their standings. But in no case do triple-A bonds receive upgrades.

In short, including a 10% allocation to high-yield bonds gives you an edge. Historically, portfolios that include exposure to this asset class have performed better than those that rely solely on investment-grade bonds for the fixed income allocation.

Incidentally, some investors may ask why our high-grade bond component consists of short-term investment-grade bonds, rather than long-term Treasurys.

The first reason is that the historical return for these has only been about 1.5% less per year than the return for long-term bonds, despite a much lower level of volatility. Another is that there is a small but fairly consistent negative correlation between short-term bonds and stocks. If we own these bonds not to boost our returns but to get us through the inevitable sinking spells in the market without abandoning our discipline, then short-term bonds are the superior choice.

Another Glittering Asset

Next let's turn to our inclusion of gold shares. This may seem questionable to some. After all, despite the sharp run-up in gold prices over the past few years, it wasn't until 2007 that gold finally surpassed the $800 mark it hit back in 1980.

As I mentioned in the section on long-term asset returns, gold has generally been dead weight in a long-term portfolio, despite flashes of brilliance from time to time.

Throughout the book, I've referred to more than 200 years of stock market returns. We have much more data on the historical price of gold. A few millennias' worth, in fact. And, in inflation-adjusted terms, the long-term return on the so-called barbarous relic is essentially *zero*. That's right, gold has worked well as a store of value, but as an investment it has been "*meh.*" (This isn't too surprising when you consider that for centuries gold *was* money.)

However, gold shares—and other precious metals equities—are another story. They have performed quite well. In fact, while gold shares have been traded on the major U.S. and foreign exchanges for several decades, until recently there has been no reliable precious metals equity index. This in itself is the reason many traditional asset allocators have excluded them from their portfolios. But I believe that's a mistake.

On his website EfficientFrontier.com, Bernstein has written a brief paper called "The Expected Return of Precious Metals Equity." In it, he says . . .

> One can cobble together a "precious metals index" which will estimate the long-term return of this asset. The Morningstar database of mutual funds has a precious metals fund index which goes back to 1976, and before that the Van Eck International Fund, which started operations in 1956, became a precious metals fund sometime in 1968. Combining the Van Eck data for 1969–75 with the Morningstar data beginning in 1976 provides a 27.75 year time series—just long enough to provide a reasonable estimate of the "true" long-term return of this asset. The results are startling— the annualized return from January 1969 to September 1996 was 12.81%. This is actually higher than the S&P 500 (11.24%), U.S. small stocks (12.44%), and the EAFE (12.52%) for the same period.
>
> Source: The Expected Return of Precious Metals Equity by William J. Bernstein © 1996, William J. Bernstein

REITs and gold shares are both good inflation hedges. And while gold bullion has generated a dismal long-term return, gold shares have a history of doing well. Better still, they tend to move independently of the stock and bond markets. Gold-related investments have a near-zero correlation with other asset classes. That makes them great portfolio diversifiers. That's especially true when you rebalance. Including a gold fund as a small component of a diversified portfolio helps you balance your overall portfolio risk. That's why I recommend a 5% gold share allocation.

The World Is Your Oyster

Lastly, some advisors may take issue with our heavy exposure to international equity markets. But U.S. stocks account for only about 40% of the world's market capitalization. The rest of the world accounts for 60%. It makes sense to build an equity portfolio that reflects the success of capitalism in our increasingly borderless world.

In the early 1980s, the United States accounted for a third of the global economy. Today it is just 15%. You want your portfolio to capitalize on that other 85%.

This is an area where John Bogle and I disagree. For example, he writes in *Common Sense on Mutual Funds: New Imperatives for the Intelligent Investor* that "overseas investments—holdings in the corporations of other nations—are not essential, nor even necessary, to a well-diversified portfolio."

Bogle and some others believe that the big U.S. multinational firms that make up a substantial percentage of U.S. stock indexes give you all the international exposure you need. As for diversification value, they argue that world markets have often fallen in concert during panics, crashes and crises.

My response is, yes, we've seen short-term panics that caused investors worldwide to rush to the sidelines in unison. But after brief periods when global markets moved in concert, individual country markets reverted to fluctuations based on events in their local markets.

If you don't diversify into foreign markets, you suffer an opportunity cost, as well as the loss of currency diversification and a potential rebalancing advantage.

Moreover, it's important to realize that the world is becoming increasingly integrated economically. Trade is increasing worldwide. Taxes and tariffs are coming down. Accounting standards are becoming more transparent.

Yes, the United States is still the world's leading economic power and likely to remain so for some years to come. But why be provincial? Americans are already patronizing hundreds of international companies, such as Royal Dutch Shell, Samsung, Sony, Nestlé and Honda, whether we recognize it or not. Why would you be willing to buy these companies' products but not the companies themselves?

For example, when you get up in the morning, you may turn on your Japanese TV to check the news, have a cup of Brazilian coffee, and put on your shirt made in Taiwan, your shoes from Italy and your Swiss watch, before getting in your German car for the commute to work.

Earnings growth, too, is often stronger in overseas markets. Stock valuations are often better. And currency fluctuations provide you with further diversification for your portfolio.

Of course, if putting half of your money in international markets is considered heresy, some investors will really flip their wigs about putting roughly 17% of your equity money—10% of your total portfolio—in emerging markets.

"If I wouldn't vacation in these places," a client once told me, "why should I send my investment capital there?" Higher potential returns and a portfolio that exhibits less overall volatility are two good reasons.

Sure, the stock markets of Latin America, Eastern Europe and Southeast Asia get bumpy occasionally. They tend to have more frequent political and economic problems. Their currencies are less secure. Their markets are often less regulated. But there are advantages, too.

Remember, 70 years ago Germany and Japan were emerging markets. Fifty years before that, the United States was an emerging market. And two centuries ago, England, France and Holland were too. Betting on these countries when they were emerging markets paid off pretty darn well.

Still, some will ask, "But why take the risk?" As I've said before, people today are living longer than ever. If you don't want your money to give out before your pulse does, you need your portfolio to do some heavy lifting. In the decades ahead, as emerging markets gradually turn into developed markets, they may well be the afterburners in your portfolio.

In short, holding riskier assets—like emerging markets, gold stocks and high-yield bonds—should give your portfolio a boost it wouldn't get holding tamer assets. And the fact that these assets are relatively uncorrelated should cause your total portfolio to experience less overall volatility, not more.

True, our particular asset allocation is a bit unconventional. That means it will have years—or a string of them—when the returns are radically different from those of the S&P 500. But over the long haul, if you've kept saving and rebalancing, your total return should be ample to meet your retirement needs.

THERE IS ONLY ONE OBJECTIVE

Lastly, I expect to catch some flak for recommending a single portfolio, rather than suggesting you customize your asset allocation based on your personal circumstances.

This is not the blasphemy some might imagine, however. The Gone Fishin' Portfolio is designed for long-term capital appreciation. It is not the way to save for a down payment on a house. It is not the way to invest your 15-year-old daughter's college money. It's not the way for a retiree to maximize monthly investment income.

It is a growth portfolio designed to keep you from outliving your money. It should give satisfactory returns for 25-year-olds just beginning to invest, as well as 65-year-olds whose retirement may realistically last three decades before they go to that big retirement home in the sky.

I'll be the first to concede that once you reach the late stage of life where your primary (or sole) objective is to structure your portfolio for maximum income and capital preservation, you need to make your asset allocation more conservative.

Still, the question remains: Does someone who realistically has a decade or more of life ahead of him truly need someone to assess his "personal risk tolerance" and design a customized asset allocation? My answer is no. As Templeton once said, "For all long-term investors, there is only one objective—maximum total return after taxes."

Yet some investment advisors seem to be planning for another objective: their clients' inability to stick with the program, even if that means they won't meet their long-term investment objectives. We all know that when the market begins acting badly, as it will from time to time, it can be stressful. However, if your choice is a few restless nights and a comfortable retirement or sleeping like a baby and waking up one day to find you're out of money and too elderly to go back to work, what is the better alternative? Unless you've accumulated enough to coast through a long retirement, you can't have it both ways.

A typical question that fund companies and financial planners ask is "During market declines, would you sell portions of your riskier assets and invest the money in safer assets?" Of course, millions of investors have done exactly this during market declines over the years. And almost as many millions have regretted it later.

For an investor to sell into a short-term market decline goes against everything the past has to teach us. We have 220 years of stock market history—valuable hindsight—demonstrating that every decline was a buying opportunity for the long-term investor, even the Great Depression.

Instead of setting up a conservative asset allocation based on the likelihood that you'll panic and sell during the next correction or bear market, why not simply resolve that you won't do it? And if you can't resist feeling panicky, at least keep yourself from selling. Instead of structuring your portfolio for future ineptitude, educate yourself now so you're able to show some backbone when the chips are down.

Another typical question from those who insist on assessing an investor's personal investment style is "Would you invest in a mutual fund based solely on a brief conversation with a friend, co-worker or relative?"

If you answer yes to this question, I applaud your honesty. But that's all I applaud. Again, the only purpose this question serves is to verify whether the advisor is dealing with someone who is unsophisticated. But unsophisticated investors generally have the same long-term financial requirements as more sophisticated ones—namely, a long and comfortable retirement.

Volatile markets create a lot of anxiety, especially when we're talking about the money that will fund your lifestyle in retirement.

But we can't eliminate volatility or uncertainty. And we can't eliminate the fearful emotions that we experience when the market swoons from time to time, as it will. I can only alert you to how you're likely to feel and suggest how you can keep these emotions from undoing your good work. (In fact, I've dedicated much of Chapter 15 to this topic.)

So why do so many financial planners insist that they need to "personalize" your long-term investment portfolio? One reason is it helps justify their fees. Another reason is it reduces their legal liabilities. Brokers and other investment advisors are supposed to "know their customers." They have a multitude of onerous regulatory requirements, some of them largely meaningless.

Listen to Jim Otar, for example, a certified financial planner, an independent advisor and the author of *High Expectations & False Dreams: One Hundred Years of Stock Market History Applied to Retirement Planning*.

He has spent a lot of time researching and writing about the perfect portfolio for retirement. He wrote a column on client strategies in the journal *Financial Planning* for fellow certified financial planners. He writes that, with very few exceptions, "the optimum asset allocation for an income portfolio has nothing to do with your client's risk tolerance, his investment knowledge or many other countless questions that your clients are forced to answer during your initial interview. Other than fulfilling the regulatory requirements, the ritual of the risk assessment has no significance to the optimum asset mix."

Some advisors will argue that their clients can't withstand the volatility inherent in stocks. Fine. But are they also telling them that they aren't likely to meet their long-term investment goals as a result? Wouldn't it be better to educate them and reassure them than to just throw in the towel with a portfolio that is too conservative from the start? Because unless you're worth so much that you have the luxury of investing purely for income and preservation of capital, you need a healthy exposure to stocks.

Rest assured, you'll still experience volatility with the Gone Fishin' Portfolio because you'll own some higher-risk assets. But as Bernstein writes in *The Intelligent Asset Allocator*, "Appreciate that diversified portfolios behave very differently than the individual assets in them, in much the same way that a cake tastes different from shortening, flour, butter, and sugar."

In other words, your whole portfolio will fluctuate less than some of its constituents. And, if the next 30 years are anything like the last 30, you'll outperform the vast majority of professional money managers. Best of all, you'll be headed down the path to financial independence—and have the satisfaction and cost savings of doing it on your own.

It's reasonable to ask how you can be sure the asset allocation I've recommended here is the very best one for the future. The truth is you can't. As with so many other factors we've discussed, you simply cannot know. The "perfect" asset allocation is something that can be recognized only in hindsight.

The most important thing is to avoid a poor asset allocation. What would that be? Easily, one of the worst is 100% cash. An allocation that is light on equities generally won't work. And an asset allocation that changes like the seasons is unlikely to get the job done, either.

The Gone Fishin' Portfolio offers you excellent prospects. It divides your investment capital among a number of high-returning but imperfectly correlated assets. It contains some more unconventional investments that should give you a performance boost over time. And the portfolio has a proven track record.

Still, you might ask, isn't recommending a single asset allocation needlessly prescriptive? Perhaps. But there's another reason I've recommended a specific portfolio.

In my experience, the more choices an investor has, the less likely he or she is to get off the dime and actually put money to work. By making things dead simple, I'm trying to give you that final nudge. In essence, I'm telling you there's nothing left to figure out. Here's the portfolio. Go do it.

UNDERSTAND THE GAME TO WIN IT

The Gone Fishin' Portfolio is designed for responsible adults. Financial freedom requires that you not only plan to do the right thing, but actually do it. This is true of every successful investment strategy.

Don't make your portfolio too conservative now to prepare for emotionally overwrought behavior later. Plan for success instead. Realize that a smiling broker or financial planner will be happy to move your money in and out of the market and hold your hand year after year. (Just don't mistake this hand-holding for love. It comes at a hefty price.)

Stock market investing is a lot like football. If you're going to play the game, you're going to get knocked down from time to time. If your son or grandson came to you and told you that he wanted to be a Heisman Trophy winner—that he dreams of running and scoring and winning—you might remind him that he's going to have a lot of sore Mondays, too. To believe otherwise wouldn't be realistic. Getting the stuffing knocked out of you is part of the game.

The same is true of investing. If you're going after the kinds of returns that only volatile assets can provide, don't be surprised when the volatility shows up. Our asset allocation will provide the pads and helmet. But you're still going to get hit from time to time. Don't let that deter you. Your long-term returns should be more than satisfactory. That's what leads to investment success . . . and a comfortable retirement.

REEL IT IN . . .

1. To put your money to work in the Gone Fishin' Portfolio, invest your money as I describe in Table 10.1.
2. Rebalance your portfolio once a year to increase returns and control risk. You can do this by adding new money to lagging assets, by selling a portion of your best-performing assets and applying the proceeds to those that have lagged, or both.
3. By rebalancing annually, you will force yourself to buy low and sell high—the essence of successful investing.
4. The makeup of the Gone Fishin' Portfolio is unconventional. But riskier assets like gold shares, emerging market stocks and high-yield bonds are included to keep future returns higher and portfolio risk lower than would be possible using a more conventional asset allocation.
5. The Gone Fishin' Portfolio is designed to reduce volatility, but it cannot eliminate it. That means you need to have realistic expectations. It's okay to have down quarters—and even down years—in the pursuit of higher long-term returns.

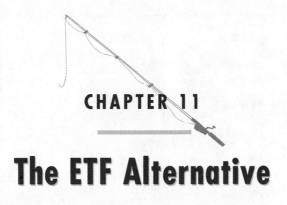

CHAPTER 11

The ETF Alternative

Stay committed to your decisions, but stay flexible in
your approach.

Source: Tony Robbins

It's important to understand that the heart and soul of the Gone
Fishin' Portfolio is the asset allocation model, as described in
Figure 9.2 (reprinted on Page 142).

In my view, The Vanguard Group is the best mutual fund
company to implement this strategy because of its size, reliability
and low-cost structure.

The mutual fund giant has never been the only way to implement the Gone Fishin' strategy. You could use other no-load
fund families, provided they offer all 10 asset classes. (Some fund
groups do not.)

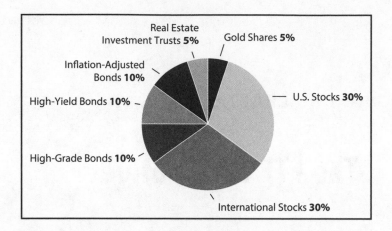

FIGURE 9.2 The Gone Fishin' Asset Allocation (repeated)

And there are a couple of potential drawbacks to using any mutual fund family, including Vanguard. As you know, a mutual fund stands ready to redeem your shares on any business day, after the market closes. Ordinarily, the cash for your redemption comes from fund inflows on the same day, the cash holdings of the fund or the manager liquidating a small portion of the fund's holdings.

If a fund were suddenly hit with massive redemptions—due to a market panic, for example—the manager could potentially need to sell a large amount of securities to meet this demand. This might mean realizing substantial capital gains, even in an index fund. Since mutual funds are required to distribute these gains to shareholders each year, it could cause even a relatively tax-efficient index fund to suddenly become tax-inefficient (provided, of course, that you own these funds outside of a tax-deferred account).

Historically, the scenario I'm describing has not been a problem. But it never hurts to expect—or at least consider—the unexpected.

With those two potential handicaps in mind, I offered an alternative version of the Gone Fishin' Portfolio in the first edition of this book. It kept our most important investment decision—the asset allocation—the same. But the funds to implement it were different. These funds will not close to new investors. They are even more tax-efficient than Vanguard mutual funds. And some have lower expenses than even Vanguard Admiral Shares.

I'm talking about exchange-traded funds, more commonly known as ETFs.

FUNDS THAT TRADE LIKE STOCKS

ETFs are essentially funds that trade on an exchange, like a stock. The first ETF was launched by State Street Global Advisors in 1993. The idea quickly caught fire. There are now thousands of ETFs representing hundreds of different market sectors and asset classes. (ETFGI, a leading independent research firm, reported that there were 7,927 global ETFs at the end of 2019 with a record $6.4 trillion in assets.)

Here's what you should know about ETFs:

- They have an exchange listing and trade continuously throughout the day, unlike ordinary mutual funds, which can be bought or redeemed only at the day's closing price.
- They may be linked to an index or actively managed (although most ETFs are index funds).
- They have much lower costs than mutual funds. According to Morningstar, the average expense ratio of an ETF is just 0.23%, while the average expense ratio for an actively managed fund is 1.45%. (Yes, more than six times higher.) And we're going to rely on some with lower costs still.
- Authorized shareholders can make redemptions on an in-kind basis, which means that rather than selling, shareholders can choose to receive large blocks of the underlying securities that make up the index in exchange for their ETF shares. (I won't go into the details here since this is not a part of our Gone Fishin' strategy.)

As you can see, ETFs offer several advantages. But there are minor potential drawbacks to these funds, too. For example, the market price and the net asset value (NAV) of an ETF can diverge temporarily. This could be a problem if you wind up buying a fund at a premium to its NAV or selling it at a discount. (The NAV is used to determine the fair value of a security. It is calculated by taking the security's total assets less liabilities and dividing by the number of shares outstanding.)

However, two things keep the NAV and market price from straying too far apart. First, since the NAV is generally quoted intraday, traders who spot the discrepancy can immediately buy or sell ETF shares to exploit the difference. In this way, self-interested investors keep the market prices relatively close to net asset values.

Also, authorized participants can buy huge blocks of ETFs and trade them back to the fund for the shares in the underlying portfolio. These mostly large, institutional investors help ensure a relatively efficient market for ETFs.

I've had a few investors tell me that they avoid ETFs because of low trading volume. They are making the mistake of equating volume with liquidity. With ETFs, trading volume and liquidity are two entirely different things. Unlike closed-end funds, ETFs are open-ended.

This is an important distinction. Even without a change in the NAV, a closed-end fund can see a sudden, dramatic change in the market price if there is a spike in trading volume. By contrast, a large number of buy or sell orders is unlikely to change the price of an ETF drastically, since new shares can always be created.

Because of their unique structure, ETFs can avoid the potential tax problem I mentioned earlier. When shares of an ETF are bought or sold, the transaction takes place on an exchange. In other words, the exchange, not the ETF's portfolio of securities, provides the liquidity. Mutual fund shareholders interact directly with the fund's portfolio when buying or selling shares. If a fund has big net redemptions, it could force the manager to sell securities, creating taxable pass-through gains for the remaining shareholders. The structure of ETFs is more tax-efficient. You should experience little or no unexpected pass-through capital gains.

Moreover, ETFs are also wonderful for tax-loss harvesting at year-end. One year, for example, you might be able to sell a broad market ETF, like the Vanguard Total Stock Market ETF (VTI), at a capital loss and immediately replace it with another broad market fund, like the iShares Core S&P Total U.S. Stock Market ETF (ITOT). Even though there will be virtually no difference in the performance of these two funds, the IRS does not disallow it since they are two different securities.

WEIGHING THE ADVANTAGES OF ETFS

Clearly, ETFs have many benefits. And there is an ETF for every asset class in our Gone Fishin' Portfolio. For some investors, these ETFs will be more advantageous than traditional Vanguard mutual funds. For others, the Vanguard funds (or some other no-load group) are the better choice. Here's how to decide.

The first thing to consider in evaluating whether ETFs are right for you is the cost ratio. I've already written about the paramount importance of running your portfolio like a penny-pincher. Using no-load index funds instead of actively managed funds can cut your average annual costs from 3% to around 1.5%. By using Vanguard funds, you can lower them to around 0.1%. Using ETFs, however, you can cut that already minuscule rate even lower. For example, the iShares Core S&P Total U.S. Market ETF that I just mentioned has an annual expense ratio of just 0.03%. That's just $30 for every $100,000 invested.

There are potential brokerage commissions to consider with ETFs. Trading an ETF is like buying or selling a stock. The order must be executed through a broker, so you may be charged a commission each time you place a trade. (However, if you're using an online or deep discount broker, that commission will be negligible or even zero.) There is also a bid–ask spread to cover with every publicly traded security, including ETFs.

These factors are relatively minor. But if you're adding money to your portfolio regularly, they can add up. At rebalancing time, too, some of your ETFs may need to be sold down and others added to, resulting in more transactions. Each time you add money to your portfolio or change its composition, you'll face commissions on the transactions. (Unless, again, you're using a zero-commission broker.)

No-load mutual fund companies like Vanguard, by comparison, will charge you nothing for transactions. They can also debit funds from your checking account each month and invest them for you automatically.

ETF performance may also suffer slightly from a cash drag. When the stocks in an ETF portfolio pay a dividend, the fund pays those dividends out to shareholders periodically. But, until the pay date, that cash sits uninvested. Mutual funds, on the other hand, can reinvest the dividends immediately or pay them out to shareholders. This allows the capital to be deployed more efficiently.

(ETF advocates often talk up the advantage of being able to buy ETFs intraday on a dip, for example. This is indeed a benefit for traders. But the Gone Fishin' Portfolio is not a short-term strategy, and intraday trading is not a factor for us.)

Clearly, both mutual funds and ETFs have their advantages and disadvantages. Deciding which to use depends on your particular situation.

There are three specific types of investors who would benefit from using ETFs:

1. Small investors who do not meet the minimum investment requirements for Vanguard (or other no-load funds) and who intend to invest through a deep discount broker annually or quarterly, not monthly.
2. Lump-sum investors who are putting most of their money to work up front and will be making few additional purchases, aside from the annual rebalancing.
3. Those who have most of their money in a brokerage account, don't want to move it and pay nothing for transactions anyway.

THE GONE FISHIN' PORTFOLIO 2.0

In short, a 100% ETF portfolio is an excellent alternative to using Vanguard mutual funds. Table 11.1 shows, for example, how you could construct the Gone Fishin' Portfolio using ETFs alone. (You'll find more complete information about each of these funds in Appendix B.)

TABLE 11.1 The Gone Fishin' Portfolio 2.0: Exchange-Traded Funds

ETF	Symbol	Allocation
Vanguard Total Stock Market ETF	VTI	15%
Vanguard Small–Cap ETF	VB	15%
Vanguard FTSE Europe ETF	VGK	10%
Vanguard FTSE Pacific ETF	VPL	10%
Vanguard FTSE Emerging Markets ETF	VWO	10%
Vanguard Short–Term Bond ETF	BSV	10%
iShares iBoxx $ High Yield Corporate Bond ETF	HYG	10%
PIMCO 15+ Year U.S. TIPS Index ETF	LTPZ	10%
Vanguard Real Estate ETF	VNQ	5%
VanEck Vectors Gold Miners ETF	GDX	5%

Please note that the asset allocation is identical to the Gone Fishin' Portfolio's as constructed with Vanguard mutual funds. You'll own the same asset classes in the very same percentages. All we're doing is using ETFs instead of mutual funds.

I should point out that I have made two somewhat substantive changes to the ETF portfolio in the first edition of the book. I originally recommended the iShares TIPS Bond ETF (TIP) for our inflation-adjusted bonds allocation.

The fund served its purpose and continues to reflect the performance of the Bloomberg Barclays U.S. Treasury Inflation Protected Securities Index.

However, the average weighted maturity of the bonds it holds is 8.3 years. A TIPS fund that holds bonds with longer-term maturities will perform better if hyperinflation rears its ugly head again in the years ahead.

(Given the tens of trillions of dollars that the United States and other nations around the world have added to their sovereign debt in recent years—in both good times and bad—it's a distinct possibility.)

So I have replaced the iShares TIPS Bond ETF with the PIMCO 15+ Year U.S. TIPS Index ETF (LTPZ).

It, too, helps investors preserve purchasing power against inflation with low default risk. But the average maturity of its bonds is

24 years. If higher inflation is coming our way, longer-term TIPS will appreciate more than shorter-term TIPS.

The fund's annual expense ratio at 0.2% is slightly higher than the category average of 0.16%. But given the performance boost we would get from a resurgence of inflation, I believe it's worth it.

The second change is the replacement of the Vanguard Total Bond Market ETF (BND) with the Vanguard Short-Term Bond ETF (BSV). This ETF better reflects our asset allocation of 10% high-quality, short-term bonds. The fund can invest in not only high-quality corporate bonds but also U.S. government and investment-grade international dollar-denominated bonds.

I like the shorter maturities for the reasons I mentioned in the last chapter. The bonds in the Vanguard Total Bond Market ETF have an average maturity of 8.5 years, whereas the bonds in the Vanguard Short-Term Bond ETF have an average maturity of just 2.9 years.

I would have used this ETF from the very beginning, except that the fund was only a few months old when I wrote the book. But the fund has passed the test of time and now has assets of nearly $60 billion.

As you can see in Table 11.2, the average annual expense ratio for the ETF version of the portfolio is only 0.16%. That's rock

TABLE 11.2 The Gone Fishin' Portfolio: ETF Expenses

ETF	Symbol	Expense
Vanguard Total Stock Market ETF	VTI	0.03%
Vanguard Small-Cap ETF	VB	0.05%
Vanguard FTSE Europe ETF	VGK	0.08%
Vanguard FTSE Pacific ETF	VPL	0.08%
Vanguard FTSE Emerging Markets ETF	VWO	0.10%
Vanguard Short-Term Bond ETF	BSV	0.05%
iShares iBoxx $ High Yield Corporate Bond ETF	HYG	0.49%
PIMCO 15+ Year U.S. TIPS Index ETF	LTPZ	0.20%
Vanguard Real Estate ETF	VNQ	0.12%
VanEck Vectors Gold Miners ETF	GDX	0.52%

bottom. (The average expenses for the Gone Fishin' Portfolio using Vanguard funds is approximately 0.25%.)

If you are in the top marginal tax bracket, you may want to substitute a Vanguard municipal bond fund for the corporate bond fund in order to reduce taxes. If that sounds like you, consider substituting the Vanguard Tax-Exempt Bond ETF (VTEB). It employs an indexing approach designed to track the Standard & Poor's National AMT-Free Municipal Bond Index. And its expense ratio is a paltry 0.06%.

Essentially, the choice is yours. You can create the Gone Fishin' Portfolio using Vanguard or other no-load fund companies. You can create it using ETFs in a discount brokerage account. Or you can create it using a combination of ETFs and mutual funds.

Expenses for ETFs were already low when the first edition of this book came out in 2008. Since then, they have only come down further. The expense ratios for the Vanguard European and Pacific funds have dropped by a third. The expense ratios for the Total Stock Market, Small-Cap and Emerging Markets funds have fallen by half. There simply is no cheaper way to create a diversified portfolio. And those cost savings go right into your pocket.

The important thing is to stick with the discipline. In other words:

1. Use the recommended funds to set up the initial asset allocation.
2. Keep taxes and operating costs to a minimum.
3. Rebalance regularly.
4. Don't abandon ship when the waves get rough. (More on this important point in Chapter 15.)

It's hard to think of an investment program much simpler than this. Or that allows you more time to go fishin' . . . or pursue your other interests.

REEL IT IN . . .

1. ETFs offer some benefits over no-load mutual funds, including slightly lower expenses and possible greater tax efficiency.
2. ETFs are available to purchase any day the nation's stock exchanges are open.
3. ETFs also have drawbacks. These include the bid–ask spreads, potential trading commissions and lack of some mutual fund conveniences, such as automatic dividend reinvestment, as well as automated purchases and withdrawals.
4. Vanguard funds may be better for some investors, especially those making regular monthly purchases.
5. ETFs may be better suited for small investors who have less than $30,000 to invest (and therefore cannot meet the minimum investment requirements to hold the 10 Vanguard funds in the Gone Fishin' Portfolio) or do not need to automate their monthly investments.

CHAPTER 12

Why the Gone Fishin' Portfolio Is Your Best Investment Plan

Over the last decade, investors increasingly recognized that portfolio construction, not security selection, drives the majority of returns.

Source: Letter to Shareholders 2020 by Larry Fink, Blackrock CEO © Larry Fink

The Gone Fishin' Portfolio is an investment system that will save you time, money and endless headaches. It's simple, yes. But don't be fooled by its simplicity.

The Yale University endowment and the California Public Employees' Retirement System, the nation's largest pension fund, are using similar systems. Run your money this way, and you can count yourself among the nation's most sophisticated investors.

The Gone Fishin' Portfolio will allow you to generate high, risk-adjusted returns for decades to come. When you put this system to work, you will be light-years ahead of the typical investor who is wondering what the heck to do, learning the hard way or turning things over to an investment professional (who, if any good, will do something similar at a much higher cost, or, if not so good, will deliver subpar returns along with high fees for as long as the client allows it).

So, congratulate yourself. You are joining an elite minority who are securing their financial futures by managing risk intelligently.

THE PLAN THAT OUTPERFORMS PROFESSIONAL MONEY MANAGERS

Before we discuss why the Gone Fishin' Portfolio is your best investment choice, let's take a moment to review what we've established so far:

1. You have a prosperity mindset, an understanding that things are getting better for most people in most places in most ways.

2. You have a real-world philosophy as the foundation of your investment strategy. (That means you acknowledge that the future is always uncertain, that no one can accurately and consistently forecast interest rates, inflation, the economy or the financial markets.)

3. You know that investment success begins with meaningful saving. You need to save as much as you can, for as long as you can and begin as soon as you can.

4. You understand that no one cares more about the net return on your portfolio than you. You should manage your money yourself.

5. Most Americans are living longer, healthier lives. Many Baby Boomers retiring at age 65 will spend up to three decades in retirement. That means unless you have an ultra-high net worth, you need to skip the ultraconservative choices and maximize your total return so your money lasts as long as you do.

6. There are seven factors that will determine the long-term value of your portfolio: the amount you save, the length of time you let it compound, your asset allocation, your security selection, your portfolio's annual returns, your investment expenses and taxes.

7. Your asset allocation is your most important investment decision. Although no one can tell you the single best asset allocation in advance, you need one that offers an excellent chance of long-term success.

8. No-load index funds and ETFs with low annual expenses and high tax efficiency are the best vehicles for implementing your investment strategy.

9. You need to rebalance approximately once a year to boost returns and reduce risk.

10. In the end, the best investors are not necessarily smarter, just more disciplined.

By sticking to the Gone Fishin' strategy—by saving, asset allocating, rebalancing, and keeping an eye on taxes and expenses—you can look forward to both reaching your long-term investment goals and outperforming the vast majority of professional money managers.

This last claim—beating the professional managers—is likely to be a sticking point with some investors. Many of them will accept the evidence that asset allocation is the primary driver of their portfolios' total returns. But wouldn't the returns be better if we searched for the best managers in each asset class instead of settling for the return of the benchmark?

The answer is no.

In Chapter 8, I cited the studies of Michael Jensen, who did a thorough survey of the performance skills of mutual fund managers. The overwhelming majority of them underperformed the S&P 500. But he learned that many of them did so because the funds they managed held high percentages of cash.

That allowed the managers to argue that they were providing greater safety, if not greater returns. So Jensen then used sophisticated statistical methods to correct for the amounts of cash held. The majority still underperformed.

In fact, out of 115 funds, only one outperformed the market by more than 3% a year while 21 underperformed by more than 3%. Of course, this was just one study, which was done more than 50 years ago. Certainly times have changed and active managers have gotten better, right?

Not so.

William Bernstein writes in *The Four Pillars of Investing*, "Since Jensen's study, literally dozens of studies have duplicated his findings and verified the last prediction: Past superior performance has almost no predictive value." In other words, just because a fund beat the market this year or over the past three years doesn't mean it's likely to beat the market over the next three years.

For the few that do, it is often because of what is known as style drift. That means your fund manager is seeking better returns by straying beyond the fund's designated asset class—and undermining your asset allocation in the process.

Let's say, for example, that for your small cap allocation you chose the mythical actively managed Fidelity Super-Duper Small Cap Fund. The fund's prospectus may well give the manager the flexibility to invest a substantial percentage of the fund's assets outside of the small cap sector. The fund manager may be able to move money into mid-caps or even large caps. Maybe he or she can buy foreign stocks or hold 25% in bonds.

In any given year, the fund may be investing fairly heavily in an asset class that performs better than small caps. As a result, the fund may wind up on the list of best-performing small cap funds. Temporarily. Because when this fund manager strays again from small caps but guesses wrong, as will eventually happen, the fund will move right back to the middle of the pack—the underperforming herd—or, even worse, toward the bottom.

Meanwhile, what has happened to your disciplined asset allocation? It's been tainted. You may want to have 15% of your portfolio in small cap stocks. But if your active small cap manager is moving money elsewhere, you stand to miss the big rally in small caps when it comes. In essence, you end up missing the rally because your manager did.

Why take that chance?

HERE TODAY, GONE TOMORROW

As we discussed, truly talented fund managers are rare. (And many of the great ones, like John Templeton and Peter Lynch, either left active fund management decades ago or are deceased.) Furthermore, fund managers who do show evidence of stock-picking skill have an unfortunate tendency to pick up and leave.

We live in an age where superstar money managers are treated like superstar athletes. In other words, they beat the market for a few years and are then given powerful monetary incentives to move around. So you may invest in a fund with a top-performing manager, only to find months later that he or she jumped ship.

I've often said that mutual funds don't have track records— fund managers do. Does it really make sense to buy, say, the Fidelity Magellan Fund due to its long-term track record? Lynch, the man primarily responsible for its exceptional record, left the helm more than 30 years ago. Many successors have since come and gone. To expect the fund to begin generating Lynch-like performance again is the triumph of hope over experience.

Some funds, like Value Line Funds, are managed by a committee or use a specific strategy. Funny, though, you rarely see a fund managed by a committee winning any long-term performance awards. As for systems, most of them fail miserably, too.

Even the Value Line Mid Cap Focused Fund, using the much-vaunted system published by the Value Line Investment Survey, has dramatically underperformed the market over the last two decades. So it behooves investors to understand that only a tiny minority of mutual fund managers demonstrate any evidence of skill.

In sum, the vast majority of mutual fund managers underperform their benchmarks. Of the ones that do outperform, it is often due to style drift rather than stock picking. And since most of these are unable to maintain their streak, their success is more often attributable to luck than skill. Finally, the handful that stick to their style discipline and outperform their benchmarks with consistency tend to be mobile. Here today, gone tomorrow.

For all these reasons, the best fund company to implement the Gone Fishin' strategy, in my view, is Vanguard or ETFs or, of course, Vanguard ETFs. These funds are inexpensive, tax-efficient and effective at capturing the performance of the asset classes in our portfolio.

The Four Biggest Investment Pitfalls

The Gone Fishin' Portfolio eliminates the four biggest investment pitfalls. Let me detail what they are and show you how our investment strategy avoids them:

1. **Being too conservative**. Investors who put their money to work exclusively in money markets, certificates of deposit and tax-free bonds generally think they're just being careful and sensible. But, unless they're already independently wealthy, they're not.

    The Gone Fishin' Response: Roman historian Tacitus rightly observed, "The desire for safety stands against every great and noble enterprise." Invest too conservatively and you risk outliving your money, especially given today's life expectancies.

    Remember, shortfall risk—the likelihood that you'll outlive your savings—is the biggest financial risk you face. Sure, no one wants to handle retirement assets foolishly. Yet being ultraconservative can be just that. Fortunately, our Gone Fishin' Portfolio contains 10 different asset classes—each of which is likely to outperform cash investments over time.

2. **Being too aggressive**. There are two reasons investors generally get too aggressive with their assets. One is that they're overconfident in their abilities or, in some cases, the abilities of their financial advisor. The other is that they realize they've fallen behind and have decided they're going to get superaggressive with their investments to make up for lost time.

    The Gone Fishin' Response: If you haven't saved enough, it's extremely unlikely that your salvation will come in the form of options, futures, day trading or margin accounts. Instead, investors need to spend less, save more and use a proven approach to grow their assets.

3. Trying—and failing—to time the market. As I mentioned before, it seems so easy when you imagine it: You'll be in the market for most of the run-up and out of the market for most of the sell-off—then back in again for the next rally.

Except it doesn't work that way. What market timers invariably find, if they keep at it long enough, is that they're out during some of the good times and in during some of the bad times. The end result is high turnover (which leads to high costs), plenty of capital gains taxes and substandard performance.

The Gone Fishin' Response: Yes, there are times when the market as a whole looks incredibly cheap. And there are times when the market appears awfully expensive. But the key to making money in the market is *time*, not timing.

However, there is a good living to be made offering market timing advice. So it shouldn't surprise you that "professional" market commentators don't see things the same way. I group these soothsayers into three categories: permabulls, permabears and roadkill. Here's how they stack up.

Permabulls and permabears give strong opinions about where the markets are heading, but they are really not market timers at all. That is because they rarely—if ever—change their points of view. They are perpetually bullish or bearish.

Since the market has historically gone up three years out of four, permabulls, on the one hand, tend to be right most of the time. There's no shame in owning stocks in a down market. That's simply part of the game. But by listening to a highly confident permabull, you may have more money invested in stocks than you're comfortable with—or might even be tempted to invest on margin.

Permabears, on the other hand, are forever seeing gloom and doom. They're wrong most of the time, but during those periods when they're right, their warnings tend to echo in your ears. "Don't be a chump . . . a sucker . . . a fool . . . a patsy." Of course, whenever we do experience a genuine bear market, or even a minor correction, they're quick to remind you that they "told you so."

No matter how low the market goes, these commentators are forever insisting that the bear market is just warming up. The last group—the true market timers—I call roadkill.

These are the timers who switch from bullish to bearish and back again. I've named them for the inevitable result of all their road crossings. (Think of the last opossum you saw that was shaped like a furry pancake.) It would be nice to think someone has this kind of clairvoyance. But as George and Ira Gershwin warned us, "It ain't necessarily so."

4. **Unwise delegation**. Delegators are investors who—fearful of being too conservative or too aggressive and rightly convinced they can't time the market—turn everything over to an insurance agent, planner or full-service broker.

The Gone Fishin' Response: Brokers sell "financial products" or trade for commissions or wrap fees. Insurance agents sell some of the highest-cost products in the financial industry. And, over the course of several years, even financial planners can convert a substantial portion of your assets into *their* assets. Fortunately, the Gone Fishin' Portfolio—which you can easily implement on your own—sidesteps the unwise delegation pitfall altogether.

STICKING TO THE TRIED AND TRUE

The beauty of this system is that you'll never be out of the market and therefore miss out on the kind of great returns that only stocks have given over the long term. You will also never be fully invested in stocks, either, and take a drubbing as many investors did in the savage bear markets of 2000–2002 and 2008–2009, and briefly in the first quarter of 2020.

Some will say that if you were fully invested in stocks and just held on during this period, everything would have worked out fine eventually. This is true, of course. But it neglects to account for human nature. We're reasoning animals, yes. But we also tend to be motivated by fear and greed. Especially fear.

Very few individuals are stoic enough to watch their life savings go through a slow-motion, multiyear meltdown. The psychological pain becomes nearly unbearable. "There goes that cabin in the mountains . . . There goes the membership to the golf club . . . There goes early retirement."

And so they abandon their discipline and sell. Wall Street is the only market where the customers don't buy when the merchandise goes on sale. And there's practically always an asset class on sale somewhere.

A balanced portfolio like ours is likely to decline less in a market downturn. That makes you more likely to stick with the program. When you rebalance your portfolio, you'll be taking advantage of the fact that different asset classes move to the beat of their own drum. You'll be buying whatever is on sale.

When U.S. stocks are weak, for instance, foreign shares are often rising. When both foreign and domestic stocks are down, bonds generally go up. Real estate investment trusts move independently of most stocks and yet have given excellent returns over the past 30 years. Junk bonds do well in an economic recovery. Inflation-adjusted bonds will protect your purchasing power when consumer prices start to rise. And gold shares act not only as an inflation hedge but also as an insurance policy against economic or political chaos.

Of course, the value of your portfolio will still fluctuate. Some years will be better than others. And occasionally, you will see negative returns. That's unavoidable. It's also a good thing. Because it allows you to load up when an asset is cheap. Once a year— or every 366 days to avoid short-term capital gains taxes—you will rebalance your portfolio, bringing each asset class back to its target allocation.

A sensible asset allocation model—with rebalancing annually— is not just a priority. It's the safest, easiest and most effective thing you can do with your serious long-term money.

Over time, investing is a process in which money is transferred to those who have a plan and can execute it from those who don't or can't.

But to earn the highest net return on your investments, you're going to need to take one other important step. You need to tax-manage your investment portfolio. That's the subject we'll turn to next.

REEL IT IN . . .

1. The Gone Fishin' Portfolio is a complete long-term investment program.
2. With the Gone Fishin' strategy, you can look forward to both reaching your long-term investment goals and outperforming the vast majority of professional money managers.
3. In addition to requiring little time and effort, this strategy allows you to avoid the four most common pitfalls of investing: being too conservative, being too aggressive, trying—and failing—to time the market, and delegating unwisely.
4. This strategy cannot promise positive returns every year. But your portfolio should do well in rising markets and will fall less than a 100% stock portfolio in a down market.

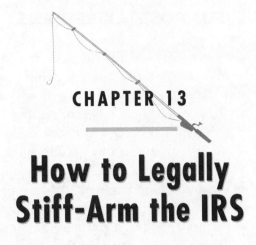

CHAPTER 13

How to Legally
Stiff-Arm the IRS

Be wary of strong drink. It can make you shoot at tax collectors . . .
and miss.

Source: Robert Heinlein

We've already discussed the crucial importance of keeping your investment expenses under control. But there is another encumbrance that can do just as much (or more) damage to the long-term value of your portfolio: taxes. As Arthur Godfrey said, "I'm proud to pay taxes in the United States; the only thing is, I could be just as proud for half the money."

If you're like most investors, there's a good chance you're paying more in taxes on your portfolio each year than is necessary. So let's look at how you can keep your tax bite to an absolute minimum—and legally stiff-arm the IRS.

PRE-TAX VERSUS POST-TAX RETURNS

Mutual fund advertisements and the financial media love to tout funds' total returns. These returns take operating costs (expenses) into account, but not taxes. However, two funds with identical gross returns can deliver drastically different returns after taxes.

Mutual funds are required by law to distribute at least 90% of their realized gains each year. You can get hit with a big tax bill even if you haven't sold a share. How? Inside the fund, the manager may be buying and selling like mad, turning over the entire portfolio in less than a year. Although this doesn't necessarily hurt the fund manager's annual bonus, it can have a dramatic effect on your net returns. After all, you may owe taxes on all those short- and long-term capital gains, even if you haven't sold a single share.

Lipper, a global leader in fund information and analytical tools, published a study that found that taxes gobbled up 15% of the gross return of the average U.S. diversified equity fund. And the tax hit was even worse for the average U.S. taxable bond fund. Here, 38% of the gross return was lost to taxes, nearly double the cost of operating expenses and loads combined.

If you are voluntarily surrendering thousands of dollars to the IRS each year, that makes it much tougher to meet your long-term financial goals. For this reason, you need to tax-manage your portfolio to increase your real-world returns. Here's how.

THE TAXMAN COMETH

The annual tax liabilities on your portfolio will depend on both your tax bracket and how much of your portfolio is held outside of qualified retirement plans. I'm going to run through a few different scenarios, allowing you to easily adopt the strategy that is closest to your own situation.

Let's start with the easiest scenario. If all your long-term money is in a tax-advantaged account like an IRA, H.R. 10 (or Keogh), 401(k), 403(b) or private pension plan, you can stop sweating. You don't have to be concerned with the tax ramifications of your asset allocation and rebalancing strategy because the investments in these vehicles feature tax-deferred compounding. That means you won't owe any taxes on these accounts until you begin making withdrawals. So if all your long-term money is in a qualified retirement plan—or at least the money you intend to use in the Gone Fishin' strategy—you can skip the rest of this chapter. You're already home free.

But, if you're like most investors, your personal situation is probably a bit more complex. You likely have liquid assets both inside and outside of retirement accounts. In that case, you'll need to do a bit of tax planning.

The first order of business is to place the appropriate mutual funds or ETFs in the right accounts to maximize after-tax returns. That means you'll need to put the most tax-inefficient funds in your tax-deferred accounts and the remaining funds in your taxable accounts.

For example, real estate investment trusts (REITs) are highly tax-inefficient. Most of your return will come in the form of dividends, and these are taxable at your income tax rate, not the lower capital gains tax rate. For this reason, your Vanguard Real Estate Index Fund or ETF should ideally be held in one of your tax-deferred accounts.

Another tax-inefficient asset is high-yield bonds. Here the majority of the return comes from interest income—and all of it is taxable. A junk bond fund will typically make capital gains distributions from time to time as well. So your high-yield fund or ETF should also be placed in your tax-deferred account, if possible.

Also highly tax-inefficient are Treasury inflation-protected securities (TIPS). The semiannual interest payments on TIPS are taxable, just as they are for other Treasury securities. However, investors are also taxed on inflation adjustments to the principal, a situation that is commonly described as taxing *phantom income*. For these reasons, you should also hold your inflation-adjusted Treasurys in your tax-deferred account.

High-grade corporate bonds pay taxable income, too. They, too, should be held in your tax-deferred account, if possible. If you're running out of room in your retirement account at this point—and especially if you reside in an upper tax bracket—you should make a substitution here. Instead of buying the Vanguard Short-Term Investment-Grade Fund, invest in the Vanguard High-Yield Tax-Exempt Fund (VWAHX). The fund is run so conservatively that Morningstar doesn't even put it in the high-yield category. You may get a slightly lower yield, but your dividends will be exempt from federal taxes. (If you reside in California, Massachusetts, New Jersey, New York, Ohio or Pennsylvania, use one of the tax-exempt bond funds or ETFs offered for your state.)

Our remaining stock index funds are fairly tax-efficient, with one exception: small caps. If a small company is successful and keeps growing, it will reach the point where it is no longer a small cap stock. (It will become large enough to be classified as a mid-cap stock and, perhaps ultimately, a large cap stock.) Those companies will eventually be removed from the small cap index. When a small cap index fund sells a holding that has grown too large, it will ordinarily generate a realized capital gain. That gain, of course, will be distributed to shareholders.

If you still have room in your tax-deferred account, own the Vanguard Small-Cap Index Fund there. If you don't have room, consider owning the Vanguard Tax-Managed Small-Cap Fund (VTMSX) in your taxable account. Again, this is especially important for investors who reside in the top tax brackets.

Let's talk about priorities. In tax-managing your assets, put your high-yield bonds and REITs in your retirement accounts first. Why? Because these are the highest-yielding components of your portfolio and there is no tax-advantaged substitution you can make. There is no tax-free substitution for inflation-adjusted Treasurys, either. So, if possible, plunk the Vanguard High-Yield Corporate Fund, Vanguard Real Estate Index Fund and Vanguard Inflation-Protected Securities Fund—or their ETF equivalents—in your retirement accounts.

Our remaining funds—Vanguard Total Stock Market Index Fund, Vanguard Emerging Markets Stock Index Fund, Vanguard European Stock Index Fund, Vanguard Pacific Stock Index Fund and VanEck Vectors Gold Miners ETF—are pretty darn tax-efficient. These are fine for your taxable accounts.

A PLACE FOR EVERYTHING . . .
AND EVERYTHING IN ITS PLACE

I've talked a lot about the supreme importance of asset allocation. Tax-managing your portfolio is essentially your asset *location* strategy. As I've described, you ideally want to own your least tax-efficient assets inside your retirement account and your most tax-efficient outside them. Effective tax management of your portfolio is critical and can dramatically increase your long-term, real-world returns.

Please don't think that this step isn't worth the trouble. It is. John Bogle often pointed out that the average mutual index fund takes 2.5% in annual costs each year. Taxes take another 2%, on average. No wonder the average mutual fund investor feels like he's on a slow boat to China. You can't reach financial independence as quickly if you're surrendering so much of your annual returns to the taxman and the mutual fund industry.

A brief illustration shows you why. Let's say one investor owns a $100,000 tax-managed portfolio of Vanguard Admiral Shares with an average expense ratio of 0.1%. Another invests the same amount but is surrendering a total of 4.5% each year in taxes and expenses. Even if both portfolios have 10% gross annual returns, the results over time become dramatically different.

As seen in Table 13.1, the investor who keeps his taxes and expenses to a minimum ends up with a portfolio worth more than three times as much—and that's without generating gross returns that are any better! Clearly, if you're not doing everything possible to minimize your investment costs and taxes, you're at a serious disadvantage.

The difference, as you can see, is not subtle. And consider what it would be if you started with a $1 million portfolio. In 30 years, you'd have nearly $17 million versus less than $5 million.

As a financial writer, I've written and spoken about this important topic many times. Occasionally, this strategy provokes anxiety from investors who see tax management strategies as an abdication of their civic responsibilities.

TABLE 13.1 Effects of Tax Management on a $100,000 Portfolio

Number of Years	Tax-Managed Portfolio	Non-Tax-Managed Portfolio
5	$ 157,424	$130,696
10	$ 247,823	$170,814
15	$ 390,132	$223,247
20	$ 614,161	$291,775
25	$ 966,836	$381,339
30	$1,522,031	$498,395

Nothing could be further from the truth. As a law-abiding U.S. citizen, you are required to pay all the taxes you are obligated to pay—and not one penny more. As Judge Learned Hand, who served for years as chief judge of the U.S. Court of Appeals for the Second Circuit, famously wrote, "Any one may so arrange his affairs that his taxes shall be as low as possible; he is not bound to choose that pattern which will best pay the Treasury. There is not even a patriotic duty to increase one's taxes."

And in a separate case, "Over and over again courts have said that there is nothing sinister in so arranging one's affairs as to keep taxes as low as possible. Everybody does so, rich or poor; and all do right, for nobody owes any public duty to pay more than the law demands."

Amen, Judge.

Let me remind you, too, that our strategy is to wait at least a year and a day before rebalancing your portfolio. That means you will never be subject to short-term capital gains taxes, which—including state taxes—can run well over 40%. If you choose to rebalance your portfolio every 18 months, you can reduce your annual tax liabilities further, as you will not be creating a taxable event each year.

As Bogle has said, "Fads come and go and styles of investing come and go. The only things that go on forever are costs and taxes."

In sum, taxes matter . . . a lot. Take the basic steps I've outlined here to tax-manage your portfolio and you're assured of higher real-world, after-tax returns.

REEL IT IN . . .

1. Voluntarily surrendering a significant percentage of your annual returns to the IRS each year makes it much tougher to meet your long-term financial goals.
2. Taxes can potentially be greater than your other annual investment costs combined. Studies show that typical investors surrender 2% of their annual returns to the taxman each year.
3. Maximizing your real-world returns means tax-managing your portfolio to minimize the annual tax liabilities.
4. Implement an asset location strategy. Keep your tax-inefficient investments—such as bonds, REITs and small cap funds—in your retirement accounts. Keep your tax-efficient investments—such as large cap stock index funds—in your nonretirement accounts.
5. If needed, substitute tax-managed funds or their ETF equivalents.
6. Wait at least a year and a day before rebalancing. If you want to be even more tax-conscious, you can choose to rebalance every 18 to 24 months, further reducing your annual tax liabilities.

PART III

Get On with Your Life

CHAPTER 14

The Last Two Essentials

Specific Goals and Realistic Expectations

Goals are dreams with deadlines.

Source: Diana Scharf-Hunt

Now that you understand what the Gone Fishin' Portfolio is and how it works, you may wonder whether it will truly help you achieve your most important financial goals. That depends.

It depends on how diligently you save, how long you let your money compound, whether you rebalance regularly, whether you can stick with the system during sudden or protracted downturns, and—not least of all—whether you have the discipline to keep from spending your fortune as it grows.

It also depends on your conception of financial freedom. The *Oxford American Dictionary* defines rich as "having a great deal of money or wealth." But then, how much is a great deal?

The Economic Policy Institute reported in December 2019 that the average annual wages for the top 5% in the United States were $309,348. For the top 1%, they were $737,697. And according to Bloomberg, the net worth of the top 10% is $1,182,390. The one-percenters? It's $10,374,030.

But it doesn't take that much to be wealthy in the eyes of the Securities and Exchange Commission (SEC). This government agency is happy to give you a very specific definition of rich. You see, the SEC restricts hedge-fund ownership and other "private money" investments to wealthy individuals, who they assume can take care of themselves.

This requires the regulatory body to define—and occasionally redefine—what it means to be rich. The current standard requires a net worth of at least $1 million, excluding the value of primary residences, or annual income of $200,000 for the previous two years. It's $300,000 for couples.

Forget keeping up with the Joneses. If you want to consider yourself well off, now you have to keep up with the SEC.

Yet, in my view, the quest for financial independence begins not with someone else's notion of affluence but with your own. That means you need a clear, specific vision of where you are trying to go.

TAKING AIM

For some people, a net worth of a few hundred thousand dollars is all they'd need to forget about money, relax and enjoy themselves. Those who are interested in high living or enjoying the finer things in life will shoot for much more.

How much is *enough* is for you to determine, not me. But I have a few thoughts on how to make your dreams a reality. And it starts with having realistic expectations.

When I was in high school, I was a low-handicap golfer. I lettered in the sport every year and alternated among the top two slots on the golf team during my senior year. However, it wasn't until I read Bob Toski's *The Touch System for Better Golf* (now out of print, unfortunately) that my game really started to improve.

Toski made a number of good suggestions, but one I found particularly helpful was his strategy for hitting off the tee. As a teenager, when I got ready to hit a tee shot, I simply aimed down the middle of the fairway and tried to hit it as far as I could without coming out of my shoes. (Plenty of other golfers do pretty much the same thing, I've noticed.) Using this approach, I did hit the ball long, but too often it wound up in the elephant grass, not on the fairway. That was costing me strokes.

Toski suggested that instead of just aiming down the middle and letting it rip, I should pick a specific spot in the fairway and hit to it as if it were a target.

The result? Instead of taking a huge wallop, I began swinging more within myself, much easier. And I couldn't argue with the results. I found the fairway more often—and my score started coming down.

I think most investors would benefit from aiming for a target as well. Too many investors simply plan (either consciously or unconsciously) to "make a whole bunch of money" or earn as high a return on their investments as they can. They're trying to kill it off the tee—and that leads to all sorts of problems. That's how they find themselves in all kinds of speculative investments like options, futures, penny stocks, private equity or hedge funds. The results are seldom salutary.

If you haven't saved enough—or your investments haven't delivered a satisfactory return—it's unlikely your salvation will come from taking a much bigger swing. Yet many investors are susceptible to this temptation.

As a money manager, I once had a retired client who was sending money out of the country to invest in—of all things—a Mexican jojoba plantation. The investment syndicate was *guaranteeing* him returns of 28% a year.

This had scam written all over it, of course. But he trusted the individual he was dealing with—whom he'd only spoken to on the phone—and he received regular statements purporting that his money was indeed compounding at a 28% annual rate. So he was a true believer.

I argued that he should show some skepticism and investigate further—and, in the meantime, stop sending money abroad.

Despite my arguments, he kept on. Finally, I suggested that he simply ask for part of his money back, as an act of good faith.

"But why would I want my money back," he asked, "especially when it's compounding at 28%? I should be sending even more."

Try it, I suggested. Something must have clicked because, eventually, he did. And, of course, he never saw a dime. Some readers will hear this story and say my client was duped, plain and simple. But he was duped because he had unrealistic expectations.

Instead of aiming for a reasonable target, he tried to just tee it high and let it fly. And, like my errant drives, he ended up in the weeds.

FINDING THE BULL'S-EYE

I can't overstate the value of having realistic expectations and a specific investment goal, something to shoot for. (Incidentally, the larger your portfolio gets, the more important this approach becomes.) To manage your serious money successfully, you need to aim at a specific target. You need a goal, a number. Without one, you may not get where you want to go.

Goals are dreams with deadlines. This is especially true in the case of financial dreams. Ideally, your financial goal should be clear and specific. It is not enough to say, "I'd like to have a lot of money some day." It is far better to say, "I intend to have $1.5 million on my 65th birthday." Now that's specific.

How you're going to get there should be quantifiable, too. For example, you can use a financial calculator to determine how to reach that $1 million goal.

Let's say that your goal is to accumulate $1 million from scratch over the next 25 years. Just visit Investor.gov and navigate to the Savings Goal Calculator. It will show you exactly how much you'd need to set aside each month in order to achieve your goal.

To keep things simple, let's say, for example, the Gone Fishin' Portfolio returns 9% a year—less than the average return of the stock market over the past 90 years. Saving and investing $891 a month each month—and letting it compound at 9% monthly—will give you over $1 million in 25 years.

The beauty of these calculators is that you can change the inputs to fit your personal circumstances. If you have more time before you retire—or less—you can adjust for that. If you are able to invest more each month—or each year—you can adjust for that as well.

The important point is that you're more likely to achieve your goal if it's specific—and you know exactly how to achieve it.

First you need to decide how much you need to retire comfortably. This is not always an easy task.

When I was growing up, a million-dollar net worth seemed unspeakably rich. People with that much money, I imagined, had no concerns about money whatsoever. (Presumably, they spent their days smiling, whistling and counting their blessings.)

Today the situation is different. Yes, a million dollars is still a substantial sum. And by the standards of most of the world's population, millionaires are not just affluent. They are exceedingly wealthy. But I can assure you that most folks with a million-dollar net worth do not consider themselves rich.

As I mentioned earlier, there are more than 11 million U.S. households with a net worth of more than $1 million, excluding home equity. That's nearly 1 in 8 households.

When I first read this, it came as a shock. Who knew there were so many affluent individuals around the country?

As I write, however, interest rates are so low that $1 million invested in 10-year Treasurys would generate annual income of just $6,000, or $500 a month. Clearly, the need to take prudent risks with your money doesn't end even when you've accumulated a seven-figure portfolio.

But it's not necessary to take extravagant risks with your investment capital in order to fund your lifestyle. The basic necessities of life just don't require that much money, especially once you qualify for Social Security and Medicare.

Just as a big house, fancy cars and luxury vacations make it hard for you to save as much as you need during your working years, an extravagant retirement lifestyle may make it tougher for you to live comfortably on what you've accumulated in your lifetime.

My favorite activities, for example, are playing golf and tennis, hiking, swimming, reading, listening to music, and spending time with my family and friends. The required annual cost of pursuing these interests—except for the occasional greens fee—is essentially zero. That has made it easy for me to live beneath my means and save regularly.

Someone whose interests lean more toward yachting, raising thoroughbreds or collecting vintage cars has a different perspective on the cost of their hobbies. If you have the income to pursue these interests and still meet your financial goals, more power to you. But, for most of us, a simpler, less materialistic lifestyle could be the biggest liberating factor in our lives.

As Albert Einstein once wrote, "I believe that a simple and unassuming manner of life is best for everyone, best both for the body and the mind."

HOW TO CALCULATE YOUR NUMBER

Ultimately, it's up to you to decide what kind of lifestyle you want to live and how much income is necessary to support it. But here's a quick-and-dirty calculation that financial planners use to determine how much money a person needs to reach financial independence. Take your required annual income—apart from Social Security and any pension income you may receive—and multiply it by 25.

Want $50,000 a year? You'll need to accumulate $1.25 million. Need $100,000 a year? Make it $2.5 million. Need $200,000 a year? It's $5 million.

Why multiply times 25? Because a good rule of thumb, if you want to be conservative, is to draw down no more than 4% of your portfolio each year in retirement.

You should expect the annual return on the Gone Fishin' Portfolio to well exceed that, of course. But the returns above 4% will keep your portfolio rising in value so that you get a cost-of-living increase over the years as you continue to make withdrawals.

Some financial advisors will argue that 4% is too conservative. They believe that takes into account too many worst-case scenarios where the market behaves badly or tanks just when you reach retirement. And they may be right. If they're wrong, however, you'll have taken a very bad gamble. You run the risk of *lifestyle relapse*. You may be unable to live in the style to which you've become accustomed.

For example, imagine drawing down your retirement portfolio while the stock market is in a multiyear tailspin. That's why 30% of our Gone Fishin' Portfolio is in various types of bonds, as well as REITs and gold shares.

So, yes, you can always draw down more than 4% of your investment in retirement. But the higher the percentage you take out, the greater the chance your portfolio will kick the bucket before you do.

How do you calculate that final sum you need to live on, your investment goal? In Lee Eisenberg's book *The Number,* he suggests the following approach:

A. Total up your invested assets.
B. Multiply A by .04, which tells you how much annual investment income you might reasonably withdraw each year.
C. Add in the annual value of any home equity you have (to do this, divide your total equity by the number of years you expect to live. For example, if your age is sixty, and you have $400,000 in home equity, and expect to live to be one hundred, the annual value of your real estate would be $10,000).
D. Add any income you expect from an inheritance (again, total inheritance divided by the number of years you expect to live).
E. Add the amount of Social Security you assume you're entitled to per year (for help, visit ssa.gov).
F. Add any expected annual pension benefits.
G. Add any remaining income you expect, such as from part-time work or other sources.
H. Total B through G, and you arrive at how much you can safely spend each year to get through the rest of your life.

Once you have the total, multiply by 25. That will give you "The Number"—the lump sum you're aiming to accumulate during your working years. People are often shocked to find out how big this number is. Shocked because life can be expensive—and it's easier to spend than to save. As Eisenberg writes, "Whatever you thought your Number was at age thirty will strike you as amusing by the time you're forty, a regular laugh riot at fifty."

Here's the good news, though. When you're in the accumulation phase, you may end up pleasantly surprised. As money compounds, it becomes the proverbial snowball rolling downhill. As I mentioned earlier, $891 a month compounded at 9% a year turns into more than $1 million in 25 years.

The goal of the Gone Fishin' Portfolio is to make sure your invested assets are doing the hard work, so you can eventually leave your job—or do only work you enjoy—and live your version of retirement heaven.

The important thing is this: Knowing exactly what you want— and how you plan to get there—will go a long way toward helping you reach your target. Make your number realistic. Make it specific. And, most importantly, give it a deadline. That's how to turn your dream of financial freedom into a reality.

REEL IT IN . . .

1. The quest for financial independence begins with having a clear, specific vision—with realistic expectations—of where you are trying to go. You're much more likely to achieve your goal once you know exactly how much is needed to retire comfortably.

2. Only you can determine how much money you'll need to achieve your dream retirement. But the more affluent your lifestyle, the harder it is to save money, which impedes the ultimate goal of financial independence.

3. Once you are retired, use 4% as a conservative estimate of how much you can draw down your retirement portfolio each year. This helps ensure your money lasts as long as you do.

CHAPTER 15

Your Most Precious Resource

Time is but the stream I go a-fishin in.

Source: Henry David Thoreau,
Walden, Volume 1, Houghton, Mifflin, 1854.

I've made it clear that I am a rational optimist. You should be, too. Yet year after year and decade after decade, Americans consistently tell pollsters that the country is on the wrong track.

Why the disconnect? As I see it, there are seven major reasons:

1. **Ignorance of the Facts**. Most of us simply aren't aware of the true state of the world. In his excellent book *Factfulness*, renowned public educator Hans Rosling explains how he posed hundreds of questions to thousands of people in dozens of countries.

    He concluded, "Everyone seems to get the world devastatingly wrong. Not only devastatingly wrong, but *systematically* wrong . . . worse than the results I would get if the people answering my questions had no knowledge at all."

2. **Lack of Perspective**. Few of us truly appreciate just how tough life was for our ancestors. Most men and women worked long hours doing hard physical labor. (That includes homemakers.) Your great-grandparents would view your life today—with all its modern conveniences (microwaves, dishwashers, coffee makers, lounge chairs that give massages)—as the realization of some utopia.

3. **Habituation**. Whenever new products or developments appear, we rapidly adopt them and just as quickly take them for granted. Heart transplants, space probes, high-speed internet connections, smartphones, 70-inch ultra-HDTVs, immunotherapies, a new cure for hepatitis. Ho-hum. What else is new?

4. **The Hedonic Treadmill**. In some ways, human beings are hardwired to feel dissatisfaction. We strive to achieve what we desire. Those things satisfy us for a while. But nothing ever quite does it. And so we yearn for something more: a better-paying job, a new car, a bigger house, a firmer abdomen, a sexier spouse. It's a recipe for unhappiness.

5. **Status Anxiety**. Researchers have discovered that, to an astonishing degree, our life satisfaction is tied to how we evaluate our position in society relative to others. Honoré de Balzac called envy "the most stupid of vices, for there is no single advantage to be gained from it." (Unless, of course, you're a politician running for office.) If you insist on doing this, at least do it right. According to the Credit Suisse 2018 Global Wealth Report, an income of $32,400 puts you in the top 1% globally. (Congratulations! You're a one-percenter.)

6. **Apprehension About the Future**. Despite peace and widespread prosperity, many cannot enjoy them thanks to the coming (take your pick) economic meltdown, currency collapse, political crisis, terrorist attack, population explosion, bird flu epidemic, mineral shortage, war in the Middle East, debt default, government shutdown, North Korean nuclear attack, global pandemic or environmental catastrophe.

7. Media Negativity. A mediocre public education system combined with biased journalism creates and reinforces an unduly pessimistic worldview.

Future peace and prosperity are not guaranteed. But we've always pulled through before.

Alarmists of all stripes have been telling us to cup our groins and curl into the fetal position for decades now, and things really haven't gone their way.

Human beings, technology and capital markets operate as an enormous problem-solving machine, improving our lives in almost every way imaginable: faster communications, more powerful computers, safer transportation, and lifesaving drugs and medical devices, to name just a few.

Of course, risk is real. And down markets—which are inevitable—inflict emotional and psychological pain.

This is part of why The Gone Fishin' Portfolio is 30% bonds. The difference between their relatively low returns and the much larger long-term returns of the equity investments in the portfolio might gnaw at you some of the time. But if they keep you from having to sell your stocks during a bear market, their actual return may be many multiples of their meager yields. The ill-timed sale of your stocks could do more damage to your long-term returns than any temporary bear market.

Remember, it isn't necessary to earn fantastic short-term returns to meet your long-term financial goals. Good returns compounded uninterrupted—especially during times of chaos—are all you need.

You can look back at every market sell-off of the last 200 years and see that it was a buying opportunity. When markets get hit hard, however, people feel emotional. They feel a strong need to do something. And that something is usually the wrong thing.

That's because down markets are almost always caused by unexpected events. I've mentioned the crash of 1987, Saddam Hussein's invasion of Kuwait and the events of 9/11 as triggers for market sell-offs. But plenty of other disasters have happened.

In *The Psychology of Money: Timeless Lessons on Wealth, Greed, and Happiness*, Morgan Housel points out that over the last 170 years . . .

- 1.3 million Americans died while fighting nine major wars.
- Roughly 99.9% of all companies that were created went out of business.
- Four U.S. presidents were assassinated.
- 675,000 Americans died in a single year from a flu pandemic.
- 30 separate natural disasters killed at least 400 Americans each.
- 33 recessions lasted a cumulative 48 years . . .
- The stock market fell more than 10% from a recent high at least 102 times.
- Stocks lost a third of their value at least 12 times.
- Annual inflation exceeded 7% in 20 separate years.

Yet life went on and our standard of living increased 20-fold in those 170 years.

It wasn't easy for investors to hang on during all this disruption. But it was crucial. Staying invested when the outlook is good and running to cash when the outlook is poor may have seemed like a safe strategy at the time. But it hasn't worked in the past. And it's unlikely to work in the future.

Most investment advice is geared toward what investors should do right now. But what you do most days isn't all that important. It's what you do—or more to the point *don't do*—during that small number of days when you're terrified that is absolutely vital.

Another potential downfall for investors is pride. After all, who doesn't like the idea of "slaying the market" with high-returning individual stocks. As someone who has owned shares of Amazon, Apple and Netflix not just for years but for decades, I get this. Owning specific companies can be exciting . . . and highly profitable.

Selecting individual stocks has nothing to do with the Gone Fishin' strategy itself. But it is not the least bit incompatible with our philosophy—that the short-term performance of the economy and markets can't be accurately predicted—or with our investment sensibility—that most things are getting better in most ways for most people in most places.

Indeed, I own plenty of individual stocks, and as Chief Investment Strategist of The Oxford Club, I recommend various portfolios of them. And they have done well.

But when it comes to owning individual stocks, there are some daunting statistics for long-term investors to consider. As Housel also writes in *The Psychology of Money* . . .

> Most public companies are duds, a few do well, and a handful become extraordinary winners that account for the majority of the stock market's returns.
>
> J.P. Morgan Asset Management once published the distribution of returns for the Russell 3000 Index—a big, broad, collection of public companies—since 1980.
>
> Forty percent of all Russell 3000 stock components lost at least 70% of their value and never recovered over this period.
>
> Effectively all of the index's overall returns came from 7% of component companies that outperformed by at least two standard deviations.
>
> That's the kind of thing you'd expect from venture capital. But it's what happened inside a boring, diversified index.
>
> This thumping of most public companies spares no industry. More than half of all public technology and telecom companies lose most of their value and never recover. Even among public utilities, the failure rate is more than 1 in 10.

At first blush this is hard to believe. Forty percent of stocks lost at least 70% of their value and never recovered. Seven percent of the 3,000 stocks in the index were responsible for essentially all of its return.

But the most important point is the bottom line: The Russell 3000 has increased more than 73-fold over the last four decades. A boring, diversified index? Most investors would disagree.

THE KEY TO LONG-TERM INVESTMENT SUCCESS

You are now ready to implement the Gone Fishin' Portfolio. Feel confident about your decision. This portfolio is based on decades of market analysis, as well as rigorous thinking about how to maximize your returns while keeping investment risk strictly limited.

The idea of diversifying broadly, asset allocating properly, cutting costs and taxes and rebalancing annually may seem elementary. But simplicity is part of its charm, its elegance. I know of no strategy that comes closer to guaranteeing long-term investment success.

The Gone Fishin' Portfolio allows you to take your financial destiny into your own hands. It requires minimal time and effort. Putting this portfolio together is a snap. Maintaining it takes just a few minutes a year.

History teaches us that, over time, bonds return more than cash, but fluctuate in value. Stocks return more than bonds, but are more volatile still. And when you blend these noncorrelated assets together, including slightly more exotic fare like REITs, junk bonds and gold shares, you are likely to capture excellent returns within an acceptable level of risk.

The pursuit of "the very best" asset allocation is not required to achieve your investment goals. What's more important is to develop a reasonable asset allocation—that includes a fair number of uncorrelated assets—and stick with your decision through thick and thin. That's what is paramount.

Heed the words of Daniel Goleman, the author who promoted the idea in the 1990s that success is more closely tied to your emotional state than education or knowledge. In his book *Emotional Intelligence: Why It Can Matter More Than IQ,* he writes, "As we all know from experience, when it comes to shaping our decisions and our actions, feelings count every bit as much—and often more—than thought . . . Passions overwhelm reason time and again." Unfortunately, passion is how great investment plans come undone.

Goleman argues that two key aspects of emotional intelligence are impulse control and persistence. These are exactly the two qualities that will keep you from letting periods of poor market performance cause you to abandon your investment strategy in a panic.

In short, investment success is more often attributable to your EQ (emotional quotient) than your IQ. Here are four ways you can keep your emotions under control:

1. **Do a reality check**. Recognize that investing in stocks means your portfolio value is bound to sustain wide

fluctuations from time to time. It's unrealistic to think that you're going to earn the superior returns only stocks can give while watching your funds rise as steadily as a savings account.

2. **Automate your investments**. If you're in the early stages of wealth accumulation, use a discipline like dollar-cost averaging—investing a consistent amount at regular intervals—to take advantage of the market's occasional swoons.

3. **Act unemotionally**. When you rebalance regularly, you check harmful emotions like fear, greed, hope, pride or envy. Buying what everyone else is running from takes courage. But if you are equal to the task, you will be well rewarded.

4. **Sit on your hands**. Warren Buffett once said, "Inactivity strikes us as intelligent behavior." During volatile periods between rebalancing, you must resist the urge to "do something." It's one thing to feel fearful about the market. It's quite another to let that fear trump your well-laid investment plans.

Studies in behavioral finance clearly demonstrate that it's not your store of market knowledge that is most likely to determine your success as an investor. It's whether you let your emotions dictate your actions.

I'm not saying you shouldn't feel emotional from time to time. That would be too much to ask. But if you let those emotions control your investment decisions, eventually you're going to feel something entirely different . . .

Regret.

This is not just my perspective, by the way. In *The Four Pillars of Investing*, William Bernstein writes . . .

It is not uncommon to meet extremely intelligent and financially sophisticated people, oftentimes finance professionals, who are still emotionally incapable of executing a plan properly—they can talk the talk, but they cannot walk the walk, no matter how hard they try. The most common reason for the "failure to execute" shortcoming is the emotional inability to go against the market and buy assets that are not doing well. Almost as common is an inability to get off the dime and commit hard cash to a perfectly good investment blueprint, also called "commitment paralysis."

Most investors don't realize that their biggest obstacle to success is not inflation, bad markets, the taxman or Wall Street. As Benjamin Graham wrote back in 1934, "The investor's chief problem—and even his worst enemy—is likely to be himself." (Or, as the comic strip *Pogo* once put it, "We have met the enemy and he is us.")

The other pitfall, one that keeps investors from even getting out of the blocks, is procrastination. Many of us have big plans that—due to a lack of action—never get beyond the planning stage. Resolve that you will take responsibility for your success by understanding the timeless principles at work here—and move forward.

Don't make the mistake of waiting until the "right time" to get started. There will always be troubles in the economy and challenges facing the stock market.

Look at Figure 15.1. It shows what your returns would have been had you had the ridiculous bad luck of buying into the market at its high point every year.

As you can see—and as I've been arguing from Page 1—over the long haul, trying to time your entry point in the market is a mug's game. There is no bad time to start a disciplined long-term investment program.

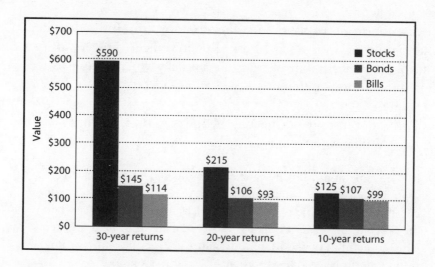

FIGURE 15.1 Average Total Returns After Major Market Peaks

Note: Major market peaks include 1901, 1906, 1915, 1929, 1937, 1946 and 1968.
Source: Jeremy J. Siegel, *Stocks for the Long Run*, 4th Ed.

A PLAN FOR ALL SEASONS

Ultimately, the Gone Fishin' strategy is about waking up and taking the reins of financial freedom. You can't live your life fully if you're a slave to your job, your financial commitments or your monthly overhead. Or, worse, if you're worried that you won't be able to maintain a comfortable retirement.

The essential truth of modern economic life is that money gives you choices. Chief among these is the opportunity to do what you want, where you want, with whom you want. That's what financial freedom is all about.

It's a shame, really, that more of us don't recognize this when we're young. But then, it's never too late to start learning—or to finish our investment education.

What will the Gone Fishin' Portfolio return in the future? The historical returns for each asset class in our portfolio are well known. It is reasonable to expect that they will be similar in the future, but certainly not in the short term. And perhaps not even over the longer term. Investing is always a challenge, and "the answer" is always qualified.

As Jeremy Siegel warns in *Stocks for the Long Run*, "The returns derived from the past are not hard constants, like the speed of light or gravitational force, waiting to be discovered in the natural world. Historical values must be tempered with an appreciation of how investors, attempting to take advantage of the returns from the past, may alter those very returns in the future."

No matter how thoroughly you understand historical asset returns and essential investment principles, it's important to realize that uncertainty will forever be your inseparable companion.

And that's okay. The Gone Fishin' Portfolio is a system that acknowledges and embraces uncertainty. Ultimately, it thrives on it. You understand that all asset classes go through up and down cycles. By investing this way, you'll always have a stake in whatever assets are performing best. And by rebalancing regularly, you'll keep buying low and selling high, preparing your portfolio for the next change in the cycle.

To gird you through the inevitable market declines—including serious bear markets—let me remind you of two important points:

1. When you own a diversified stock portfolio, you own an interest in a broad selection of the world's biggest and most profitable companies. If you take a moment to recognize, for example, that your holdings include a slug of Amazon, Apple, Procter & Gamble, McDonald's, Johnson & Johnson, and other high-quality companies, you're likely to sleep better and hang in there long enough for time to work its magic.

2. Don't waste time looking at your portfolio too often. Sure, it's fun to watch your account rise when times are good. But it does no good whatsoever to dwell on your portfolio's daily fluctuations in a market downturn, watching in anguish as your net worth declines—at least temporarily.

When I worked as a money manager, many of my clients would take a mental snapshot—if not an *actual* one—of the best statement they ever received. During market corrections, they would often remind me how much they had "lost in the market," failing to understand that nothing was truly lost unless they panicked and abandoned their equity allocation. They also apparently forgot that their account would never have reached that high-water mark if they hadn't been invested in stocks to begin with.

With an investment strategy that is designed to last decades, you will see your share of bear markets. If it makes you feel better, remember that every one for the past 200 years was a buying opportunity. Recognize this and it becomes tougher to believe that the next one is any different.

As an investment advisor, I tried valiantly to get clients to increase their exposure to stocks during market downturns. The ones who did prospered. But, for many, hanging on was all I could get them to do. Adding to assets that were down was often out of the question.

Of course, when times in the market were good, many assured me they would welcome the chance to buy in a downturn. But that's when we were talking in the abstract. When the bear market actually showed up, they sang a different tune. "I never imagined that 'this' would happen!" they'd say in frustration. And, of course, "this" is something different every time.

Yet history demonstrates that common stocks are nothing if not resilient. That's why I refer to them as the greatest wealth creators of all time.

Yes, the economy will suffer the occasional recession. And the market will stumble. Expect it. And remember that you're using a system that allows you to capitalize on these inevitable downturns. In fact, the odds are good that the long-term value of your portfolio will be greater because of them. After all, it's during down markets that you get an opportunity to buy what's cheap and prosper during the recovery that follows.

Over the last 80 years, the average U.S. recession has lasted less than 11 months. (You have to go back to the Great Depression to find an economic downturn that lasted longer than 18 months.) Enduring a downturn like this hardly requires superhuman resolve. And yet so many investors fail to do it . . . including professional money managers.

In a study published in *The Journal of Portfolio Management*, Christophe Faugère, Hany Shawky and David Smith—finance professors at the State University of New York at Albany—researched the performance of money managers who oversee pension funds, endowments and high-net-worth accounts. Because most institutions work under strict investment guidelines, these academics were able to analyze performance based on different approaches to selling stocks.

The result? The institutional managers who fared best were those with restrictive rules that did not allow for emotional decision making. The managers who relied on "flexible" sell strategies did far worse. Count me unsurprised. Institutional money managers are prone to rationalizing—and making emotional mistakes—just like amateurs.

Our Gone Fishin' strategy—if you follow it—enables you to check these reactions at the door. Expect the market to decline sharply sometimes. And abide by the one action you need to take each year—rebalancing—to take advantage of it.

To succeed with this strategy, only two things are truly essential: a thorough understanding of the system and the discipline to follow through.

TIME IS ON YOUR SIDE

As I've tried to make clear in these pages, genius is not the key to investment success. And neither is timing. Rather, patience and discipline are.

However, the Gone Fishin' Portfolio is designed to deliver something even more important than superior investment returns. A reader who owns the portfolio once sent me the following quote from an unknown author.

> Imagine there is a bank that credits your account each morning with $86,400, carries over no balance from day to day, allows you to keep no cash balance, and every evening cancels whatever part of the amount you had failed to use during the day.
> What would you do?
> Draw out every cent, of course!
> Well, everyone has such a bank. Its name is time.
> Every morning, it credits you 86,400 seconds.
> Every night it writes off, as lost, whatever of this you have failed to invest to good purpose.
> It carries over no balance. It allows no overdraft.
> Each day it opens a new account for you.
> Each night it burns the records of the day.
> If you fail to use the day's deposits, the loss is yours.
> There is no going back. There is no drawing against tomorrow.
> You must live in the present on today's deposits.
> Invest it so as to get from it the utmost in health, happiness, and success.

Time, not money, is your most precious resource. It is the most valuable thing you have. It is perishable, irreplaceable and, unlike money, cannot be saved. The beauty of the Gone Fishin' Portfolio is that it allows you to redirect your time to high-value activities, whether it's work you enjoy, your favorite pastimes, or just relaxing with your friends and family.

In *The Pleasures of Life,* Sir John Lubbock writes, "All other good gifts depend on time for their value. What are friends, books, or health, the interest of travel or the delights of home, if we have not time for their enjoyment? Time is often said to be money, but it is more—it is life; and yet many who would cling desperately to life, think nothing of wasting time."

The Gone Fishin' Portfolio gives you an excellent opportunity to increase your wealth. But it *guarantees* you more time to devote to the people and pastimes you love.

Perhaps that is what recommends it most.

AFTERWORD

The Gone Fishin' strategy may be different from any investment portfolio you've owned or considered owning. Yet the idea of asset allocating and rebalancing using low-cost, tax-efficient index funds is hardly unique.

As I made clear in earlier chapters, there are good reasons to use mainly index funds.

This way, we don't have to worry about a fund manager's misguided attempts to time the market. We don't have to worry about picking the wrong stocks or holding too much cash. We don't have to worry about style drift. We don't have to keep checking to make sure the original manager is still at the helm. We know index funds are low cost and tax-efficient. They take very little time to analyze and monitor. And they outperform the vast majority of actively managed funds.

However, I want readers to understand that I have serious philosophical differences with asset allocators who recommend index funds because they believe it is impossible to beat the market by selecting and monitoring individual stocks.

That's simply not so. I have beaten the market soundly with my own stock portfolio over the past three decades. (And not by a small amount. A recent brokerage statement showed that my shares of Apple alone are up over 62,000%.) I did it for clients as an investment advisor. And I have done it with stock portfolios that I direct for The Oxford Club as well. (*The Wall Street Journal* put my letter on its Honor Roll of the top-performing investment letters in the nation for both bull and bear markets.)

I'm making this clear because I don't want readers to infer that I subscribe to the efficient market hypothesis (EMH) or its sister, modern portfolio theory (MPT), whose followers also advocate index funds.

EMH is the theory that all public information is immediately discounted into share prices by rational, self-interested investors. Therefore, its proponents argue, it is futile to try to outperform the market by selecting individual stocks.

EMH and MPT have much of value to say about risk and return, the benefits of diversification, and effective portfolio construction. But let's look at the basic premise of MPT. We're all self-interested, yes. But are we entirely rational?

Is a young woman thinking rationally when she marries the troubled guy who promises to change his ways and hew to the straight and narrow? Is a young couple thinking logically when they buy more house than they can afford so they can live up to a certain image of success? Is a balding, middle-aged man thinking rationally when he plunks down hard cash for an expensive convertible to impress women half his age?

Perhaps not.

You may want to read Michael Shermer's excellent book *The Mind of the Market: How Biology and Psychology Shape Our Economic Lives*. Shermer, a columnist for *Scientific American* and the founder of *Skeptic* magazine, writes, "We are remarkably irrational creatures, driven as much (if not more) by deep and unconscious emotions that evolved over the eons as we are by logic and conscious reason developed in the modern world."

He backs up this claim with plenty of examples from the new science of behavioral economics. Studies show, for example, that most people are willing to drive five blocks if they can buy a $100 cellphone for half price. But they are far less willing to drive five blocks to save $50 on a new HDTV that costs $1,000. Why? After all, 50 bucks is 50 bucks, no matter how you spend it—or save it. But, according to Shermer, *mental accounting* makes us reluctant to make the effort to save money when the relative amount we're dealing with is small.

Or take the sunk-cost fallacy. Objectively, a company with lousy business prospects is not worth holding, no matter what you paid for it. Yet many investors will hold on to a losing stock for years, even when it's clearly unprofitable. Shermer correctly points out, "Rationally, we should just compute the odds of succeeding from this point forward." Yet investors who have sunk a lot into a stock—including a fair amount of ego—have trouble doing this.

Mental accounting and the sunk-cost fallacy are just the tip of the iceberg. Shermer shows that consumers and investors also fall prey to cognitive dissonance, hindsight bias, self-justification, inattentional blindness, confirmation bias, the introspection illusion, availability bias, self-serving bias, representative bias, the law of small numbers, attribution bias, the loss aversion effect, the framing effect, anchoring bias, the endowment effect and the bias blind spot. (And you thought most of us had only a couple small glitches upstairs.)

By the time Shermer is done exposing all the flaws in our mental machinery, you feel inclined to put MPT right up there with the "stork theory" in sex education.

Okay, I'm exaggerating . . . a little. Every experienced investor knows that shares of most publicly traded companies are fairly efficiently priced most of the time. But that's a whole lot different than saying *all* shares are efficiently priced *all* the time, the foundation stone of efficient market theory.

Warren Buffett summed up my view nicely—if not entirely accurately—when he once remarked, "I'd be a bum on the street with a tin cup if the markets were always efficient."

I make this distinction because EMH proponents often point to much of the same data I've used about the poor performance of actively managed mutual funds. But as we've seen, there are plenty of reasons—many of them related to operating costs, cash holdings and blinkered attempts to time the market—that cause actively managed funds to founder in their quest to beat their benchmarks.

It's true that the stock market is efficient at absorbing and discounting news and opinions. But that doesn't mean that attractive buying opportunities don't develop with individual stocks. If this were true, no investment strategy would be better than a coin toss.

Yet that's exactly what hard core EMH and MPT advocates argue. Listen to just a few of the EMH proponents whom I've quoted favorably throughout the book:

- In *What Wall Street Doesn't Want You to Know*, Larry Swedroe writes that "current market prices reflect the total knowledge and expectations of all investors, and no investor can consistently know more than the market does collectively."
- In *The Intelligent Asset Allocator*, William Bernstein writes that "mutual fund manager performance does not persist and the return of stock picking is zero."
- In *The Coffeehouse Investor: How to Build Wealth, Ignore Wall Street, and Get On with Your Life*, Bill Schultheis writes that "any attempt to beat the market is likely to prove disastrous to your long-term financial health."

Efficient market advocates begrudgingly acknowledge a few famous investors who have beaten the market over a period of decades. But they rationalize that if enough money managers try to beat the market, the law of averages says a lucky handful will succeed over the long haul.

By this reasoning, Warren Buffett is just one of the 1 in 300 million guys who bought the right lottery ticket. But that's absurd. Buffett is a financial genius who has forgotten more about successful stock picking than most investment analysts will ever know.

Efficient market theorists do concede that investors chase prices too high and the market goes "barking mad" from time to time. But does it make sense to you that the market at any given moment is either "perfectly efficient" or "barking mad"?

The eggheads do have it partially right. You're not going to beat the market over the long haul by trying to guess what the market's likely to do next. But to say you can't beat the market through superior stock selection is naïve.

I'm not saying it's easy. It's not. It requires knowledge, discipline and, sometimes, nerves of steel. But it's certainly possible.

Yes, the overwhelming majority of active fund managers do fail to beat the market. But as an individual investor trading for your own account, you don't have the same handicaps they do.

You are not managing an enormous sum of money, hundreds of millions or billions of dollars. You do not have to worry about the market-impact cost of your trades. You do not face the pressures not to disappoint your clients with this quarter's results. You do not have to pay Wall Street specialists to accumulate or unwind your positions. And you do not have to deduct active management fees from your returns.

Having said this, I'm ready to concede that beating the market over the long haul is harder than it looks—and many if not most amateur investors will fail. Still, for those investors who truly enjoy hunting big game and devoting the hours required to become good at selecting stocks, there is no reason to be pessimistic.

Allow me a few caveats, however.

I learned most of my investment lessons the hard way. And they took years to sink in. Plenty of individual stock traders—even ones who wind up doing well—report similar experiences. It may be possible to learn how to trade stocks by simply reading a book or listening to someone else's experience, but I've never met anyone who's actually done it.

When it comes to investing in individual stocks, the only lessons that stick, it seems, are those that come with a kick in the pants.

Fortunately, I learned most of them when I was investing relatively small sums. And I was young enough that I had plenty of time to make up for my mistakes. The older and closer to financial independence you are, the less attractive this path becomes.

Remember, too, I worked in the financial industry, spending thousands of hours watching traders, reading, studying the great investors and practicing what I learned.

Most people don't have this kind of time to devote to stock picking. And, even if they do, there's no guarantee they will get the results they're seeking. Sometimes all they get is an expensive education.

So how have I been able to select stocks that earn higher-than-average returns? That would take another book. And, even then, I'm not sure I could explain it all.

Being a successful investor takes experience. It means comprehending business and the economy. It means understanding human psychology. But a large part, perhaps the biggest part of all, is temperament, an Asperger's-like emotional detachment.

Obviously, there is a lot more to selecting stocks than I can relate in a few pages here. If you're interested in trading individual stocks, feel free to subscribe to *The Oxford Communiqué,* my monthly investment newsletter. Or you can read my market commentary for free at LibertyThroughWealth.com.

Modern portfolio theorists claim that my personal winning streak—and my investment letter's—are due to luck, not skill. Fine. I keep beating the market. They keep calling me lucky.

I hope nothing ever changes.

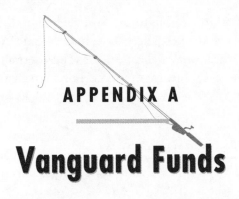

APPENDIX A

Vanguard Funds

VANGUARD TOTAL STOCK MARKET INDEX FUND

Overview

Symbol	VTSAX
Expense Ratio	0.04%
Inception Date	11/13/2000
Yield	1.57%

Description

The Vanguard Total Stock Market Index Fund is designed to provide investors with exposure to the entire U.S. equity market, including small cap, mid-cap, and large cap growth and value stocks. The fund employs an indexing investment approach designed to track the performance of the CRSP U.S. Total Market Index, which represents approximately 100% of the investable U.S. stock market and includes large cap, mid-cap, small cap, and micro-cap stocks regularly traded on the New York Stock Exchange and Nasdaq. The fund invests by sampling the index, meaning that it holds a broadly diversified collection of securities that, in the aggregate, approximates the full index in terms of key characteristics. These key characteristics include industry weightings and market capitalization, as well as certain financial measures, such as price-to-earnings ratio and dividend yield.

Performance

TABLE A.1 After-Tax Returns as of 9/30/2020

	1-Year	3-Year	5-Year	10-Year	Since Inception 11/13/2000
Total Stock Market Index Adm					
Returns before taxes	14.99%	11.64%	13.68%	13.48%	7.18%
Returns after taxes on distributions	14.47%	11.13%	13.14%	12.99%	6.77%
Returns after taxes on distributions and sales of fund shares	9.15%	9.00%	10.85%	11.21%	5.94%
Average Large Blend Fund					
Returns before taxes	10.70%	9.55%	11.77%	11.96%	—
Returns after taxes on distributions	—	—	—	—	—
Returns after taxes on distributions and sales of fund shares	—	—	—	—	—

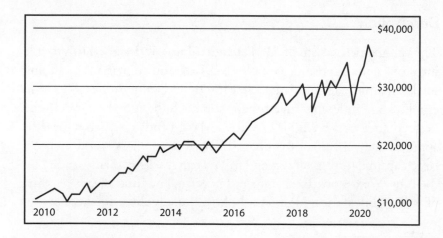

FIGURE A.1 Hypothetical Growth of $10,000 Invested in Vanguard Total Stock Market Index Fund Through September 30, 2020

Holdings

Number of Holdings   3,566

Total Net Assets $937.6 billion

Top 10 Holdings as of 9/30/2020

1. Apple Inc.
2. Microsoft Corp.
3. Amazon.com Inc.
4. Alphabet Inc.
5. Facebook Inc.
6. Berkshire Hathaway Inc.
7. Johnson & Johnson
8. Procter & Gamble Co.
9. Visa Inc.
10. Tesla Inc.

Risk Attributes

TABLE A.2   Historical Volatility Measures as of 9/30/2020

Benchmark	R-squared[*]	Beta[*]
Spliced Total Stock Market Index	1.00	1.00

[*]R-squared and beta are calculated from trailing 36-month fund returns relative to the associated benchmark.

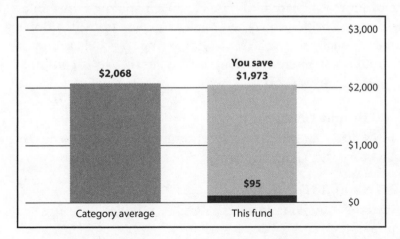

FIGURE A.2   Hypothetical Fees on $10,000 Invested in Vanguard Total Stock Market Index Fund Over 10 Years

Management

Gerard C. O'Reilly, Principal
- Portfolio manager
- Advised the fund since 1994
- Worked in investment management since 1992
- BS, Villanova University

Walter Nejman
- Portfolio manager
- Advised the fund since 2016
- Worked in investment management since 2008
- BA, Arcadia University
- MBA, Villanova University

Investment Policy

The fund reserves the right to substitute a different index for the index it currently tracks if the current index is discontinued, if the fund's agreement with the sponsor of its target index is terminated or for any other reason determined in good faith by the fund's board of trustees. The fund may invest in foreign securities to the extent necessary to carry out its investment strategy. To track its target index as closely as possible, the fund attempts to remain fully invested in stocks. The fund's daily cash balance may be invested in one or more Vanguard CMT funds, which are low-cost money market funds. The fund may temporarily depart from its normal investment policies and strategies when doing so is believed to be in the fund's best interest, so long as the alternative is consistent with the fund's investment objective.

Who Should Invest
- Investors seeking the broadest exposure to the U.S. stock market
- Investors with a long-term investment horizon (at least five years)

Who Should Not Invest
- Investors unwilling to accept significant fluctuations in share price
- Investors seeking significant dividend income

Minimums

TABLE A.3 Minimums

	Initial Minimum	Additional Investments
Minimum investment	$3,000	$1

Expenses

TABLE A.4 Expenses

	Expense Ratio
Vanguard Total Stock Market Index Adm	0.04%
Average Large Blend Fund	0.91%

VANGUARD SMALL-CAP INDEX FUND

Overview
Symbol   VSMAX
Expense Ratio   0.05%
Inception Date   11/13/2000
Yield   1.47%

Description

This low-cost index fund provides broad exposure to the small cap U.S. equity market. The fund employs an indexing investment approach designed to track the performance of the CRSP U.S. Small Cap Index, a broadly diversified index of stocks of smaller U.S. companies. The fund attempts to replicate the target index by investing all, or substantially all, of its assets in the stocks that make up the index, holding each stock in approximately the same proportion as its weighting in the index.

TABLE A.5 After-Tax Returns as of 09/30/2020

	1–Year	3–Year	5–Year	10–Year	Since Inception 11/13/2000
Small–Cap Index Fund Adm					
Returns before taxes	1.34%	4.39%	8.95%	10.95%	8.49%
Returns after taxes on distributions	0.93%	3.95%	8.47%	10.48%	7.91%
Returns after taxes on distributions and sales of fund shares	0.97%	3.29%	6.94%	8.94%	7.00%
Average Small Blend Fund					
Returns before taxes	-6.56%	-0.86%	5.68%	8.66%	—
Returns after taxes on distributions	—	—	—	—	—
Returns after taxes on distributions and sales of fund shares	—	—	—	—	—

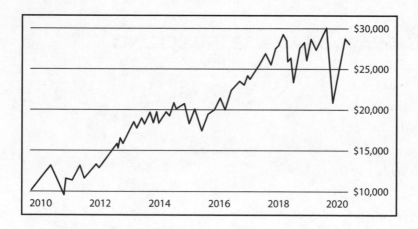

FIGURE A.3 Hypothetical Growth of $10,000 Invested in Vanguard Small-Cap Index Fund Through September 30, 2020

Holdings

Number of Holdings	1,405
Total Net Assets	$89.8 billion

Top 10 Holdings as of 9/30/2020

1. Immunomedics Inc.

2. Horizon Therapeutics PLC

3. Insulet Corp.

4. STERIS PLC

5. Etsy Inc.

6. PerkinElmer Inc.

7. Catalent Inc.

8. IDEX Corp.

9. Zebra Technologies Corp.

10. Teradyne Inc.

Risk Attributes

TABLE A.6 Historical Volatility Measures as of 9/30/2020

Benchmark	R-squared*	Beta*
Spliced Small–Cap Index	1.00	1.00

*R-squared and beta are calculated from trailing 36-month fund returns relative to the associated benchmark.

Management

Gerard C. O'Reilly, Principal
- Portfolio manager
- Advised the fund since 2016
- Worked in investment management since 1992
- BS, Villanova University

William Coleman, CFA
- Portfolio manager
- Advised the fund since 2016
- Worked in investment management since 2006
- BS, King's College
- MS, Saint Joseph's University

Investment Policy

The fund reserves the right to substitute a different index for the index it currently tracks if the current index is discontinued, if the fund's agreement with the sponsor of its target index is terminated or for any other reason determined in good faith by the fund's board of trustees. The fund may invest in foreign securities to the extent necessary to carry out its investment strategy of holding all, or substantially all, of the stocks that make up the index it tracks. To track its target index as closely as possible, the fund attempts to remain fully invested in stocks. To help stay fully invested and to reduce transaction costs, the fund may invest, to a limited extent, in derivatives. The fund will not use derivatives for speculation or for the purpose of leveraging (magnifying) investment returns. The fund's daily cash balance may be invested in one or more Vanguard CMT funds, which are low-cost money market funds. The fund may temporarily depart from its normal investment policies and strategies when doing so is believed to be in the fund's best interest, so long as the alternative is consistent with the fund's investment objective.

Who Should Invest
- Investors seeking a simple, low-cost way to invest in small cap stocks
- Investors with a long-term investment horizon (at least five years)

Who Should Not Invest
- Investors unwilling to accept significant fluctuations in share price
- Investors seeking significant dividend income

Minimums

TABLE A.7 Minimums

	Initial Minimum	Additional Investments
Minimum investment	$3,000	$1

Expenses

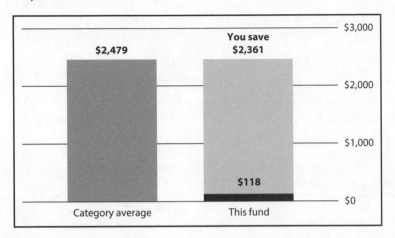

FIGURE A.4 Hypothetical Fees on $10,000 Invested in Vanguard Small-Cap Index Fund Over 10 Years

TABLE A.8 Expenses

	Expense Ratio
Vanguard Small-Cap Index Fund Adm	0.05%
Average Small Blend Fund	1.10%

VANGUARD EUROPEAN STOCK INDEX FUND

Overview

Symbol	VEUSX
Expense Ratio	0.10%
Inception Date	8/13/2001
Yield	N/A

Description

This index fund provides investors low-cost exposure to the European stock markets. The fund holds more than 1,200 stocks across the European region, which makes up roughly half of the non–U.S. equity marketplace. The fund employs an indexing investment approach by investing all, or substantially all, of its assets in the common stocks included in the FTSE Developed Europe All Cap Index. The FTSE Developed Europe All Cap Index is a market-capitalization-weighted index that is made up of approximately 1,307 common stocks of large cap, mid-cap, and small cap companies located in 16 European countries—mostly companies in the United Kingdom, Germany, France and Switzerland. Other countries represented in the index include Austria, Belgium, Denmark, Finland, Ireland, Italy, the Netherlands, Norway, Poland, Portugal, Spain and Sweden.

TABLE A.9 After-Tax Returns as of 9/30/2020

	1-Year	3-Year	5-Year	10-Year	Since Inception 8/13/2001
European Stock Index Adm					
Returns before taxes	0.33%	−0.40%	4.55%	4.63%	5.05%
Returns after taxes on distributions	−0.26%	−1.09%	3.81%	3.83%	4.33%
Returns after taxes on distributions and sales of fund shares	0.55%	−0.27%	3.52%	3.67%	4.12%
Average Europe Stock Fund					
Returns before taxes	2.46%	−0.17%	4.82%	4.87%	—
Returns after taxes on distributions	—	—	—	—	—
Returns after taxes on distributions and sales of fund shares	—	—	—	—	—

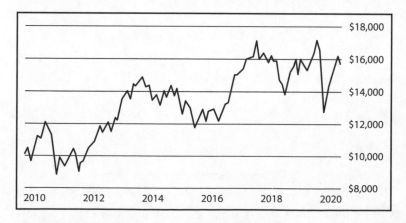

FIGURE A.5 Hypothetical Growth of $10,000 Invested in Vanguard European Stock Index Fund Through September 30, 2020

Holdings

Number of Holdings   1,310
Total Net Assets $17.2 billion

Top 10 Holdings as of 9/30/20

1. Nestlé SA
2. Roche Holding AG
3. Novartis AG
4. SAP SE
5. Unilever
6. ASML Holding NV
7. AstraZeneca PLC
8. LVMH Moët Hennessy Louis Vuitton SE
9. Novo Nordisk A/S
10. Sanofi

Risk Attributes

TABLE A.10   Historical Volatility Measures as of 9/30/2020

Benchmark	R-squared*	Beta*
Spliced European Stock Index	0.99	1.02

*R-squared and beta are calculated from trailing 36-month fund returns relative to the associated benchmark.

Management

Christine D. Franquin, Principal

- Portfolio manager
- Advised the fund since 2016
- Worked in investment management since 2000
- BA, Universitaire Faculteiten Sint Ignatius, Antwerpen, Belgium
- JD, University of Liège, Belgium
- Master of Science in Finance, Clark University, Massachusetts

Justin E. Hales, CFA, CFP
- Portfolio manager
- Advised the fund since 2016
- Worked in investment management since 2006
- BA, University of Maryland

Investment Policy

The fund reserves the right to substitute a different index for the index it currently tracks if the current index is discontinued, if a fund's agreement with the sponsor of its target index is terminated or for any other reason determined in good faith by the fund's board of trustees. The fund may invest, to a limited extent, in derivatives but will not use derivatives for speculation or for the purpose of leveraging (magnifying) investment returns. Investments in derivatives may subject the fund to risks different from, and possibly greater than, those of the underlying securities, assets, or market indexes. The fund may enter into forward foreign currency exchange contracts, which are types of derivative contracts, in order to maintain the same currency exposure as its respective index. The fund's daily cash balance may be invested in one or more Vanguard CMT funds, which are low-cost money market funds. The fund may temporarily depart from its normal investment policies and strategies when doing so is believed to be in the fund's best interest, so long as the alternative is consistent with the fund's investment objective.

Who Should Invest
- Investors seeking to further diversify a portfolio of U.S. securities
- Investors seeking long-term growth of capital
- Investors with a long-term investment horizon (at least five years)

Who Should Not Invest
- Investors unwilling to accept significant fluctuations in share price
- Investors seeking significant dividend income

Minimums

TABLE A.11 Minimums

	Initial Minimum	Additional Investments
Minimum investment	$3,000	$1

Expenses

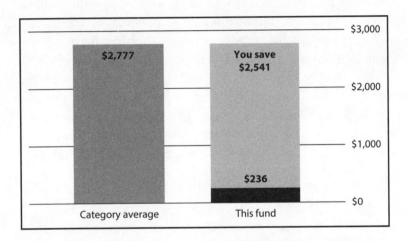

FIGURE A.6 Hypothetical Fees on $10,000 Invested in Vanguard European Stock Index Fund Over 10 Years

TABLE A.12 Expenses

	Expense Ratio
Vanguard European Stock Index Adm	0.10%
Average Europe Stock Fund	1.24%

VANGUARD PACIFIC STOCK INDEX FUND

Overview
Symbol   VPADX

Expense Ratio   0.10%

Overview

Inception Date   8/13/2001
Yield   N/A

Description

This index fund provides investors low-cost exposure to companies in developed countries of the Pacific region. The fund invests in about 2,400 stocks throughout the region, which makes up roughly a quarter of the non-U.S. equity marketplace. The fund employs an indexing investment approach by investing all, or substantially all, of its assets in the common stocks included in the FTSE Developed Asia Pacific All Cap Index. The FTSE Developed Asia Pacific All Cap Index is a market-capitalization-weighted index that is made up of approximately 2,313 common stocks of large cap, mid-cap and small cap companies located in Japan, Australia, South Korea, Hong Kong, Singapore and New Zealand.

TABLE A.13 After-Tax Returns as of 9/30/2020

	1-Year	3-Year	5-Year	10-Year	Since Inception 8/13/2001
Pacific Stock Index Adm					
Returns before taxes	5.75%	2.65%	7.66%	5.50%	5.25%
Returns after taxes on distributions	5.13%	1.99%	6.96%	4.78%	4.71%
Returns after taxes on distributions and sales of fund shares	3.79%	1.99%	5.93%	4.29%	4.26%
Average Pacific/Asia Stock Fund					
Returns before taxes	9.37%	3.06%	9.31%	7.59%	—
Returns after taxes on distributions	—	—	—	—	—
Returns after taxes on distributions and sales of fund shares	—	—	—	—	—

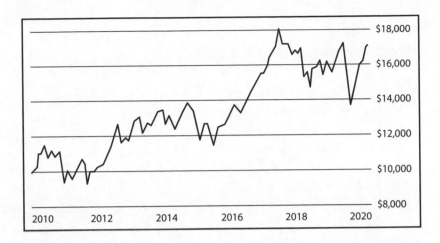

FIGURE A.7   Hypothetical Growth of $10,000 Invested in Vanguard Pacific Stock Index Fund Through September 30, 2020

Holdings

Number of Holdings   2,410
Total Net Assets $6.4 billion

Top 10 Holdings as of 9/30/2020

1. Samsung Electronics Co. Ltd.
2. Toyota Motor Corp.
3. AIA Group Ltd.
4. CSL Ltd.
5. Sony Corp.
6. SoftBank Group Corp.
7. Keyence Corp.
8. Commonwealth Bank of Australia
9. BHP Group Ltd.
10. Nintendo Co. Ltd.

Risk Attributes

TABLE A.14   Historical Volatility Measures as of 9/30/2020

Benchmark	R-squared*	Beta*
Spliced Pacific Stock Index	0.97	0.99

*R-squared and beta are calculated from trailing 36-month fund returns relative to the associated benchmark.

Management

Michael Perre, Principal
- Portfolio manager
- Advised the fund since 2016
- Worked in investment management since 1990
- BA, Saint Joseph's University
- MBA, Villanova University

Jeffrey D. Miller
- Portfolio manager
- Advised the fund since 2016
- Worked in investment management since 2007
- BA, Pennsylvania State University
- MBA, Drexel University

Investment Policy

The fund reserves the right to substitute a different index for the index it currently tracks if the current index is discontinued, if a fund's agreement with the sponsor of its target index is terminated, or for any other reason determined in good faith by the fund's board of trustees. The fund may invest, to a limited extent, in derivatives but will not use derivatives for speculation or for the purpose of leveraging (magnifying) investment returns. The fund may enter into forward foreign currency exchange contracts, which are types of derivative contracts, in order to maintain the same currency exposure as its respective index. The fund's daily cash balance may be invested in one or more Vanguard CMT funds, which are low-cost money market funds. The fund may temporarily depart from its normal investment policies and strategies when doing so is believed to be in the fund's best interest, so long as the alternative is consistent with the fund's investment objective.

Who Should Invest
- Investors seeking to further diversify a portfolio of U.S. securities
- Investors seeking long-term growth of capital
- Investors with a long-term investment horizon (at least five years)

Who Should Not Invest
- Investors unwilling to accept significant fluctuations in share price
- Investors seeking significant dividend income

Minimums

TABLE A.15 Minimums

	Initial Minimum	Additional Investments
General Account	$3,000	$1

Expenses

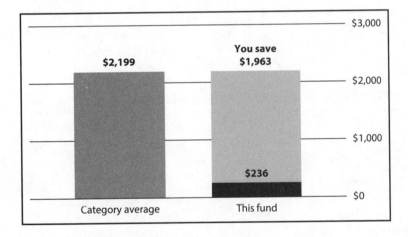

FIGURE A.8 Hypothetical Fees on $10,000 Invested in Vanguard Pacific Stock Index Fund Over 10 Years

TABLE A.16 Expenses

	Expense Ratio
Vanguard Pacific Stock Index Adm	0.10%
Average Pacific/Asia Stock Fund	0.97%

VANGUARD EMERGING MARKETS STOCK INDEX FUND

Overview

Symbol	VEMAX
Expense Ratio	0.14%
Inception Date	6/23/2006
Yield	N/A

Description

This fund offers investors a low-cost way to gain equity exposure to emerging markets. The fund employs an indexing investment approach designed to track the performance of the FTSE Emerging Markets All Cap China A Inclusion Index, a market-capitalization-weighted index that is made up of approximately 4,018 common stocks of large cap, mid-cap and small cap companies

TABLE A.17 After-Tax Returns as of 9/30/2020 (Fee-Adjusted)

	1-Year	3-Year	5-Year	10-Year	Since Inception 6/23/2006
Emerging Markets Stock Index Adm					
Returns before taxes	9.75%	2.50%	8.20%	2.26%	5.27%
Returns after taxes on distributions	8.80%	1.72%	7.40%	1.55%	4.65%
Returns after taxes on distributions and sales of fund shares	6.04%	1.75%	6.27%	1.62%	4.19%
Average Diversified Emerging Markets Fund					
Returns before taxes	9.11%	1.73%	8.08%	2.46%	—
Returns after taxes on distributions	—	—	—	—	—
Returns after taxes on distributions and sales of fund shares	—	—	—	—	—

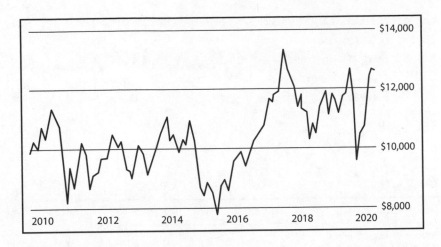

FIGURE A.9 Hypothetical Growth of $10,000 Invested in Vanguard Emerging Markets Stock Index Fund Through September 30, 2020

located in emerging markets around the world. The fund invests by sampling the index, meaning that it holds a broadly diversified collection of securities that, in the aggregate, approximates the index in terms of key characteristics. These key characteristics include industry weightings and market capitalization, as well as certain financial measures, such as price-to-earnings ratio and dividend yield.

Holdings

Number of Holdings	5,030
Total Net Assets	$85.8 billion

Top 10 Holdings as of 9/30/2020

1. Alibaba Group Holding Ltd.
2. Tencent Holdings Ltd.
3. Taiwan Semiconductor Manufacturing Co. Ltd.
4. Meituan Dianping
5. Reliance Industries Ltd.

6. Naspers Ltd.
7. JD.com Inc.
8. Ping An Insurance Group Co. of China Ltd.
9. China Construction Bank Corp.
10. Infosys Ltd.

Risk Attributes

TABLE A.18 Historical Volatility Measures as of 9/30/2020

Benchmark	R-squared*	Beta*
Spliced Emerging Markets Index	0.99	1.01

*R-squared and beta are calculated from trailing 36-month fund returns relative to the associated benchmark.

Management

Michael Perre, Principal
- Portfolio manager
- Advised the fund since 2008
- Worked in investment management since 1990
- BA, Saint Joseph's University
- MBA, Villanova University

Jeffrey D. Miller
- Portfolio manager
- Advised the fund since 2016
- Worked in investment management since 2007
- BA, Pennsylvania State University
- MBA, Drexel University

Investment Policy

The fund reserves the right to substitute a different index for the index it currently tracks if the current index is discontinued, if a fund's agreement with the sponsor of its target index is terminated or for any other reason determined in good faith by the fund's board of trustees. The fund may invest, to a limited extent, in derivatives but will not use derivatives for speculation or for the purpose of leveraging (magnifying) investment returns. The fund may enter into forward foreign currency exchange contracts, which are types of derivative contracts, in order to maintain the same currency exposure as its respective index. The fund's daily cash balance may be invested in one or more Vanguard CMT funds, which are low-cost money market funds. The fund may temporarily depart from its normal investment policies and strategies when doing so is believed to be in the fund's best interest, so long as the alternative is consistent with the fund's investment objective.

Who Should Invest
- Investors seeking to further diversify a portfolio of U.S. securities
- Investors seeking long-term growth of capital
- Investors with a long-term investment horizon (at least five years)

Who Should Not Invest
- Investors unwilling to accept significant fluctuations in share price
- Investors seeking significant dividend income

Minimums

TABLE A.19 Minimums

	Initial Minimum	Additional Investments
Minimum investment	$3,000	$1

Expenses

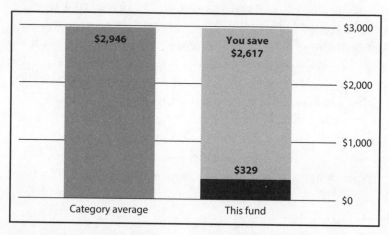

FIGURE A.10 Hypothetical Fees on $10,000 Invested in Vanguard Total Stock Market Index Fund Over 10 Years

TABLE A.20 Expenses

	Expense Ratio
Vanguard Emerging Markets Stock Index Adm	0.14%
Average Diversified Emerging Market Fund	1.32%

VANGUARD SHORT-TERM INVESTMENT-GRADE FUND

Overview

Symbol	VFSTX
Expense Ratio	0.20%
Inception Date	10/29/1982
Yield	0.97%
Admiral Shares	VFSUX

Description

This fund is designed to give investors exposure to high- and medium-quality investment-grade bonds with short-term maturities. The fund invests in a variety of high- and medium-quality fixed income securities, at least 80% of which will be short- and intermediate-term investment-grade securities. High-quality fixed income securities are those rated the equivalent of A3 or better by Moody's Investors Service Inc., or another independent rating agency; medium-quality fixed income securities are those rated the equivalent of Baa1, Baa2 or Baa3 by Moody's or another independent rating agency. (Investment-grade fixed income securities are those rated the equivalent of Baa3 and above by Moody's.) The fund is expected to maintain a dollar-weighted average maturity of one to four years.

TABLE A.21 After-Tax Returns as of 9/30/2020

	1-Year	3-Year	5-Year	10-Year	Since Inception 10/29/1982
Short-Term Investment-					
Grade Fund Inv					
Returns before taxes	4.79%	3.54%	3.02%	2.55%	5.88%
Returns after taxes on distributions	3.74%	2.45%	2.01%	1.58%	—
Returns after taxes on distributions and sales of fund shares	2.82%	2.23%	1.86%	1.55%	—
Average					
Short-Term Bond Fund					
Returns before taxes	3.30%	2.76%	2.39%	1.99%	—
Returns after taxes on distributions	—	—	—	—	—
Returns after taxes on distributions and sales of fund shares	—	—	—	—	—

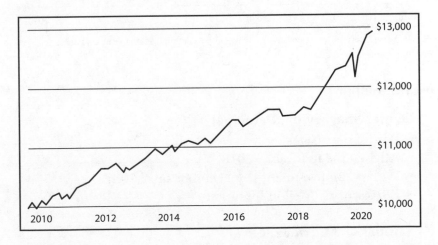

FIGURE A.11 Hypothetical Growth of $10,000 Invested in Vanguard Short-Term Investment-Grade Fund Through September 30, 2020

Holdings

Number of Holdings   2,469
Total Net Assets $66.8 billion

Bond Distribution by Issuer as of 9/30/2020

Asset-backed	7.0%
Commercial mortgage-backed	8.0%
Finance	28.2%
Foreign	5.6%
Government mortgage-backed	1.7%
Industrial	36.9%
Other	0.2%
Short-term reserves	2.4%
Treasury/agency	6.1%
Utilities	3.9%

Risk Attributes

TABLE A.22   Historical Volatility Measures as of 9/30/2020

Benchmark	R-squared*	Beta*
Bloomberg Barclays US 1–5 Year Credit Bond Index	0.98	1.00

*R-squared and beta are calculated from trailing 36-month fund returns relative to the associated benchmark.

Management

Daniel Shaykevich, Principal
- Portfolio manager
- Advised the fund since 2018
- Worked in investment management since 2001
- BS, Carnegie Mellon University

Samuel C. Martinez, CFA
- Portfolio manager
- Advised the fund since 2018

- Worked in investment management since 2010
- BS, Southern Utah University
- MBA, The Wharton School of the University of Pennsylvania

Arvind Narayanan, CFA
- Portfolio manager
- Advised the fund since 2019
- Worked in investment management since 2002
- BA, Goucher College
- MBA, New York University Stern School of Business

Investment Policy

The fund may invest in derivatives only if the expected risks and rewards of the derivatives are consistent with the investment objective, policies, strategies, and risks of the fund as disclosed in the prospectus. The fund may invest up to 15% of its net assets in illiquid securities. The fund may invest in shares of bond exchange-traded funds (ETFs). ETFs provide returns similar to those of the bonds listed in the index or a subset of the index.

Who Should Invest
- Investors seeking a high level of interest income and only slight fluctuations in the market value of their investment
- Investors seeking to balance a stock portfolio with a fixed income investment

Who Should Not Invest
- Investors seeking long-term growth of capital

Minimums

TABLE A.23 Minimums

	Initial Minimum	Additional Investments
General Account	$3,000	$1
IRA	$3,000	$1
UGMAs/UTMAs	$3,000	$1

Expenses

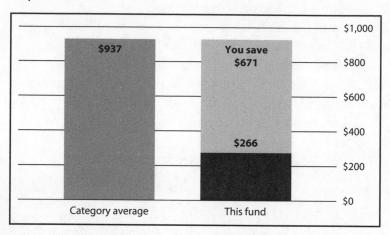

FIGURE A.12 Hypothetical Fees on $10,000 Invested in Vanguard Short-Term Investment-Grade Fund Over 10 Years

TABLE A.24 Expenses

	Expense Ratio
Vanguard Short–Term Investment-Grade Fund Inv	0.20%
Average Short–Term Investment-Grade Bond Fund	0.72%

VANGUARD HIGH-YIELD CORPORATE FUND

Overview

Symbol	VWEHX
Expense Ratio	0.23%
Inception Date	12/27/1978
Yield	3.74%
Admiral Shares	VWEAX

Description

The fund invests mainly in a diversified group of high-yielding, higher-risk corporate bonds—commonly known as junk bonds—with medium- and lower-range credit-quality ratings. The fund invests at least 80% of its assets in corporate bonds that are rated below Baa by Moody's Investors Service, Inc., have an equivalent rating by any other independent bond-rating agency, or, if unrated, are determined to be of comparable quality by the fund's advisor. The fund's 80% policy may be changed only upon 60 days' notice to investors. The fund may not invest more than 20% of its assets in any of the following, taken as a whole: bonds with credit ratings lower than B or the equivalent, convertible securities, and preferred stocks.

TABLE A.25   After-Tax Returns as of 9/30/2020

	1-Year	3-Year	5-Year	10-Year	Since Inception 12/27/1978
High-Yield Corporate Fund Inv					
Returns before taxes	3.16%	4.21%	6.02%	6.11%	8.19%
Returns after taxes on distributions	1.08%	1.97%	3.63%	3.66%	—
Returns after taxes on distributions and sales of fund shares	1.84%	2.23%	3.55%	3.65%	—
Average High-Yield Bond Fund					
Returns before taxes	1.33%	2.89%	5.18%	5.29%	—
Returns after taxes on distributions	—	—	—	—	—
Returns after taxes on distributions and sale of fund shares	—	—	—	—	—

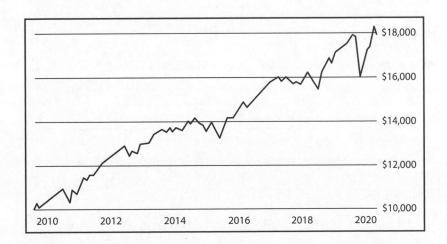

FIGURE A.13   Hypothetical Growth of $10,000 Invested in Vanguard High-Yield Corporate Fund Through September 30, 2020

Holdings

Number of Holdings	574
Total Net Assets	$27.2 billion

Bond Distribution by Issuer as of 9/30/2020

Basic industry	4.5%
Capital goods	11.9%
Communication	19.4%
Consumer cyclical	12.9%
Consumer noncyclical	15.1%
Energy	9.5%
Finance	8.1%
Industrial other	0.4%
Other corporate	3.1%
Reserves	-2.9%
Technology	11.5%
Transportation	0.2%
Treasury/agency	5.4%
Utilities	0.9%

Risk Attributes

TABLE A.26 Historical Volatility Measures as of 9/30/2020

Benchmark	R-squared*	Beta*
High-Yield Corporate Composite Index	0.98	1.01

*R-squared and beta are calculated from trailing 36-month fund returns relative to the associated benchmark.

Management

Michael L. Hong, CFA, Senior Managing Director

- Portfolio manager
- Advised the fund since 2008

- Worked in investment management since 1997
- AB, Harvard College

Investment Policy

The fund may invest in derivatives only if the expected risks and rewards of the derivatives are consistent with the investment objective, policies, strategies and risks of the fund. The fund's daily cash balance may be invested in one or more Vanguard CMT funds, which are low-cost money market funds. The fund may temporarily depart from its normal investment policies and strategies when doing so is believed to be in the fund's best interest, so long as the alternative is consistent with the fund's investment objective.

Who Should Invest
- Investors seeking a high level of dividend income
- Investors seeking modest long-term growth of capital
- Investors with a long-term investment horizon (at least five years)

Who Should Not Invest
- Investors unwilling to accept significant fluctuations in share price
- Investors seeking an investment in high-quality bonds

Minimums

TABLE A.27 Minimums

	Initial Minimum	Additional Investments
General Account	$3,000	$1
IRA	$3,000	$1
UGMAs/UTMAs	$3,000	$1

Expenses

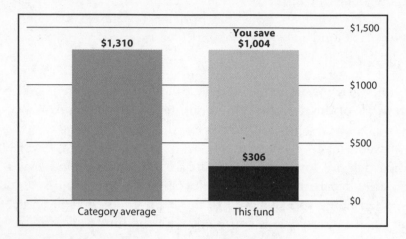

FIGURE A.14 Hypothetical Fees on $10,000 Invested in Vanguard High-Yield Corporate Fund Over 10 Years

TABLE A.28 Expenses

	Expense Ratio
Vanguard High-Yield Corporate Fund Inv	0.23%
Average High-Yield Bond Fund	1.02%

VANGUARD INFLATION-PROTECTED SECURITIES FUND

Overview

Symbol	VIPSX
Expense Ratio	0.20%
Inception Date	6/29/2000
Yield	−1.18%
Admiral Shares	VAIPX

Description

This fund is designed to protect investors from the eroding effect of inflation by investing primarily in securities that seek to provide a "real" return. The fund focuses on investments in inflation-protected bonds that are backed by the full faith and credit of the federal government and whose principal is adjusted based on inflation. The fund invests at least 80% of its assets in inflation-indexed bonds issued by the U.S. government, its agencies and instrumentalities, and corporations. The fund may invest in bonds of any maturity; however, its dollar-weighted average maturity is expected to be in a range of seven to 20 years. At a minimum, all bonds purchased by the fund will be rated "investment grade" or, if unrated, will be considered by the advisor to be investment grade.

TABLE A.29 After-Tax Returns as of 9/30/2020

	1-Year	3-Year	5-Year	10-Year	Since Inception 6/29/2000
Inflation-Protected Securities Fund Inv					
Returns before taxes	9.64%	5.53%	4.35%	3.36%	5.33%
Returns after taxes on distributions	9.03%	4.54%	3.43%	2.42%	4.06%
Returns after taxes on distributions and sales of fund shares	5.68%	3.79%	2.93%	2.21%	3.74%
Average Inflation-Protected Bond Fund					
Returns before taxes	8.79%	5.00%	4.02%	2.96%	—
Returns after taxes on distributions	—	—	—	—	—
Returns after taxes on distributions and sales of fund shares	—	—	—	—	—

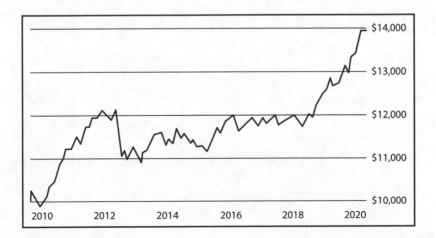

FIGURE A.15 Hypothetical Growth of $10,000 Invested in Vanguard Inflation-Protected Securities Fund Through September 30, 2020

Holdings

Number of Holdings   49

Total Net Assets $33.0 billion

Risk Attributes

TABLE A.30 Historical Volatility Measures as of 9/30/2020

Benchmark	R-squared*	Beta*
Bloomberg Barclays US Treasury Inflation Protected Index	0.98	0.94

*R-squared and beta are calculated from trailing 36-month fund returns relative to the associated benchmark.

Management

Gemma Wright-Casparius, Principal
- Portfolio manager
- Advised the fund since 2011
- Worked in investment management since 2005
- BBA, Bernard M. Baruch College of The City University of New York
- MBA, Bernard M. Baruch College of The City University of New York

Investment Policy

Up to 20% of the fund's assets may be invested in holdings that are not inflation-indexed. The fund will make such investments primarily when inflation-indexed bonds are less attractive. The fund's non–inflation-indexed holdings may include the following:

- Corporate debt obligations
- U.S. government and agency bonds
- Cash investments
- Futures, options, and other derivatives
- Restricted or illiquid securities
- Mortgage dollar rolls

The fund may invest up to 20% of its total assets in bond futures contracts, options, credit swaps, interest rate swaps and other types of derivatives. These contracts may be used to keep cash on hand to meet shareholder redemptions or other needs while simulating full investment in bonds, to reduce transaction costs, for hedging purposes, or to add value when these instruments are favorably priced. Losses (or gains) involving futures can be substantial— in part because a relatively small price movement in a futures contract may result in an immediate and substantial loss (or gain) for the fund. Similar risks exist for other types of derivatives. For this reason, the fund will not use derivatives for speculative purposes or as leveraged investments that magnify the gains or losses of an investment.

Restricted securities are privately placed securities that generally can only be sold to qualified institutional buyers and, hence, could be difficult for the fund to convert to cash, if needed. The fund will not invest more than 15% of its assets in such illiquid securities.

Mortgage dollar rolls are transactions in which a fund sells mortgage-backed securities to a dealer and simultaneously agrees to purchase similar securities in the future at a predetermined price. These transactions simulate an investment in mortgage-backed securities and have the potential to enhance a fund's returns and reduce its administrative burdens, compared with holding mortgage-backed securities directly. These transactions may increase a fund's portfolio turnover rate. Mortgage dollar rolls will be used only if consistent with a fund's investment objective and risk profile.

Who Should Invest
- Investors seeking a bond fund that provides inflation protection
- Investors seeking additional portfolio diversification that inflation-indexed securities can offer

Who Should Not Invest
- Investors unwilling to accept some volatility in income distributions

- Investors unwilling to tolerate modest fluctuations in share price
- Investors seeking long-term growth of capital

Minimums

TABLE A.31   Minimums

	Initial Minimum	Additional Investments
General Account	$3,000	$1
IRA	$3,000	$1
UGMAs/UTMAs	$3,000	$1

Expenses

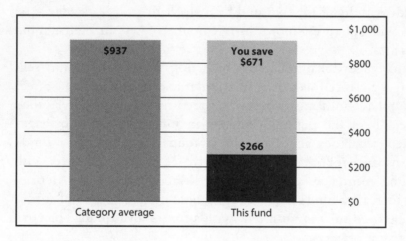

FIGURE A.16   Hypothetical Fees on $10,000 Invested in Vanguard Inflation-Protected Securities Fund Over 10 Years

TABLE A.32   Expenses

	Expense Ratio
Vanguard Inflation-Protected Securities Fund Inv	0.20%
Average Inflation-Protected Bond Fund	0.72%

VANGUARD REAL ESTATE INDEX FUND

Overview

Symbol	VGSLX
Expense Ratio	0.12%
Inception Date	11/12/2001
Yield	3.63%

Description

This fund invests in real estate investment trusts—companies that purchase office buildings, hotels and other real estate property. The fund employs an indexing investment approach designed to track the performance of the MSCI US Investable Market Real Estate 25/50 Index. The MSCI US Investable Market Real Estate 25/50 Index is made up of stocks of large, mid-size and small U.S. companies within the real estate sector, as classified under the Global Industry Classification Standard (GICS). The GICS real estate sector is composed of equity real estate investment trusts (known as REITs), which includes specialized REITs, and real estate management and development companies. The fund attempts to replicate the index by investing all, or substantially all, of its assets—either directly or indirectly through a wholly owned subsidiary (the underlying fund), which is itself a registered investment company—in the stocks that make up the index, holding each stock in approximately the same proportion as its weighting in the index. The fund may invest a portion of its assets in the underlying fund.

TABLE A.33   After-Tax Returns as of 9/30/2020

	1-Year	3-Year	5-Year	10-Year	Since Inception 11/12/2001
REIT Index Fund Adm					
Returns before taxes	−12.19%	2.37%	5.22%	8.50%	9.41%
Returns after taxes on distributions	−13.37%	1.05%	3.86%	7.24%	7.96%
Returns after taxes on distributions and sales of fund shares	−7.20%	1.26%	3.46%	6.30%	7.28%

(continued)

TABLE A.33 After-Tax Returns as of 9/30/2020 (*Continued*)

	1-Year	3-Year	5-Year	10-Year	Since Inception 11/12/2001
Average Real Estate Fund					
Returns before taxes	−13.44%	1.17%	4.28%	7.80%	—
Returns after taxes on distributions	—	—	—	—	—
Returns after taxes on distributions and sales of fund shares	—	—	—	—	—

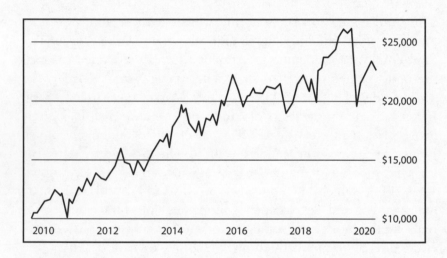

FIGURE A.17 Hypothetical Growth of $10,000 Invested in Vanguard Real Estate Index Fund Through September 30, 2020

Holdings

Number of Holdings   181
Total Net Assets $55.2 billion

Top 10 Holdings as of 9/30/2020

1. Vanguard Real Estate II Index Fund
2. American Tower Corp.
3. Prologis Inc.
4. Crown Castle International Corp.

5. Equinix Inc.
6. Digital Realty Trust Inc.
7. SBA Communications Corp.
8. Public Storage
9. Welltower Inc.
10. Weyerhaeuser Co.

Risk Attributes

TABLE A.34 Historical Volatility Measures as of 9/30/2020

Benchmark	R-squared*	Beta*
Real Estate Spliced Index	1.00	1.00

*R-squared and beta are calculated from trailing 36-month fund returns relative to the associated benchmark.

Management

Gerard C. O'Reilly, Principal
- Portfolio manager
- Advised the fund since 1996
- Worked in investment management since 1992
- BS, Villanova University

Walter Nejman
- Portfolio manager
- Advised the fund since 2016
- Worked in investment management since 2008
- BA, Arcadia University
- MBA, Villanova University

Investment Policy

The fund reserves the right to substitute a different index for the index it currently tracks if the current index is discontinued, if the fund's agreement with the sponsor of its target index is terminated or for any other reason determined in good faith by the fund's board of trustees. The fund may invest in foreign securities to the extent necessary to carry out its investment strategy of holding all, or substantially all, of the stocks that make up the index it tracks. Besides investing in common stocks of REITs, the fund may make other kinds of investments to achieve its objective. The fund may invest in derivatives only if the expected risks and rewards of the derivatives are consistent with the investment objective, policies, strategies, and risks of the fund as disclosed in the prospectus. The advisor will not use derivatives to change the risk exposure of the fund. The fund's daily cash balance may be invested in one or more Vanguard CMT funds, which are low-cost money market funds. The fund may temporarily depart from its normal investment policies and strategies when doing so is believed to be in the fund's best interest, so long as the alternative is consistent with the fund's investment objective.

Who Should Invest
- Investors seeking a high level of dividend income and long-term growth of capital
- Investors with a long-term investment horizon (at least five years)
- Investors seeking to add real estate exposure to their mix of stock, bond and money market mutual funds

Who Should Not Invest
- Investors unwilling to accept significant fluctuations in share price
- Investors seeking a mutual fund that invests in a variety of industries

Minimums

TABLE A.35 Minimums

	Initial Minimum	Additional Investments
General Account	$3,000	$1

Expenses

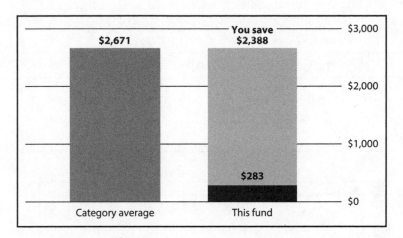

FIGURE A.18 Hypothetical Fees on $10,000 Invested in Vanguard Real Estate Index Fund Over 10 Years

TABLE A.36 Expenses

	Expense Ratio
Vanguard REIT Index Fund Adm	0.12%
Average Real Estate Fund	1.19%

VANECK VECTORS GOLD MINERS ETF

Overview

Symbol	GDX
Expense Ratio	0.52%
Inception Date	5/16/2006
Yield	0.37%

Description

VanEck Vectors® Gold Miners ETF (GDX®) seeks to replicate as closely as possible, before fees and expenses, the price and yield performance of the NYSE Arca Gold Miners Index (GDMNTR), which is intended to track the overall performance of companies involved in the gold mining industry.

TABLE A.37 Performance Returns as of 9/30/2020

	1-Year	3-Year	5-Year	10-Year	Since Inception 5/16/2006
Gold Miners ETF					
Returns before taxes	47.01%	20.26%	24.07%	−2.88%	0.52%

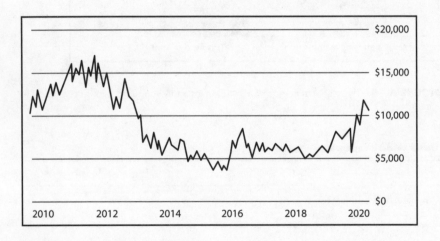

FIGURE A.19 Hypothetical Growth of $10,000 Invested in VanEck Vectors Gold Miners ETF Through September 30, 2020

Holdings

Number of Holdings   54

Fund Total Net Assets $16.1 billion

Top 10 Holdings as of 9/30/2020

1. Newmont Corp.
2. Barrick Gold Corp.
3. Franco-Nevada Corp.
4. Newcrest Mining Ltd.
5. Wheaton Precious Metals Corp.

6. Agnico Eagle Mines Ltd.
7. Kirkland Lake Gold Ltd.
8. Kinross Gold Corp.
9. Anglogold Ashanti Ltd.
10. Gold Fields Ltd.

Risk Attributes

TABLE A.38   Historical Volatility Measures as of 9/30/2020

Benchmark	Beta*
S&P 500 Index	0.86

*Beta is calculated from trailing 36-month fund returns relative to the associated benchmark.

Management

Peter H. Liao
- Portfolio manager
- Advised the fund since 2005
- BA, mathematics and economics, New York University

Investment Policy

The fund, using a passive or indexing investment approach, attempts to approximate the investment performance of the NYSE Arca Gold Miners Index by investing in a portfolio of securities that generally replicates the Gold Miners Index. The fund normally invests at least 80% of its total assets in common stocks and depositary receipts of companies involved in the gold mining industry. Such companies may include small cap and medium cap companies and foreign issuers. The Gold Miners Index is a modified market-capitalization weighted index primarily composed of publicly traded companies involved in the mining for gold and silver. The weight of the companies whose revenues are more significantly exposed to silver mining will not exceed 20% of the Gold Miners Index at rebalance.

Who Should Invest
- Investors seeking long-term growth of capital
- Investors with a long-term investment horizon (at least five years)

Who Should Not Invest
- Investors unwilling to accept significant fluctuations in share price
- Investors seeking a mutual fund that invests in a variety of industries

Expenses

TABLE A.39 Expenses

	Expense Ratio
VanEck Vectors Gold Miners ETF	0.52%

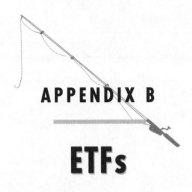

APPENDIX B

ETFs

Exchange-traded funds (ETFs) are a relatively new investment vehicle, as you can see from the inception dates for the funds included in this section. You may notice that the stated performance of these funds varies greatly in some cases from the performance of similar mutual funds offered by The Vanguard Group. Please understand that these discrepancies are due primarily to the ETFs' short life spans and not to any dramatic difference in their composition or management. Going forward, the annual returns generated by these ETFs and the Vanguard mutual funds should be similar.

VANGUARD TOTAL STOCK MARKET ETF

Overview

Symbol   VTI
Expense Ratio   0.03%
Inception Date   5/24/2001

Description

The Vanguard Total Stock Market ETF is an exchange-traded share class of the Vanguard Total Stock Market Index Fund, which employs an indexing investment approach designed to track the

TABLE B.1 Performance Returns Before Taxes

1-Year	3-Year	5-Year	10-Year	Since Inception
14.98%	11.66%	13.70%	13.48%	7.60%

performance of the CRSP U.S. Total Market Index. This index represents approximately 100% of the investable U.S. stock market and includes large cap, mid-cap, small cap and micro-cap stocks regularly traded on the New York Stock Exchange and Nasdaq. The fund invests by sampling the index, meaning that it holds a broadly diversified collection of securities that, in the aggregate, approximates the full index in terms of key characteristics. These key characteristics include industry weightings and market capitalization, as well as certain financial measures, such as price-to-earnings ratio and dividend yield.

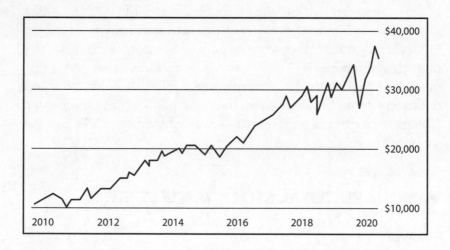

FIGURE B.1 Hypothetical Growth of $10,000 Invested in Vanguard Total Stock Market ETF Through September 30, 2020

Holdings

Number of Holdings	3,566
Median Market Cap	$108.4 billion
Fund Total Net Assets	$937.6 billion

Top 10 Holdings as of 9/30/2020

1. Apple Inc.
2. Microsoft Corp.
3. Amazon.com Inc.
4. Alphabet Inc.
5. Facebook Inc.
6. Berkshire Hathaway Inc.
7. Johnson & Johnson
8. Procter & Gamble Co.
9. Visa Inc.
10. Tesla Inc.

VANGUARD SMALL-CAP ETF

Overview

Symbol	VB
Expense Ratio	0.05%
Inception Date	1/26/2004

Description

The Vanguard Small-Cap ETF is an exchange-traded share class of the Vanguard Small-Cap Index Fund, which employs an indexing investment approach designed to track the performance of the CRSP U.S. Small Cap Index, a broadly diversified index of stocks of smaller U.S. companies. The fund attempts to replicate the target index by investing all, or substantially all, of its assets in the stocks that make up the index, holding each stock in approximately the same proportion as its weighting in the index.

TABLE B.2 Performance Returns Before Taxes

1–Year	3–Year	5–Year	10–Year	Since Inception
1.39%	4.39%	8.95%	10.96%	8.42%

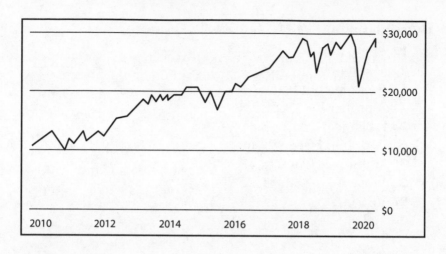

FIGURE B.2 Hypothetical Growth of $10,000 Invested in Vanguard Small-Cap ETF Through September 30, 2020

Holdings

Number of Holdings	1,405
Median Market Cap	$4.9 billion
Fund Total Net Assets	$89.8 billion

Top 10 Holdings as of 9/30/2020

1. Immunomedics Inc.
2. Horizon Therapeutics PLC
3. Insulet Corp.
4. STERIS PLC
5. Etsy Inc.
6. PerkinElmer Inc.
7. Catalent Inc.
8. IDEX Corp.
9. Zebra Technologies Corp.
10. Teradyne Inc.

VANGUARD FTSE EUROPE ETF

Overview

Symbol	VGK
Expense Ratio	0.08%
Inception Date	3/4/2005

Description

The Vanguard FTSE Europe ETF is an exchange-traded share class of the Vanguard European Stock Index Fund, which employs an indexing investment approach by investing all, or substantially all, of its assets in the common stocks included in the FTSE Developed Europe All Cap Index. The FTSE Developed Europe All Cap Index is a market-capitalization-weighted index that is made up of approximately 1,200 common stocks of large cap, mid-cap and small cap companies located in 16 European countries—mostly companies in the United Kingdom, Germany, France and Switzerland. Other countries represented in the index include Austria, Belgium, Denmark, Finland, Ireland, Italy, the Netherlands, Norway, Poland, Portugal, Spain and Sweden.

TABLE B.3 Performance Returns Before Taxes

1-Year	3-Year	5-Year	10-Year	Since Inception
0.33%	−0.40%	4.55%	4.65%	3.97%

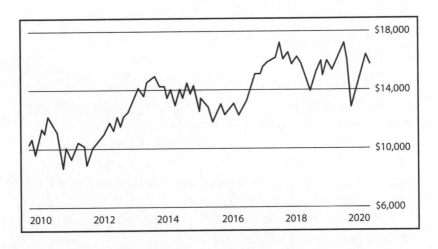

FIGURE B.3 Hypothetical Growth of $10,000 Invested in Vanguard FTSE Europe ETF Through September 30, 2020

Holdings

Number of Holdings	1,310
Median Market Cap	$35.6 billion
Fund Total Net Assets	$17.2 billion

Top 10 Holdings as of 9/30/2020

1. Nestlé SA
2. Roche Holding AG
3. Novartis AG
4. SAP SE
5. Unilever
6. ASML Holding NV
7. AstraZeneca PLC
8. LVMH Moët Hennessy Louis Vuitton SE
9. Novo Nordisk A/S
10. Sanofi

VANGUARD FTSE PACIFIC ETF

Overview

Symbol	VPL
Expense Ratio	0.08%
Inception Date	3/4/2005

Description

The Vanguard FTSE Pacific ETF is an exchange-traded share class of the Vanguard Pacific Stock Index Fund, which employs an indexing investment approach by investing all, or substantially all, of its assets in the common stocks included in the FTSE Developed Asia Pacific All Cap Index. The FTSE Developed Asia Pacific All Cap Index is a market-capitalization-weighted index that is made up of approximately 2,313 common stocks of large cap, mid-cap and small cap companies located in Japan, Australia, Korea, Hong Kong, Singapore and New Zealand.

TABLE B.4 Performance Returns Before Taxes

1–Year	3–Year	5–Year	10–Year	Since Inception
5.52%	2.63%	7.65%	5.49%	4.62%

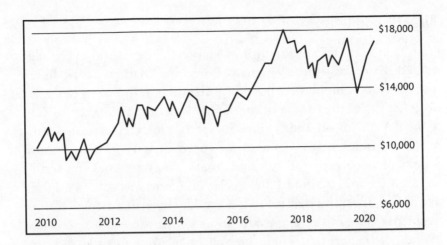

FIGURE B.4 Hypothetical Growth of $10,000 Invested in Vanguard FTSE Pacific ETF Through September 30, 2020

Holdings

Number of Holdings	2,410
Median Market Cap	$20.1 billion
Fund Total Net Assets	$6.4 billion

Top 10 Holdings as of 9/30/2020

1. Samsung Electronics Co. Ltd.
2. Toyota Motor Corp.
3. AIA Group Ltd.
4. CSL Ltd.
5. Sony Corp.
6. SoftBank Group Corp.
7. Keyence Corp.
8. Commonwealth Bank of Australia
9. BHP Group Ltd.
10. Nintendo Co. Ltd.

VANGUARD FTSE EMERGING MARKETS ETF

Overview

Symbol	VWO
Expense Ratio	0.10%
Inception Date	3/4/2005

Description

The Vanguard FTSE Emerging Markets ETF is an exchange-traded share class of the Vanguard Emerging Markets Stock Index Fund, which employs an indexing investment approach designed to track the performance of the FTSE Emerging Markets All Cap China A Inclusion Index. The index is a market-capitalization-weighted index that is made up of approximately 4,018 common stocks of large cap, mid-cap and small cap companies located in emerging markets around the world. The fund invests by sampling the index, meaning that it holds a broadly diversified collection of securities that, in the aggregate, approximates the index in terms of key characteristics. These key characteristics include industry weightings and market capitalization, as well as certain financial measures, such as price-to-earnings ratio and dividend yield.

TABLE B.5 Performance Returns Before Taxes

1-Year	3-Year	5-Year	10-Year	Since Inception
10.43%	2.48%	8.29%	2.28%	6.14%

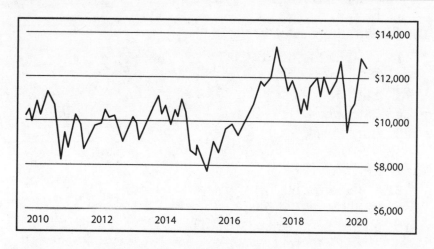

FIGURE B.5 Hypothetical Growth of $10,000 Invested in Vanguard FTSE Emerging Markets ETF Through September 30, 2020

Holdings

Number of Holdings	5,030
Median Market Cap	$23.7 billion
Fund Total Net Assets	$85.8 billion

Top 10 Holdings as of 9/30/2020

1. Alibaba Group Holding Ltd.
2. Tencent Holdings Ltd.
3. Taiwan Semiconductor Manufacturing Co. Ltd.
4. Meituan Dianping
5. Reliance Industries Ltd.
6. Naspers Ltd.
7. JD.com Inc.
8. Ping An Insurance Group Co. of China Ltd.
9. China Construction Bank Corp.
10. Infosys Ltd.

VANGUARD SHORT-TERM BOND ETF

Overview

Symbol	BSV
Expense Ratio	0.05%
Inception Date	4/3/2007

Description

The fund employs an indexing investment approach designed to track the performance of the Bloomberg Barclays U.S. 1–5 Year Government/Credit Float Adjusted Index. This index includes all medium and larger issues of U.S. government, investment-grade corporate, and investment-grade international dollar-denominated bonds that have maturities between one and five years and are publicly issued. The fund invests by sampling the index, meaning that it holds a range of securities that, in the aggregate, approximates the full index in terms of key risk factors and other characteristics. All of the fund's investments will be selected through the sampling process, and at least 80% of the fund's assets will be invested in bonds held in the index. The fund maintains a dollar-weighted average maturity consistent with that of the index.

TABLE B.6 Performance Returns Before Taxes

1-Year	3-Year	5-Year	10-Year	Since Inception
4.80%	3.42%	2.51%	2.00%	2.97%

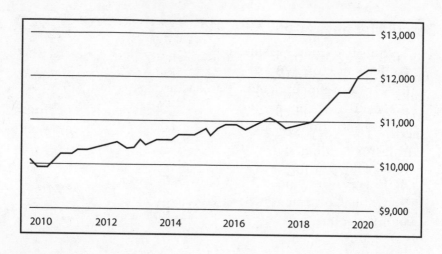

FIGURE B.6 Hypothetical Growth of $10,000 Invested in Vanguard Short-Term Bond ETF Through September 30, 2020

Holdings

Number of Holdings	2,655
Fund Total Net Assets	$27.3 billion

Holdings—Types of Bonds

1. Asset-backed
2. Commercial mortgage-backed
3. Finance
4. Foreign
5. Government mortgage-backed
6. Industrial
7. Other
8. Treasury/agency
9. Utilities

ISHARES IBOXX $ HIGH YIELD CORPORATE BOND ETF

Overview

Symbol	HYG
Expense Ratio	0.49%
Inception Date	4/4/2007

Description

This fund seeks to track the investment results of the Markit iBoxx® USD Liquid High Yield Index. The underlying index is a rules-based index consisting of U.S. dollar-denominated, high-yield corporate bonds for sale in the United States. The fund generally will invest at least 90% of its assets in the component securities of the underlying index and may invest up to 10% of its assets in certain futures, options and swap contracts, cash and cash equivalents, as well as in securities not included in the underlying index.

Holdings

Number of Holdings	1,250
Fund Total Net Assets	$25.7 billion

TABLE B.7 Performance Returns Before Taxes

1-Year	3-Year	5-Year	10-Year	Since Inception
1.21%	3.34%	5.55%	5.29%	5.18%

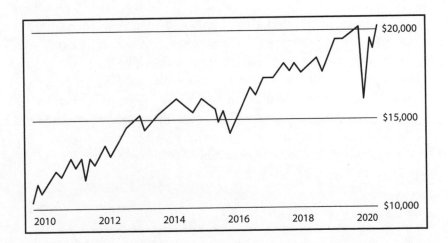

FIGURE B.7 Hypothetical Growth of $10,000 Invested in iShares iBoxx $ High Yield Corporate Bond ETF Through September 30, 2020

Top 10 Holdings as of 9/30/2020

1. Altice France SA
2. Sprint Corp.
3. Transdigm Group Inc.
4. Ford Motor Co.
5. Ford Motor Co.
6. Centene Corp.
7. CCO Holdings LLC
8. Tenet Healthcare Corp.
9. Caesars Entertainment Inc.
10. Bausch Health Companies Inc.

PIMCO© 15+ YEAR U.S. TIPS INDEX ETF*

Overview

Symbol	LTPZ
Expense Ratio	0.20%
Inception Date	9/3/2009

Description

The fund seeks to provide a total return that closely corresponds, before fees and expenses, to the total return of the ICE BofAML 15+ Year US Inflation-Linked Treasury Index. The fund invests at least 80% of its total assets (exclusive of collateral held from securities lending) in the component securities of the ICE BofAML 15+ Year US Inflation-Linked Treasury Index (the underlying index). The underlying index is an unmanaged index composed of Treasury Inflation-Protected Securities (TIPS) with a maturity of at least 15 years.

TABLE B.8 Performance Returns Before Taxes

1-Year	3-Year	5-Year	10-Year	Since Inception
21.18%	12.16%	9.71%	6.66%	7.39%

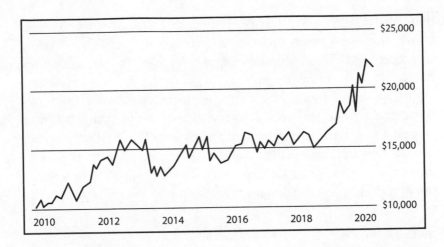

FIGURE B.8 Hypothetical Growth of $10,000 Invested in PIMCO 15+ Year U.S. TIPS Index ETF Through September 30, 2020

Holdings

Number of Holdings	10
Fund Total Net Assets	$583.5 million

*PIMCO is a trademark of Allianz Asset Management of America L.P. in the United States and throughout the world. © 2020 PIMCO.

VANGUARD REAL ESTATE ETF

Overview

Symbol	VNQ
Expense Ratio	0.12%
Inception Date	9/23/2004

Description

The Vanguard Real Estate ETF is an exchange-traded share class of the Vanguard Real Estate Index Fund that employs an indexing investment approach designed to track the performance of the MSCI US Investable Market Real Estate 25/50 Index. The MSCI US Investable Market Real Estate 25/50 Index is made up of stocks of large, mid-size and small U.S. companies within the real estate sector, as classified under the Global Industry Classification

Standard (GICS). The GICS real estate sector is composed of equity real estate investment trusts (known as REITs), including specialized REITs, and real estate management and development companies. The fund attempts to replicate the index by investing all, or substantially all, of its assets—either directly or indirectly through a wholly owned subsidiary (the underlying fund), which is itself a registered investment company—in the stocks that make up the index, holding each stock in approximately the same proportion as its weighting in the index. The fund may invest a portion of its assets in the underlying fund.

TABLE B.9 Performance Returns Before Taxes

1–Year	3–Year	5–Year	10–Year	Since Inception
−12.26%	2.34%	5.21%	8.49%	7.68%

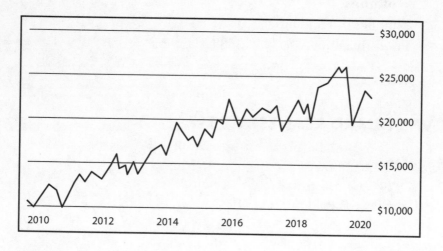

FIGURE B.9 Hypothetical Growth of $10,000 Invested in Vanguard Real Estate ETF Through September 30, 2020

Holdings

Number of Holdings	181
Average Market Cap	$19.1 billion
Fund Total Net Assets	$55.2 billion

Top 10 Holdings as of 9/30/2020

1. Vanguard Real Estate II Index Fund
2. American Tower Corp.
3. Prologis Inc.
4. Crown Castle International Corp.
5. Equinix Inc.
6. Digital Realty Trust Inc.
7. SBA Communications Corp.
8. Public Storage
9. Welltower Inc.
10. Weyerhaeuser Co.

VANECK VECTORS GOLD MINERS ETF

Overview

Symbol	GDX
Expense Ratio	0.52%
Inception Date	5/16/2006

Description

The VanEck Vectors® Gold Miners ETF (GDX®) seeks to replicate as closely as possible, before fees and expenses, the price and yield performance of the NYSE Arca Gold Miners Index (GDMNTR), which is intended to track the overall performance of companies involved in the gold mining industry.

TABLE B.10 Performance Returns Before Taxes

1-Year	3-Year	5-Year	10-Year	Since Inception
47.01%	20.26%	24.07%	−2.88%	0.52%

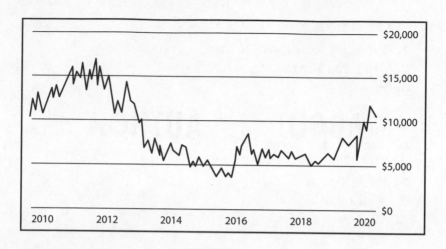

FIGURE B.10 Hypothetical Growth of $10,000 Invested in VanEck Vectors Gold Miners ETF Through September 30, 2020

Holdings

Number of Holdings	54
Fund Total Net Assets	$16.1 billion

Top 10 Holdings as of 9/30/2020

1. Newmont Corp.
2. Barrick Gold Corp.
3. Franco-Nevada Corp.
4. Newcrest Mining Ltd.
5. Wheaton Precious Metals Corp.
6. Agnico Eagle Mines Ltd.
7. Kirkland Lake Gold Ltd.
8. Kinross Gold Corp.
9. AngloGold Ashanti Ltd.
10. Gold Fields Ltd.

ABOUT THE AUTHOR

Alexander Green is the Chief Investment Strategist of The Oxford Club. He has more than three decades of experience as an investment analyst, portfolio manager and financial writer.

Under his direction, The Oxford Club's portfolios have beaten the Wilshire 5000 Index by a margin of more than 2 to 1. He directs a monthly financial newsletter, *The Oxford Communiqué*, along with three specialized trading services: *The Insider Alert*, *The Momentum Alert* and *Oxford Microcap Trader*.

Alex has written for several leading financial publications and has appeared on many radio and television shows, including Fox News, CNBC and *The O'Reilly Factor*. He has also been profiled by *The Wall Street Journal*, *Forbes*, *Kiplinger's Personal Finance*, MarketWatch and other major media.

He is a main contributor to *Liberty Through Wealth*, an investment e-letter with more than 600,000 readers.

Alex is also the bestselling author of three other books: *The Secret of Shelter Island: Money and What Matters*; *Beyond Wealth: The Road Map to a Rich Life*; and *An Embarrassment of Riches: Tapping Into the World's Greatest Legacy of Wealth*.

INDEX